An Unlikely Audience

An Unlikely Audience

AL JAZEERA'S STRUGGLE IN AMERICA

WILLIAM LAFI YOUMANS

Oxford University Press is a department of the University of Oxford. It furthers
the University's objective of excellence in research, scholarship, and education
by publishing worldwide. Oxford is a registered trade mark of Oxford University
Press in the UK and certain other countries.

Published in the United States of America by Oxford University Press
198 Madison Avenue, New York, NY 10016, United States of America.

Library of Congress Cataloging-in-Publication Data
Names: Youmans, William Lafi author.
Title: An unlikely audience : Al Jazeera's Struggle in America / by William Lafi Youmans.
Description: New York, NY : Oxford University Press, 2017. |
Includes bibliographical references and index.
Identifiers: LCCN 2016038025 (print) | LCCN 2016052210 (ebook) |
ISBN 9780190655723 (cloth : alk. paper) | ISBN 9780190655730 (epdf) |
ISBN 9780190655747 (ebook) | ISBN 9780190655754 (online course)
Subjects: LCSH: Al Jazeera America (Television network) | Television
broadcasting of news—United States.
Classification: LCC PN1992.92.A392 Y68 2017 (print) |
LCC PN1992.92.A392 (ebook) | DDC 384.5506/5—dc23
LC record available at https://lccn.loc.gov/2016038025

9 8 7 6 5 4 3 2 1
Printed by Sheridan Books, Inc., United States of America

Contents

Preface

When I received my first gate pass granting me access to enter Al Jazeera's compound in Doha back in 2010, I could not anticipate where it would eventually take me. I was a graduate student just beginning my dissertation research. I was fascinated by Al Jazeera English (AJE) from a distance, as a viewer. It was an experiment in international journalism that offered a notably divergent editorial perspective on a world, especially by staking out an interest in the parts of the world neglected by western news channels that claim a global expanse, namely the BBC and CNN. Al Jazeera English claimed to be a direct challenge to the traditional patterns in the flows of global news, producing news from the global south and making it available to viewers around the world, but most subversively, those of the global north. As a budding scholar concerned with the world's inter-relations through media, this was an alluring promise.

The more time I spent at AJE's headquarters in Doha, the more I appreciated the magnitude of the technical, reportorial, and managerial complexities behind making good, international television. It was my first extended exposure to the innards of a daily TV news operation. It all began with a degree of awe at the spectacle of television production. I was struck by the ongoing coordination of so many individuals in a bewildering, nonstop manufacturing process.

The Doha headquarters was a research site where the professional practices of journalism met the unique, and seemingly contradictory, politics of a mission aiming to subvert the global news order—to generate reporting from a conscientious position of alterity. The channel could reconcile these purposes through an embedded multi-perspectivality, identifiable both in the channel's distributed organizational map that had personnel all around the world and in the makeup of the workforce. In the channel's headquarters, I found a distinctly multinational medley of professionals with very different personalities, political outlooks, career paths, backgrounds, visions, and job descriptions. It was among the most diverse institutional settings I ever witnessed at work. Yet, this heterogeneous group managed to put out a continuous series of news packages, reports, programs, and documentaries. That astounded me, as did the contentiousness and creativity of the news-making I witnessed. The employees, being journalists, were naturally opinionated, disputatious, and committed enough to transparency to air those sentiments freely to this curious researcher. It was eye-opening to witness how vivacious debates over "the news" were behind the scenes. The relative seamlessness of the broadcast obscured a complex social machinery of production. This made studying it all the more tantalizing, but also speaks to the difficulty of imposing a straightforward narrative on how media like Al Jazeera are made. I try to justify my necessary simplification in this book by focusing on one main factor, geography, because it interweaves many others.

This book was only possible because I enjoyed a privileged view of subsequent developments around my chief interest, the network's struggle in the US market, from the launch of AJE in 2006, to its "moment" covering the Egyptian revolution to the establishment of Al Jazeera America and AJ+. With my dissertation, I was primarily fascinated in what AJE's entry into the United States said about both the network and the country as a polity and world power. As the network moved quickly into the launch of Al Jazeera America and then AJ+, my basic research question about how the network competes in a difficult US news market and post-9/11 political context became even more pertinent. As I observed the channels from up close as a researcher and from afar as a viewer, my thinking on the geographic aspects of AJ's three services—the subject of the book—came into sharp relief. It was not my first focus, but a discovery that came about much later. The "aha" moment arrived in the fall of 2015 when I was returning to my home department, Communication Studies at the University of Michigan, to deliver a talk based on my fieldwork at AJ+'s offices in San Francisco.

Over the years, I returned to Doha multiple times for research, and was lucky to have emails and phone calls returned. Conducting close observation of, and interviews with, present and former staff at all levels of AJ's organization, I depended very much on a cadre of willing participants, more than sixty in total, to demystify what I observed and to open up about their own sense-making. Many of them graciously gave me hours of their very busy, deadline-obsessed schedules, and were, from as best as I can tell, candid with me. To prevent them from any harm that might result from my research, I offered them confidentiality as a matter of course, even though I disclosed this book is an academic treatment rather than a journalistic expose. Many of them said they would speak on the record, but others required I protect their identities. For the purpose of consistency and to minimize any potential harms from participation with my research, as unlikely as it appears, I do not provide the names of my interviewees. Without their openness and participation, this book could not have been possible.

   Although I had a clear interest in contributing to international communication theory when I started this study, I quickly realized how incomplete discipline or research methodology would be for really making sense of this question before me. Over the more than five years I've spent studying AJ's expansion into the US market, I've had to broaden my theoretical and methodological arsenal into a tableau that may frustrate the purists in both realms. While this book is primarily geared toward those interested in media and international affairs, I draw piecemeal and incompletely from economics, business, political science, sociology, anthropology, law, philosophy, history, and Middle East studies. Methodologically, I deployed semi-structured interviews, surveys, content analysis, legal analyses, and an experiment (explained in appendix A). I am guilty of jumping between and then denying the separability of geographic scales of analysis, from the global, to the transregional, international, and local. This eclecticism is part of who I am. A book, after all, is always a reflection of the author's worldview and its necessarily disjointed components. It is also justified by the book's subject being a complex organization that defies any single, neat lens.

Acknowledgments

This book would not have been possible without the care, encouragement, and inspiration I received from so many people, peers, friends, mentors, and family. The saying that "it takes a village to raise a child" is just as apt to describe the community it takes for an author to complete a book. I could not name everyone, so excuse any absences.

No one sacrificed as much for the book as did my great partner, Sharon, who gave up many evenings and weekends with me in support of what must have seemed a never-ending project. As she observed, she is present in this book, between the lines and in its spaces, holding it all together because without her loving support and forgiveness I could not have completed it. I must also thank my immediate family—Ed, Nadia, Samer, and Scott—and my extended relatives who all saw me a little less than I would have liked in order for me to produce this manuscript. My closest friends who were patient with me as I became a hermit are also owed a debt of gratitude. Dr. Ammar Askari, in particular, was a great help in always asking about the book's progress, giving thoughtful remarks on draft chapters, and inducing me to meet deadlines.

Of course, I could not have written this book, literally speaking, without the many Al Jazeera personnel, present and former, who spoke with me, provided me information, and gave me so much time and attention in the process. Some of them were much more instrumental to this book than this flat acknowledgment admits, but for the sake of protecting their identities, they must go unnamed.

Also, this book could only exist in this form thanks to my editor Hallie Stebbins and her diligent team at Oxford University Press. I am honored they believed in this project. Their touch on the manuscript improved it greatly. The book's reviewers were also especially influential in directing me to strengthen the book's arguments and flow.

The project's seeds lay in my time in graduate school at the University of Michigan. The Department of Communication Studies supported me tremendously, beginning first and foremost with the faculty and mentors who educated me: Susan Douglas and Robin Means Coleman taught me how to teach and research, and championed me through the doctoral program. I also called upon various other faculty members during my time there and in the years after for advice, support, and education: Nojin Kwak, Shazia Iftkhar, Nick Valentino, Sean Jacobs, Amanda Lotz, Sonya Dal Cin, Rowell Huesmann, Josh Pasek, Julia Sonnenvend, Mike Traugott, and Derek Valiant. Amy Eaton and Orlandez Huddleston were also very supportive. My classmates and friends there were instrumental, especially Katie Brown for our collaborative research on AJE and other topics that informed parts of this book.

Deserving of special thanks are my dissertation advisers, who set me on this path and shaped my scholarly identity. W. Russell Neuman crucially set my sights on studying Al Jazeera English when I was searching for an idea and offered instrumental advice on all matters of graduate student existence. Paddy Scannell greatly expanded my theoretical horizons as my teacher, adviser and inspiration, and he encouraged me with his continued, engaged passion for my work. Aswin Punathambekar's generous commitment of time and wisdom as a mentor and friend and his scholarship were formative in my development (and he introduced me to many of the core concepts in the book). Finally, my outside committee member Andrew Shryock did so much to push my thinking and taught me to strive for more complexity.

The book's authoring really began while I was an assistant professor at the School of Media and Public Affairs at George Washington University. I owe so much to the excellent encouragement, constructive feedback, and occasional interventions I received from my colleagues. Kim Gross's support and mentorship, as well as Steven Livingston's critical reminders and generous book-lending, supplemented their gracious commitment of time to reading and editing my proposal early on, and then giving me useful guidance on the whole book process. The SMPA's tireless director Frank Sesno was a champion, offering his assistance, as well as commiseration, as he completed his own book. I would be negligent to exclude a special note of appreciation for Jason Osder, my collaborator on another project, who both let me neglect our work so I could complete this book, and offered terrific feedback and inspiration. Babak Bahador also let me shelve our coauthored work and gave me intellectual encouragement during our many lunches. Nikki Layser, Silvio Waisbord, Dave Karpf, Bob Entman, Kerric Harvey, Janet Steele, Pat Phalen, and Matt Hindman coached me through various stages of this book and energized me with occasional pep talks. I received kernels of wisdom, inspiration and substantive feedback from my outstanding colleagues Nina Seavey, Catie Bailard, Imani Cheers, Steve Roberts, Sean Aday, Al May, Lee Huebner, Cheryl Thompson, Ethan Porter, Chris Sterling, and Mike Shanahan, my departed colleague. Maria George, the heart of the SMPA, was of course essential to so many facets of this work, as well as my sanity.

The SMPA, the Columbian College, and the Institute for Middle East Studies in the Elliott School of International Affairs provided funding for the research, writing and formatting of this book. Various student researchers helped along the way, most notably: Rawan Alkhatib, Phillip Waller, Lenin Hernandez, and Rania Said Abdalla.

Other GWU colleagues helped me with the book a great deal. Libby Anker provided spirited mentorship and excellent feedback on both prospective titles and drafts of chapters. Dawn Nunziato and Arturo Carrillo, my friends and co-conspirators in the law school, cheered me on through this and allowed me to slack in our collaboration to see the book through. They also gave me a vital social outlet.

I enlisted help and support from outside my home institutions, as well. My friend and colleague, Niki Akhavan, met with me occasionally to share her insights on book-writing and served as an occasional sounding board. Shawn Powers and Mohamed Zayani read drafts of chapters and improved them greatly with feedback. I am indebted to Monroe Price, who took me under his wing in many ways and is a role model. Many more inflected the project's development in their own ways, indirectly and directly: Shakuntala Rao, Nasir Khan, Bilge Yesil, Raed Jarrar, Amelia Arsenault, Rhonda Zaharna, Daya Thussu, Terry Flew, Phil Seib, Adel Iskander, Marwan Kraidy, and many others.

Although this village is an expansive one, I am responsible for the book's shortcomings and oversights.

An Unlikely Audience

Introduction

> First then we must understand that place would not have been
> inquired into, if there had not been motion with respect to place.
> —Aristotle, *Physics IV.4*

It was remarkably ambitious. The Qatar-owned Arab news network Al Jazeera hoped to fully reverse its status as a virtual *medium non grata* in the United States in the early 2000s. By 2004, it began planning an English-language channel to become a mainstream source of news for viewers around the world. Once it launched in 2006, the channel put a special emphasis on reaching American viewers. This turnabout should have been unimaginable under the presidency of George W. Bush. He and his administration displayed open hostility against the company's flagship Arabic-language news channel, tarnishing the brand as a virtual enemy combatant. American leaders were upset by the relatively young network's highly critical reporting and oppositional editorial vantage point during the early years of the Iraq and Afghanistan wars. It reported on civilian casualties, put a spotlight on allied forces' military setbacks and interviewed members of the Taliban and Iraqi insurgency groups. Government officials feared Al Jazeera endangered the wars' missions by threatening to erode international and domestic public support and inflaming regional passions against the United States. They answered with sharp rhetoric against Al Jazeera. In his 2004 State of the Union address, the president disparaged the news operation as a source of "hateful propaganda." Secretary of Defense Donald Rumsfeld called its reporting "vicious, inaccurate, and inexcusable." This antipathy trickled down into the public's enmity, drawing on popular anxieties and suspicions toward all things Middle Eastern that defined the war on terror's zeitgeist. The American public and much of the commentariat were outraged that Al Jazeera aired some of Osama bin Laden's post-9/11 video messages and later showed video of captured US and allied soldiers. Many Americans came to associate Al Jazeera with Al Qaeda. There were equally false perceptions that it aired militant groups' beheading videos and glorified mob violence against American troops and contractors in Iraq.

Still, American reactions to Al Jazeera's Arabic news reporting were layered and surprisingly diverse. The young network received a surge in interest from many inclined to distrust the president and oppose the wars he prosecuted. A DC-based producer with the Arabic channel estimated they "were fielding an average of 60 calls a day from American viewers wanting to know what Al Jazeera was saying."[1] Well-known in media circles for its close-up coverage of the wars, AJ's footage made its way into US news media reports frequently.[2] It was impossible to ignore that the channel's reporting of the wars from the ground was unique and rich; its on-the-ground vantage point contrasted with the embedded perspectives of western news media participating in the US military's press control system. The military placed reporters within allied forces' units.

Before the wars, Al Jazeera's Arabic service had some fans in the United States. Outside of Arabic-speaking communities, regional experts in the government and academia relied on the channel for information and analysis about the region. It won praise for breaking new ground in the Arab satellite-news sphere by, for example, giving airtime to banned dissidents, covering taboo topics, and thereby widening the range of topics in public discourse. Its political talk shows featured guests who vigorously debated and aired live, uncensored callers— revolutionary by the region's television news standards.[3] In the years before the US invasion in Afghanistan, State Department officials made positive remarks about the station, and the government-funded broadcaster *Voice of America* even sought to carry some of its programs (Al Jazeera declined).[4]

By the time Al Jazeera was looking to reach English-speaking audiences around the world, it was unquestionably a contentious source in the United States. The built-up public and official resentment against its brand naturally burdened the network's efforts to build an American audience with its English language service. Its investment to expand into the country was astounding.

Al Jazeera in the United States

President Bush's and Secretary Rumsfeld's denunciations had the surprising consequence of boosting Al Jazeera's already swelling international reputation. Their animosity only escalated demand for the type of reporting the Arabic channel pursued—bold, visually compelling, challenging, and directly from the scenes of war. When employees traveled around the world, they heard robust praise, even, surprisingly, in countries where Arabic was not a common language. They observed cafe-goers watching for the gripping imagery alone in South Africa, India, and Indonesia, among other places.[5] This indicated to them the existence of large untapped demand. The network's calligraphic, tear-drop-shaped logo was already one of the world's most recognizable.[6] To capitalize on its improving visibility outside its home geo-linguistic region, AJ commenced a strategy of globalization. After experimenting with a website that offered translations of its Arabic reports, the network launched a major project to expand to new TV markets: a full news broadcasting service in the modern lingua franca, English.

The network established the editorially independent channel *Al Jazeera English* (*AJE*) in November 2006 after two years of planning and preparation. Designed to compete with global news giants like CNN and the BBC, it differed from them with its avowed "global south" orientation. It would cover the parts of the world to which the global news titans gave scant attention: Southwest Asia, Sub-Saharan Africa, Latin America, and urban ghettoes in the West. Issues that the incumbent news agencies underreported were to compose its news agenda, from poverty and the plight of minority groups, to the social, cultural, and environmental costs of global capitalism and power politics. Its mantra of giving "voice to the voiceless" was to be a fresh news perspective on the world.

Being on American soil positioned it to speak back to the empire, as it proclaimed, but there were also strategic and practical reasons. Al Jazeera English valued penetrating the American news market as a step to emerging as a preeminent, global media organization. Finding success in the world's power would boost its standing elsewhere. At the same time, the United States was a central fixture in international news; AJE had to be able to cover the country's seat of government. To these ends, the Doha-headquartered network built an editorial and production hub in *Washington, DC*. It was one of the channel's four regional broadcasting centers when it started broadcasting, and became the office from which AJE covered all of the Americas.

This aspiration to go from a loathed enemy castigated as a propaganda medium to a staple of the American TV news diet was made possible by the network's sponsor, the government of Qatar, which enjoyed deep pockets and was willing to fund the channel's rapid spread to benefit its own prominence. It was an investment in that the Al Jazeera brand elevated the small country's stature. Despite Al Jazeera's rich resources, however, reaching Americans with its news was no easy task. The US news market was virtually impenetrable for foreign news outlets. After four years of struggling to make headway, AJE's best chance finally came. In early 2011, the channel emerged as the indispensable source of news for the major news event of the year: the Arab Spring, a series of popular uprisings across the Middle East. In particular, its reporting on Egypt's mass protests that toppled longtime dictator Hosni Mubarak captivated American news viewers and won wide accolades. Al Jazeera English enjoyed a momentous boost in its online audience. However, due to the political stigma and doubt that Americans would tune in, the vast majority of American cable and satellite providers decided against offering the channel.

Without TV distribution agreements in place, AJE did not have the reach of the mainstream cable news companies it wanted to compete with: namely, MSNBC, Fox News, and CNN. With the Arab Spring moment, AJE hoped to convert the carriers to gain substantially wider television distribution, which was still the primary means of reaching American news viewers. It failed to convince them; the channel was absent from almost all American television sets. Being widely available online was no substitute for placement on cable and satellite TV listings. After years of floundering to grab an audience share in the coveted American news market, the network gave up on the idea of AJE being widely seen in the United States and adopted another market entry strategy.

In the first days of 2013, the Al Jazeera Media Network announced that it bought Current TV, an American youth-oriented news channel cofounded by former Vice President Al Gore and a few others. The deal for the flailing outlet gave the Arab network what its English enterprise could not obtain—a sizable cable and satellite TV distribution footprint. Rather than keeping the acquired property in place as it was or simply replacing its signal with AJE's to get the international channel on air, Al Jazeera adapted it into a US-only operation, rebranding it as Al Jazeera America (AJAM). The network converted Current TV's offices in *New York City* to AJAM's headquarters. After only eight months of preparation and test piloting, AJAM's first programs went live in August 2013. Despite its cable and satellite availability—60–65 million households—the channel only pulled in a minuscule audience in the low tens of thousands after nearly two years.[7] It was too little to show for the estimated $2 billion expended up to that point. In late 2015, the network faced budget cuts due to diminished financial support from Qatar. It shuttered the channel in April 2016, after less than three years of broadcasting.

The network was not completely out of the American news market. It had a side-bet in place. Starting with the Current TV purchase in early 2013, Al Jazeera also developed a digital media channel, AJ+. The network transformed Current TV's *San Francisco* offices into the home base for this project. Empowered to operate independently of AJAM and AJE, AJ+ assumed a unique editorial voice, one that was not typical of traditional journalism. The news presenters spoke to the younger generation of 18- to 35-year-olds, addressing them colloquially, as peers. AJ+ videos are opinionated, humorous, and even activist at times, a far cry from the objective news voice of its sister channels. That was not the only difference. Rather than relying on cable and satellite companies to reach the public, AJ+'s primary distribution modes were custom mobile phone and tablet apps, social media platforms and YouTube. This self-identified "start-up" was designed to be future facing, ahead of the news-technology curve, in contrast to AJAM's assumption of the form, style, and distribution modes of a traditional news broadcaster. In contrast to AJE's exit and AJAM's closing, AJ+ became something of a smash hit, amassing billions of online video views in its first two years. The network hailed AJ+ as a success, and it launched other language versions, chiefly in Arabic and Spanish.

An Incomplete Globalization

On its surface, the story of Al Jazeera in the United States reveals an under-appreciated tension between two orthodox theories from different corners of social science. On the one hand, we have heard so much about the vigorous power of communication technology to expand news and information flows around the world; this conception has come to define media globalization as an era of unfettered access to knowledge. On the other, Al Jazeera is irretrievably ensnared in the volatile US–Arab relations of the war on terror era, which undoubtedly militates against its market success. These two forces give us differing guidance about what we should have expected with Al Jazeera's arrival in the United States. Yet, we can see why these lenses are ultimately dissatisfactory starting points for this analysis.

Media and communication scholarship and popular thought have been so dazzled by the seeming dominance of networked logics underpinning Internet technology, which followed a prior history of techno-bewilderment at the vast capacity of satellites, concerns about the magical powers of broadcasting, and before then, how the telegraph would change the world. There tend to be grand pronouncements about the newest mechanisms that provide access to media content. At the same time, the conventional view of globalization is that borders have weakened greatly under a constant pluralism brought on by the rapid flows of people, information, goods, and services, altering the relationships between places, arguably making them more networked and interconnected across space. These come together in the idiomatic terminology to describe forms of mediated experience like online community, network society, virtual worlds, cyberspace, and telecommuting. They reflect a re-conceptualization of media geography that collapses traditional categories of social life, such as the distinct lifeworlds of places, into wider, technologically hosted spaces.* The transnationalized media lifeworld is the new normal.

This case of Al Jazeera in the United States calls into question positive prognostications about the cosmopolitan openness of the information society, or the imagined emboldening of the public sphere often thought to characterize this

---

* David Seamon, borrowing on Buttimer (1976), defined the lifeworld as the "taken-for-granted pattern and context of everyday life through which the person routinely conducts his day-to-day existence without having to make it an object of conscious attention" (1979, 20).

era of the connected world. As a case of media globalization, Al Jazeera's entry has been rough, contested, and ultimately incomplete. This is a far cry from the seamlessness of media circulation imagined by visions of a borderless world of information currency enabled by the proliferation of networked information and communication technologies.

Of course, Al Jazeera suffered a brand problem due to the political climate under the Bush administration. Still, as much as its US foray was disputed and costly, it was not a simple tale of prohibition, as one may expect due to phenomena energized as a result of the war on terror, such as Islamophobia, the national security state, post-9/11 geopolitical competition, or other ideological closures that presumably work to keep Al Jazeera out of the United States. These do not clearly explain how AJE experienced a "moment" of rapid acceptance in 2011 or why AJ+ is a relative success, nor why the most Americanized channel, AJAM, closed down. Too many analyses of Al Jazeera in America overstated the influence, and consequentially the scale, of the country's exclusive impulses by attributing AJE's absence to a ban, for example.[†] Despite the lack of formal closures, it is impossible to deny that historical obstacles and sociopolitical tensions stood in the way of a case exemplifying a modern techno-economic process like media globalization.

Neither the theorizing on expanding global flows through online platforms, nor the expected impediments built into US–Arab relations, offer the full story then. As general theories they are bound to overdetermine, that is, generate simplistic, exaggerated predictions. While both dynamics touch upon AJ's ambitions in countervailing ways, they are too macro to be fully explanatory on their own. The inadequacy of the media globalization and US–Arab relations frameworks calls for a more refined view of where AJ's services actually were in the country. The book's beginning was a recognition that this global news operation's most integral work was carried out at various localities, the places of its facilities: the cities of Washington, DC, New York, and San Francisco. These were the sites where this news network's US services landed, making them the network's most direct meeting points with the forces of inclusion that offered routes to circumvent exclusionary barriers. Al Jazeera's expedition into the US market, then, can be fruitfully investigated through the channels' presence in the American cities where they located and worked to reach the country at-large.

[†] Popular articles such as the 2011 "Al Jazeera English Blacked Out Across Most of U.S." (Grim 2011) and network officials, like longtime director-general Wadah Khanfar (2011) furthered this impression by using words like "banned" to describe AJE's lack of cable and satellite distribution. Bloggers also characterized AJE as being blocked for similar political reasons (Bebawi 2016, 87).

The Book's Argument

The book's central contention is that the three US-facing subsidiaries were indelibly shaped by the respective places that hosted their operations: AJE in Washington, DC; AJAM in New York City; and AJ+ in San Francisco. These media capitals inflected the channels' ingress into the country through the assimilative power of their main, pertinent industries: DC's media-politics, New York City's traditional TV news, and San Francisco's technology–new media. To convey how these key cities in effect modulated, attenuated, and domesticated an avowedly global media network, this book proposes we understand these urban formations as *media ports of entry*. This term is adapted from the maritime, transportation context to express how these centers are formative for resident, multinational media seeking expansion into new markets. The ports are not just neutral, logistical re-transmission points in globalization patterns. As Aristotle's quotation that is the epigraph of this introduction insinuates, we are interested in these cities as places with respect to how Al Jazeera moved through them, and how they gave form to its services. The media ports of entry framework is fully explained in chapter 2.

What follows is an effort to position this interest within several conceptual lines of inquiry in international communication. Delving into micro-scale forces at the level of key cities, with their industries and unique sociopolitical and cultural components, is based on recognition that the global is translated through localities—a premise of the literature on "glocalization." Centering cities, as this book proposes, challenges the primacy of methodological nationalism in cross-border communication research, and does so borrowing from the research tradition on global cities as the vital points of transmission in globalization. Media capitals are the places where agglomerated media industries are found, and they assist external firms in their market expansion. This theoretical mosaic combines the many geographies of Al Jazeera, descending through scalar levels from the global to the national and the local.

GLOCALIZATION: THE GLOBAL IN THE LOCAL, AND VICE VERSA

Corporate media have long embraced the practical imperatives of customization that expansion to external markets warrants. In the 1990s, the founder of News Corporation, Rupert Murdoch, said that global media networks had to adjust by presenting the "best international programming and mixing it with local content." That was why "[l]ocalization is playing an increasingly crucial role" in the growth of global news institutions.[8] The awkward portmanteau "glocalization" refers to the co-occurrence of "universalizing and particularizing" forces in the international movement of goods, people, and services.[9] Tailoring to markets was commonplace among transnational broadcasters due to heterogeneous language needs.[10]

From where did the notion of "glocalization" as business logic arise? The common genesis story, which Robertson and others traced, was that it was an explicit strategy of Japanese corporations that sought new foreign markets by tailoring products for their idiosyncratic preferences.[11] This principle was expressed in Japanese as "*dochakuka.*" Meaning "living on one's own land," the term was likened to taking root, or "adapting farming techniques to local conditions."[12] As Murdoch's business wisdom demonstrated, this became a near necessity for international media. This incentive to localize was an outcome of accelerated development of national media systems around the world. For expanding media companies, the greater complexity of target-country markets required adept differentiation to compete with emergent domestic media better equipped to meet the news needs of their compatriots. National audiences, likewise, tended to prefer domestic news sources. Powerful western media companies could no longer dominate foreign markets so easily as when their national industries were sparse and underfunded.[13]

As Roudometof noted, ascribing glocalization to corporate strategy is misleading and constrains its application to more critical research. It can be more than a strategic business principle. In his archaeological recovery of utterances of "glocal," he found it was first put into print in a 1990 art installation in Bonn, Germany. The piece, an orthogonal cube, was intended as a statement on the interconnectedness of the various ecological scales from the local to global, in effect modelling how we must think of the intertwined geographies of environmental issues. Roudometof advocated returning to this original usage to think of the various spatial scales as simultaneous, interconnected, mutually constituted fields of social, political, economic, and cultural action.[‡] The ecological metaphor pushes us to acknowledge the complex, borderless interlinkages that reveal the old caricature of top-down globalization as rare. We are forced to admit the ubiquity of strange fusions of goods, ideas, and meanings both produced and consumed between variable distances. Our transnational lives are more multiform than simple categorical thinking about global–local permutations allows.

The distinction in the two tales of this admittedly awkward term's origins is pertinent because construing it within the purely business context of multinational corporate strategy gives way to an overemphasis on actors at the global scale, making the local a subject that the global works upon. This is a

---

[‡] Scholars who deployed glocalization stressed the sorts of global-local interplay and interpenetration Robertson (1995; 2014) emphasized. Rosenau (2003), Waisbord (2004), Holton (2005), Sreberny (2006), and Jijon (2013), among many others, represent a broad range of disciplines of study and also differ in how they describe the dynamics of "glocalization."

formula for "a superficial 'façade' of diversity."[14] However, Al Jazeera's three enterprises based in US media capitals betray an iterative, tactical glocalization neither stemming purely from a calculated business strategy nor typifying the sort of organic, cultural blending of pluralistic, horizontal complexity. This book explores AJ's three channels as outcomes of transnational processes negotiating the global force of AJ's institutional mandate with local industries and norms sited in the American media capitals, all within unfolding sociopolitical, techno-economic and journalistic settings.

Glocalization usefully draws attention to the mutual interaction of multi-sited influences, not just Doha as the central administrative site emanating its own version of globality in the shape of this network, but those of the media capitals in which Al Jazeera established facilities. Framing this study narrowly around AJ's agency draws upon the business strategy notion of glocalization, which prioritizes the institutional entity as relatively autonomous. This implies its decisions are the main deciding factors in its fate. Al Jazeera's pursuit of American viewership was far from a straightforward case of a business actor seeking new customers in a normal, competitive market. AJ's subsidiaries operated in a trying sociopolitical context burdened by historical, intercultural, symbolic baggage, not to mention the inhospitable political economy of oligopolistic gatekeepers in the form of cable companies. It also faced a public culture characterized by rampant disinterest in world news that does not implicate American national interests or center on natural disasters. These structural points of resistance—further explored in chapter 1—only pushed this news network to acclimate to the uncertain US market, to more deeply hybridize as simultaneously Arab, global south, and international/foreign, as well as American.§ The three cities of production were the primary arenas through which Al Jazeera's hybridization took place. The three subsidiaries Americanized in ways steered by the cities, their media industries, and other attributes of them as places of creative work.

METHODOLOGICAL NATIONALISM

Layered between the global and the local scales is the nontrivial authority of the state and the still-potent identity of the nation. Privileging national boundaries and media flows between them has been at the core of thinking about how media move in the world. The nation-state is often the primary unit of analysis.[15] The earliest research on "news flows" tracked the circuitry of news around

---

§ Kraidy (2005) operationalized hybridity to analyze media as the integration of multiple, distant contexts in a state of admixture. Its adoption in this book is noteworthy because as a conceptual tool "hybridity" traditionally features more prominently in cultural studies than journalism and news media research.

the world. Studies like the International Press Institute's *The Flow of News*, published in 1953, set the level of analysis of "where" news is made and consumed only "in terms of states," thus highlighting "the geopolitical borders of (nation-) states drawn in maps."[16] There was presumed flow in countries' domestic news media covering other parts of the world, though skews in international coverage created imbalances in representations.[17] Media imperialism and other models premised on international hierarchy, including the accounting of contra-flow[18] in media, emphasized the nation-state to account for how more powerful countries set the international news agendas and dominated export of media. Even in much of the media glocalization research, the included "local" usually refers to the national, as Annabelle Sreberny observed.[19] This shows how foundational the national level is to thinking about media and communication.

Admittedly, there is cause for "thinking nationally" about media like AJ, given that most media markets are national, governed by national regulations, such that the state and national media systems have not withered away.[20] No assessment of Al Jazeera in the United States can deny that its perceived foreignness from a nationalist perspective was a primary factor in its US market challenges. The prevailing political context AJ navigated in the United States was largely defined by the national government. The Bush administration framed AJ as hostile to the country's interests. On the sending side, Qatar's national goals of soft power and visibility imbue AJ's expansionism.[21] Yet, as the quick review of Al Jazeera's inflow into the United States shows, its performance was incomplete and variable through different parts of the country and at various times. If we only approach Al Jazeera in the United States purely through the lens of the national, then we miss vital, analyzable nuance at both the sub- and supranational arenas of action.

Thinking "glocally" about Al Jazeera in the United States requires what Ingrid Volkmer described as a methodological transition from the frame of "'national'/ 'foreign'" to "relativistic processes of local/global, space/place."[22] This permits a downward shift in the scale of focus to AJ's services in their respective cities, as well as analytical openness to the interregional dimension, rather than starting and ending with the country at large. This move, however, must be carried out with an eye toward multi-scalar analysis, even if the local is the focus. It cannot be divorced from the others, as national, regional, and global phenomena also manifest in localities. There is no segregation between the scales, making complete isolation of one level against the others an inherently artificial exercise; we can only emphasize the unique attributes of action at one scale in relation to the others. I take Volkmer's call to suggest an instructive epistemological-methodological shift from the language of flat generalities of national containers that standard assessments of international communication tend to presume. This is tied to a methodological nationalism that Ulrich Beck identified as equating "societies with nation-state societies" such that "states and their governments [are] the cornerstones of a social sciences analysis."[23]

Methodological nationalism is an ill-fitting approach for inquiry into AJ's services, which sprawl beyond the normal units of territoriality, being globalized, interregional and multinational, but with concentrated editorial, production, and marketing functions in predominant cities. As intuitive as it is to contemplate AJ's services in terms of Qatari sponsorship and American receivership as a nation—even in an intensified political atmosphere like the "war on terror"—it is incomplete for understanding the fuller breadth of how the subsidiaries unfolded, as their particular urban contexts proved deeply influential. They defied the categories of the national dimension, being neither excluded nor fully welcome. This realization motivates the book's orientation to the inflective power of the three cities.

GLOBAL CITIES AND THE SPACE OF FLOWS

Examining the influence of cities on Al Jazeera draws from prior theorizing about the import of the metropole on social phenomena, political might, and economic power—processes in which media are intertwined. In traditional urban sociology, the city was a self-enclosed unit defined by inherent, intrinsic structural dynamics as a social realm. It was a place on its own, and fit within a clear ordering of cascading geographic scales: below the international and national. Inter-city research in the 1960s began construing cities as related to each other. Rather than being totally discrete, interconnected cities composed interdependent systems.[24] Under this paradigm, the performances of cities impacted each other; this required assessing their linkages and interworkings.[25] The primary model was of hierarchical relations. Efforts to measure and comparatively rank cities guided much of the empirical work.

City research opened up further with critical research that denaturalized urban formations and submitted that they actualized larger, spatial processes, such as globally expansive political economies. David Harvey's and Manuel Castells's works in the early 1970s followed Henri Lefebvre's conception that "(Social) space is a (social) product."[26] Castells's early interrogation, *La question urbaine*, examined how cities were spatially altered as a consequence of macro-level phenomena like capitalism, making civic cultural divides not natural but "problematic" and ideologically produced to privilege dominant class interests.[27] The "inhabiting" of space through the social practices of "everyday life" defined the urban milieus. Crucially, these forces also engendered trends in municipal planning, from the limited quality and scale of free public space to structuring street life to encourage consumerism. Capitalism construed the physics of city life and design. For Harvey, space and the social were subject to mutually constitutive tendencies.[28] That is, the spatial life of cities reflected and in turn projected a range of social, economic and political forces. The spatial arrays of cities gave shape to the local arenas of action. This laid the foundation for his later work on the outcomes of capitalist accumulation on cities, arguing that surplus capital fixed into new spatial formations; capital-intensive investments from distant companies transformed urban architectures.[29]

Yet, cities contain their own relative economic power as centers of trade, finance and other activities in the global economy. Jane Jacobs's *Cities and the Wealth of Nations* declared cities the prime moving units within national and international economies to the extent their vitality is the barometer for broader economic health.[30] Research on "world cities" measured and identified major cities that serve as the most important connected points in the global economy's spatial architecture. It emphasizes inward/outward mobility between them while recognizing that the metropoles possessed authorities and economic might vis-à-vis national governments.[31] Saskia Sassen depicted such global cities as the networked command and control centers in the world's finance-driven economy; they could be identified by their clusters of advanced producer services that complement global firms.[32] In this strain, media industries, Stefan Krätke and P. J. Taylor found, helped elevate global cities through their own arrangements as agglomerated multinational firms.[33] Cities exercise independent influence within spatializing processes then.

Cities have historically been principal hubs for trade. Janet Abu-Lughod showed the linkages between great cities of Europe, the Middle East and Asia through trade patterns in the 13th and 14th centuries.[34] She likened the centers of the day, such as Genoa, Damascus and Peking, to an economic "archipelago," or series of islands. Those pre-modern urban formations did not form an integrated, unified network, but were autonomous routing points distinct on their own; trade merely linked them.[35] This historical snapshot gestures toward a prevailing interest in the work on cities: whether the movement of flows and systemic inter-linkages diminish the unique placeness and potencies of cities. This is a salient concern because the book contends that cities leave their mark on foreign media firms setting up shop within them. To do so, they must have their own identifiable traits and means of leverage. They must be distinct—as places—from the structural processes that tie them.

Manuel Castells eloquently captured this tension between the realm of quickly circulating movement and the place of the city in *The Rise of the Network Society*.[36] He articulated it though the difference between the "space of flows" and the "space of places." His distinction contrasted the effects of technologically driven transformations in media ecologies, among other facets, with the persistent role of place, constituted by legacy geographic concepts. For Castells, "a place is a locale whose form, function, and meaning are self-contained within the boundaries of physical contiguity."[37] Historically, place contained the universe of human interaction." For many people in the world, place is still determinant, but increasingly, power and social life are channeled through the space of flows, which in turn "essentially alters the meaning and dynamic of places."[38] Thus, he predicted the connective logic of flows to prevail over places, restructuring them and redefining them; places become defined by where they fit within the space of flows. Castells admitted the constitutional organization of this network age functions through urban "nodes and hubs"—meaning the space of flows "is not placeless," after all its connective infrastructure is emplaced.[39] The space of flows thus routes through the places hosting the intertwined activities of flow-making—"the production, transmission and processing of ... information."[40] These are the integrated activities of media industries, which tend to be centrally located in particular built-up tech centers. Still, Castells discounted the placeness of cities and asserted they are best understood as networked processes, that is, spatially.[41]

This book proposes that the place characteristics of the metropoles Al Jazeera co-located within made an appreciable mark on this case of institutional media flow. The places where AJ's American services are located are in some ways "bubbles," as one Al Jazeera employee noted.[42] For example, New York is a media capital due its outgoing publication, broadcasting, and advertising might, which inversely draws in investments, talent, and other resources. There are unique facets of New York that idiosyncratically shape media production processes there. This is best demonstrated in contrast with media-making in other, competing media capitals. This book pursues this point through a comparative examination of the three outlets that are subsets of the same conglomerate. The sustained placial[††] integrity and unique touch of these cities are in part due to the distinct prominence of their media industry cores.

MEDIA INDUSTRIES AND CAPITALS

The subfield of research on media industries examines the clustered, internetworked complexes of similar business entities, supra-organizational associations, and complementary services and firms.[43] Industrial effects on constituent firms are by definition environmental, so they are magnified where firms are geographically concentrated, as in media cities. Industrially central zones attract

---

" Think of the Turkish villagers Daniel Lerner chronicled (1958). They were so wholly invested in the place of their village, Balgat, they could not imagine life elsewhere—a symptom of what the modernization theorist described as the traditional way of life.

†† Casey (1997) introduced "placial" as a term. Hardy (2000) noted that "placial" and "placiality" are not recognized words, but should be as the equivalents of "spatial" and "spatiality." He suggested that the absence of these derivations of place hints at the generalized prioritization of space over place in western thinking.

and ground agencies in milieus of action. In such places, business transactions, learning, and competition are intensely localized. Castells acknowledged that flows produce built-up centers of concentrated industries, but such clustering dynamics occurred historically due to space of place dynamics. Economic research on clusters highlighted the economic benefits of firm and service proximity due to lowered transaction costs, desires to be near transportation infrastructure and populations, and other benefits of contiguity.[44] The three cities under consideration had developed industrial formations in media-politics, television broadcasting, and technology before the rise of network society.

Industries are attractive objects of scholarly attention because they are definable, characterized by linkages and shared practices, and they produce and circulate their own texts, such as trade publications. Thinking about Al Jazeera's component channels through the lens of industries does not necessarily require interpreting them as the dominant concern. We can recognize that industrial structure and firm agency are mutual, approximating what Anthony Giddens referred to as structuration.[45] Industries are systems resulting from induced and incentivized patterns of agentic coordination among competing and collaborating firms, and they further guide, constrain, or encourage the decisions of strategic, competing, and cooperating actors.[46] Firms like Al Jazeera's subsidiaries maneuver through crowded fields of competitors and collaborators, who in turn influence the norms and rules of doing business, thus feeding back into the industries. Furthermore, industries are the consequences of analyzable historical, political, economic, and cultural processes and can therefore pertain to how firms fit into their respective industries. Industrial analysis does not supplant interests in other factors.

The global media cities that house media industries are mappable. P. J. Taylor graphed these cities out, based on the presence of media conglomerates in publishing, video, cinema, print, advertising, and Internet firms.[47] He drew on data Stefan Krätke collected to identify the prime locations of 33 global media companies.[48] Of 196 cities with a media conglomerate presence, 104 of them were housing at least 5 of the top 33 companies. Many national markets are served by one main media city, but some larger countries, and the regional language markets, have a few. Entering firms looking to plant in-market facilities must decide from which cities to launch into the larger market of aspiration. For example, Taylor identified Italian media centers such as Turin, Milan, and Rome.[49] China could be approached through Beijing, Shanghai, or Hong Kong.[50] As Krätke and Taylor wrote elsewhere, companies undertaking a market differentiation strategy will tend to co-locate in the "production centers," making them akin to "anchoring points."[51] They identified the three cities Al Jazeera moved to as media cities. This study advances media cities scholarship by underscoring how the locational advantages and disadvantages of particular media ports of entry differentially mold resident firms.

The cities that host concentrated media industries have been referred to as "media capitals." In *Playing to the World's Biggest Audience: The Globalization of Chinese Film and Television*, Michael Curtin traced the expansion of Chinese film and television firms through various nuclei of media-making in Hong Kong, Taiwan, and Singapore.[52] His work emphasized the power of location in industries' migratory expansion. Media capitals have a particular power vis-à-vis transnational media flows, rather than simply being overrun by them. Cairo, Mumbai, and Hong Kong were industrially concentrated cities that helped domestic companies resist foreign competitors.[53] *An Unlikely Audience* looks at what urban-industrial formations mean for weaker, extra-national media companies with aspirations in a dense national market. An industrial focus allows us to analytically ground Al Jazeera's subsidiaries in their respective places.

MATERIALITY AND PLACE

Industrial clustering is the primary draw for a foreign firm's emplacement in media cities. But an industry is not the most immediate basket positioning firms in particular milieus. Al Jazeera's offices, studios, and buildings—its operating facilities—directly emplaced its work in a given city, giving it an address and structuring it as a creative environment. The three channels were not staffed by teleworkers spread around the world. The brick-and-mortar structures physically planted AJ as a corporation in the respective cities, but also in industrial districts where neighborhood effects—quintessentially space of place dynamics—take hold. There were other material attributes pertinent to their immersion in these sites; place was, for example, actualized through the internal layout of workspaces, which reflected localized, industrial norms. For example, AJ+'s old warehouse office incarnated Silicon Valley's typical open-air, vertically organized, and intentionally playful workspace designs.

It is not a given that accounting for materiality only affirms the space of places. Castells referred to physical communication infrastructure as a layer of material support for networked social practices through the space of flows. Al Jazeera's Intranet, for example, could have served as an infrastructure through which news-making work among different sections of Al Jazeera as a conglomerate could occur between different places. This would be expected to more effectively transnationalize internal company flows and spatialize its work. However, access to the Intranet was structured hierarchically; it reified Doha as the top of the chain of command, the main administrative site. Distant offices had fewer permissions in the company's information technology system. Connectivity to the company's resources, including video libraries, was then place-contingent.

By referring to materiality, this book offers a contra-view to the fixation on the seemingly fluid, borderless mobility of data, our networked lifeworlds, and the symbolic hyper-currencies of communication depicted in much of media scholarship today. This emanates from the excitement over novel technologies that appear transformative. It is also rooted in a deeper legacy in the history of thought. In the longer trajectory of western philosophy and social science, place fell to subordinate status as a category of analysis due to the epistemological preference for spatiality in grand theorizing; general laws of the social realm meant to span both time and space minimized appreciation for differentiation by place.[54] In his commanding overview of place from the time of the ancients up to postmodern philosophy, Edward Casey wrote that place was treated as a "dormant" concept.[55] Place represented a tilt to particularity and idiosyncrasy; this was at odds with the scientific imperative of generalized theory-building. In this book, place is revitalized as an analytical unit through the argument that cities attenuate spatial phenomena like a media practicing international journalism and creating news to circulate in the world.

Urging attention to the skews of geographic factors in our media environment is a reminder of the disciplinary myopia David Morley diagnosed, that media and communication research is overly attentive to the "symbolic, institutional and technological dimensions" at the expense of recognizing the spatial and material facets, including transportation and infrastructure, through which media content originates, flows, and is finally consumed.[56] It is easy to forget that the "soft infrastructure," or executive decision-makers, productive labor, and creative talent, and "hard infrastructure" of plants, communication systems, and offices, are personified and take physical form, and are therefore located somewhere to meaningful effect.[57] Data, news, and information are not placeless in authorship or interpretation just because they have the potential to circulate instantaneously and appear to flow through a spatial ether. To attend to AJ's geographic, material, and industrial underpinnings of a complex news institution is to assert the continued power of place. Each of the cases in chapters 3–6 starts with references to the channels' office spaces since they materially anchor each outlet's being-in-place in their respective ports of entry.[‡‡]

Al Jazeera Research

How does this book's focal point, the Al Jazeera Media Network's performance in America, relate to the small body of Al Jazeera scholarship? While most of

---

[‡‡] This attention to materiality was inspired by a line of scholarship interested in the material and socio-technological aspects of hardware and software industries like in science and technology studies (STS) and in human geography (Pratt 2002; Gillespie et al. 2014). Brian Larkin's writing on cinemas in Kano, Nigeria, was also instructive as a "ground up" starting point for understanding mediated experiences in social context, and he traces material edifices to deeper historical encounters, including colonialism (2008, 15).

the primary research on Al Jazeera covered the Arabic channel, subsequent scholarship on AJE further extended the original theoretical interests rooted in the meeting point between international communication and international relations—through such theoretical concerns as geopolitics, international hegemony, and intercultural reconciliation. Overall, AJ research has engaged the network on global, regional, and national scales exclusively. Drawing from this body of literature, we would accentuate the exceptional qualities of Al Jazeera's US market expansion. This book's city-centric approach is different than most AJ scholarship and offers a novel framework for understanding the nuances of its troubled market entry.

On the global or interregional level, Al Jazeera presented a notable challenge to prevailing theories that stressed the centricity of American political and media hegemony on the international stage.[58] The lens of counter-hegemony has been deployed frequently in Al Jazeera research to examine what the rise of non-western, critical news means for the distribution of world power.[59] Kai Hafez considered AJ's reporting on the Afghanistan war that commenced in 2001 a "reversal of the international news flow that usually runs from the West to the East."[60] Daya Thussu called this "contra-flow" and echoed his assessment by enumerating AJ as exemplary.[61] That a marginal, historic receiver of news like Qatar could sponsor a news juggernaut sufficiently free and empowered to report unfavorably on the world's superpower seemed improbable. Reaching mass audiences in the modern media power, the United States, did as well. Naomi Sakr's description of Al Jazeera English as broadcasting back at "the empire" unintentionally indicated the dim prospects of its success.[62] Saba Bebawi challenged, however, the perception that AJE offered a distinct perspective on news.[63] Her analysis of a set of stories found that much of AJE's news reporting closely resembled the BBC's and CNN's. It presented alternative framing occasionally on important stories from the Middle East, she noted. Tine Figenschou, by contrast, found—drawing on a content-analysis study of a wider breadth of stories—that the channel was more prone to cover underreported stories from its advertised "global south" perspective, which "broadened the range of elite sources" and "documented civilian suffering, anger, and protest."[64]

An alternative theoretical interest emphasized what AJ could mean for intercultural reconciliation and understanding, as a metaphoric bridge between cultures.[65] Phil Seib raised the prospects of Al Jazeera and other new media defusing the notion that the West and the Islamic East are on a collision course.[66] Could watching AJE diminish intercultural hostilities? Mohammed El-Nawawy and Shawn Powers interrogated this through survey research of Americans who watched AJE.[67] They found a positive correlation between viewing the channel and showing tolerance to other ethno-religious groups. Other researchers depicted Al Jazeera as a representative of the Arab or Muslim world that conveyed its sentiments to global publics unfamiliar with its views and perspectives.[68] Another perspective held that Al Jazeera's Arabic channel played a deliberative function in the Middle East in the late 1990s and early 2000s. Lynch considered the Arabic channel a mediated public sphere that served as a forum for popular contestation over regional, pan-Arab politics.[69] Various geo-political or political economy accounts appropriately placed AJ vis-à-vis Qatari foreign policy in both international and regional contexts, stressing that the agenda of the owners mattered for the sorts of stories that ran on the network.[70]

The prevailing scholarship on Al Jazeera prioritizes grand-level politics, the national, regional, and global, with an interest in how its channels contributed to conflict, peace, and understanding.[§§] The network's subsequent English-language properties and their performance in the United States suggest the need for research at smaller scales that can account for the English-language offshoots' basic characteristics—the cosmopolitan diversity of the workforce, the persistent "global south" editorial agenda, the breadth and complexity of its content, and other facets that made the English channels difficult to classify through broader categories where media meets politics.[71] Al Jazeera America and AJ+ evade straightforward application of concepts like hegemony and traditional lenses such as Qatari foreign policy; AJ's endeavors have proven too complex, hybrid, and nuanced for the preexisting media-politics toolkit. Their existence has been driven and shaped by more than a national agenda of enhancing Qatar's soft power and visibility, as important as it has been. To make sense of what the channels became specifically, their modes of produc-tion, perspectivality, and content, their identities in practice and execution, and their performances, it is necessary to attend to the specificities of city-level differentiations. In concert with institutional decisions and other factors, place accounts for the radically variable forms its US-facing services took. This is the story of how AJ's three subsidiaries became embedded in and reflective of three US media capitals.

Book Outline

The first chapter overviews the obstacles to Al Jazeera's plans to penetrate the US TV news market. Some of the barriers to entry descend from historical patterns in international communication and legacy paradigms of US–Arab relations, largely formed around imperial power, conflict, and cultural misunderstanding. There are also small-scale constraints, both particular and generic, that foreign

---

[§§] There are exceptions, including audience research among Arab Diaspora populations, signify-ing a transnational focus (Miladi 2006). Institutional studies have looked into AJ through an orga-nizational lens (Zayani 2008; Zayani and Sahraoui 2007).

media firms come up against in the United States: an insular, nationalist political culture and the structurally exclusive attributes of the TV distribution and news industries. This chapter establishes the severity of the task before AJ. The pressures it faces as a market entrant help us understand why the network would invest in US-based facilities located within industrial centers.

Chapter 2 presents in detail the book's theoretical framework, *media ports of entry*. Highlighting the locational aspects of media industries, the chapter offers a guide for how the cities where AJ's three services are headquartered deeply influence this global media network's internal organization, production, marketing, as well as their conceptions of the audience. Each of the various ports—Washington, DC, New York City, and San Francisco—is a media capital that localized AJ's branches through broader social, cultural, and political acclimation: processes of domestication.

Chapter 3 introduces AJE, an international channel that saw the inability to gain cable distribution as a political rather than a commercial issue initially. It estimated that validation from Washington's establishment elite was prerequisite, assuming the media-politics logic that energizes DC as a media capital and the political capital. Al Jazeera English plugged into this nexus of industries in a city with its own culture and norms around official access, recognition, and legitimation that shape "Beltway journalism."

By 2011, AJE finally had its "moment," when it shed the negative associations of the war on terror decade. This is the focus of chapter 4. With the start of the Arab Spring, the sequential popular uprisings in North Africa and the Middle East, AJE became DC's darling news channel, praised widely as a force for reform and indispensable viewing for news from the region. The change in the politics around AJE suggested that the political context was not as important as other factors in gaining cable and satellite carriage, revealing the political capital's limited utility for AJ's US market entry.

Unlike its predecessor, AJAM was customized to specifically speak to an American news audience. Based in New York City, the operation was thoroughly embedded in the traditional US TV news industry. Its earliest hires were veteran US news media executives and familiar on-camera talent. Al Jazeera America resembled a copy of a US TV news giant, though it aimed to replicate a "golden age" of TV broadcast journalism with longer features, coverage devoid of spectacle, and more hard than soft news. Its location in Manhattan signified its attempted integration within an incumbent, commercial TV news industry en route to the national market. This is the subject of chapter 5.

When Al Jazeera acquired Current TV, it also took possession of its San Francisco office space. The network dedicated it to a separate and editorially independent project, AJ+. It is the focus of chapter 6. After a year of preparation, it was rolled out in 2014 as a digital news operation, appropriately, first in "beta" form. Being in San Francisco, AJ+ operates within a larger tech-sector milieu. The project characteristically fashioned itself as a start-up designed to rethink news creation, packaging, and delivery. Its content and style of presentation is indicative of its proximity to the tech industry of northern California.

For an explanation of the multiple methodologies used in this study, see Appendix A.

1

The Obstacles to Al Jazeera in America

If it's been "market forces" that have kept Al Jazeera English
from an American audience—fears that it would have no
audience, or that it would be "terror TV"—it is time to
readjust to reality. If it's been political pressure that has kept
Al Jazeera English off America's cable and satellite servers, it's
time to reject such literal "know-nothing-ism."
—Former AJE anchor Dave Marash.[1]

Under the direction of Tony Burman, the second managing director, a team of AJE staff began the "Americas Project" to examine how to attract more interest in the United States. The participants brainstormed ideas about what hindered the company. They drafted a memo, and raised as a chief concern the branding problem. In the United States, there is "confusion about the relationship between 'Al Jazeera' and 'Al Jazeera English.'"[2] American commentators, politicians, cable executives, and the public frequently posed this question as a coded means of finding out whether AJE would assume a similar editorial outlook—implying adversarial, rebellious, or anti-American. This incentivized the channel to distinguish itself from the separate Arabic channel. But this presented AJE with a quandary. If it tried to emphasize its independence to appear more palatable to American tastes, it would appear apologetic and might validate misperceptions of the Arabic content held by many who could not even understand the content. Internally, this was a sensitive issue. Stressing the differences would insult the Arabic channel's personnel—some of whom were arrested, injured, or saw colleagues such as Tareq Ayyoub killed reporting for the network. They sacrificed to build the very brand some saw as a liability to AJE's market aspirations.[3] The confusion about the relationship between the Arabic and English channels was more than a symbolic problem. It interfered with AJE's distribution efforts. As the memo related: "[o]ne result is that distributors are wary of the potential commercial and PR risks of carrying the channel."

About a year after that memo was distributed internally, Tony Burman appeared on the radio and TV program *Democracy Now* to discuss Al Jazeera English's prospects in the United States after the Egyptian revolution, which boosted American interest in the channel.[4] Since AJE was still not widely available on TV, those looking for news out of Egypt tuned in to the Internet livestream. Amy Goodman, the show's host, asked why AJE had such poor TV distribution. Burman surmised there were both commercial and political reasons. He referred to "resistance on the part of the cable and satellite companies at the launch of Al Jazeera English in 2006." It was during the "Bush administration," and "there was a fear on [the companies'] part that Americans don't want more international news, that perhaps they'd lose more subscribers than they would gain."

The explanations for AJE's struggles outlined in the 2010 memo and Burman's comments during his appearance on *Democracy Now* hinted at the impressive scale of the obstructions standing against AJ's success in the US news market. Despite the conventional thinking about the fluidity of media globalization and the open sphere created by new media technology—both of which presume that content moves through the world—AJE's expansion to the United States was improbable, expensive, and ultimately incomplete. It faced tremendous barriers. Since incumbent firms are not hindered by these, new-comers like AJ's subsidiaries are at a competitive disadvantage.[5] In an intense TV newscape, such barriers can be nearly insurmountable. In general, news media firms face an uphill climb in the United States. Nigel Parsons, AJE's first managing director and a principal planner of the network, noted that "[a]ll foreign news channels find this market difficult."[6]

Al Jazeera also faced the obstacles common to foreign companies expanding into other markets. They have to adjust to what international business research-ers refer to as the "liabilities of foreignness." These entail the extraneous busi-ness costs wrought by distance, novelty, and inexperience. Zaheer identified four generic types.[7] First, "travel, transportation, and coordination over dis-tance and across time zones" is resource-draining, in terms of both money and time. Second, fixing problems linked to a firm's unfamiliarity with target market environments requires adjustment, incurs learning costs, and results in inef-ficiencies. Third, multinationals must comply with home *and* receiving country rules pertaining to foreign trade, as well as informal political or cultural pres-sures. Compliance is resource-intensive. Finally, firms must attempt to reconcile themselves to sociopolitical or cultural particularities in the receiving market's environment, including latent opposition to foreign firms. One example of this is what Tunstall and others referred to as media nationalism, which involves popular hostility to foreign media and an automatic preference for one's own national media products.[8] These liabilities certainly impeded Al Jazeera in its American endeavor. The network, however, is not merely foreign. It is a Middle Eastern company, reviled for its oppositional reportage of US war efforts and therefore deeply politicized in ways France24, Euronews, or News Corp. were not. Its affiliation with the region of particular sensitivity in post-9/11 America meant Al Jazeera grappled with distinct stumbling blocks linked to longer histories of encounter between the United States and the Arab region.

Why are both the generic and idiosyncratic barriers to entry germane to the book's focus on Al Jazeera in three American media capitals? The magnitude and nature of these market curbs pushed the determined network to double down on its in-country presence through a strategy of foreign direct investment in key American cities. This chapter presents both the macro- and micro-level obstructions, starting with the grand-historical and civilizational, before moving to the national hurdles.

The Legacies of Media Imperialism and US–Arab Relations

Al Jazeera's expansion to the United States is momentous because it directly confronts two deep-seated historical legacies. First, AJ tested the prospects of upending the tradition of *unidirectional patterns in news and information flows* in the world. There is no precedent for a global south, let alone Middle Eastern, media company making such a sustained push for a mass TV audience in the world's leading media power. Second, AJ implicates the cultural and ideational dimensions of traditionally complex, typically rancorous *bilateral US–Arab relations*.

REVERSING NORTH–SOUTH INFORMATION FLOWS

On its face, Al Jazeera appears to defy the modern history of advanced, industrialized countries dominating the realm of international news, both as producers and subjects. The historical formations that gave the most powerful countries the greatest voices in news media persist. However, as legacy patterns of dominance have broken down, the histories of international imbalance in news-making still present a tide Al Jazeera must swim against; the strongest globally present news organizations it contends with are western.

Starting in the 1970s, after the recently decolonized countries of the Non-Aligned Movement (NAM) strove to remain independent of both sides of the Cold War—the mainly capitalist West led by the United States and the Soviet Union-centered cluster of communist states. This third bloc of developing countries began objecting to structural inequity in the international traffic of media products and services.[9] The 1976 "New Delhi Declaration" laid out the rationale for a New World in Information and Communication Order (NWICO) to address underlying imbalances in media and cultural arts. It problematized the overwhelming influx of programming, films, and other media produced in the most powerful countries, namely the United States. The statement objected to media-receiving countries being made into "passive recipients of information" by a concentrated few media powers and analogized it to colonial-era economic, political, and social dependencies.[10] Furthermore, it raised concerns about diversity and representation, fearing that the heavy flow of imports weakened their national fabric by ignoring or misrepresenting their societies and undermining their collective identities. Adapting language from the developmentalist agenda, the statement claimed this harmed their "political and economic growth." Asserting "information sovereignty," these countries set systematically uneven media import/export on the international agenda. The NAM countries took this issue to the United Nations in the hopes of finding recourse.

This political agenda on the international stage had a corollary in media and communication research, which interrogated this inequity under the critical paradigm of "media imperialism." Following the lead of dependency theory, scholars showed how political, economic, and military domination by a small number of powerful countries led by the United States perpetuated underdevelopment elsewhere through communicative means, among others.[11] The media imperialism thesis held that western media were disproportionately powerful, and their governments worked to sustain this advantage because media furthered the ideological project against the threat of communism. Media were the cultural front in the economic colonization of, and aggression against, poorer, weaker countries.[12] World Systems Theory proposed that the relations of dependency and dominance could be structurally mapped.[13] It categorized countries into a hierarchy of core, semi-periphery, and periphery zones to reflect their positionality in the international political-economic power order. Media imperialism research applied this hierarchy to international communication.

Over time, communication scholars contested this notion of one-way media and communication. As international economic trade accelerated in the 1990s and new media producers began to emerge in historic importing nations, the media mix in most countries showed less dependence on western sources, giving rise to what looked like a metamorphosed, complex media ecology. As Marc Raboy observed, rising "pan-regional and international news services (on television and online) on the global media scene" hastened a "shift away from the monopoly long held by dominant, Western-based news media."[14] These developments gave way to a "post-imperialist" era of media pluralism. Globalizing flows were increasingly complicated, along various disjointed scapes, as Arjun Appadurai described as his conceptual architecture of the cultural logic of globalization.[15] South–south, regional, and neighboring media traffic eroded the centrality of the global north. Cross-national media projects became more complicated ventures. Stressing the array of "complex possibilities" that globalization engendered, Joe Straubhaar argued that patterns in international media movement were "hard to predict."[16] The multi-directionalities of media in motion flouted the simple descriptive models of the past.

This disorganized pluralism is more apparent in cultural media, such as entertainment, than in news media. Generally, the liabilities of foreignness are greater for news than entertainment and cultural media given the political and nationalistic implications. Publics tend to seek, trust and prefer their national news sources over foreign ones, a sort of media nationalism.[17] There are gray areas. While developing countries' news media are still reliant on largely western wire agencies and other foreign sources, they filter, repackage, and repurpose these sources' raw materials—domesticating news from abroad to make it more palatable to national or local inclinations.[18] Western news companies could not gain or maintain wide market shares as easily once domestic news sources emerged. Jeremy Tunstall estimated domestic media were 6 to 12 times more consumed than global media in countries around the world—with smaller countries being the most dependent on foreign-made media.[19]

One indication that this phenomenon of news media organizations traversing borders was comparatively scant was that the small body of news flow research did not bother gauging the institutional expansion of foreign news companies into domestic markets. Foreign direct investment (FDI), therefore, was not considered "news flow," despite it being a rich and deep form of international communication. This line of scholarship measured the far more frequent instances of foreign reporting carried out by domestic news organizations instead.[20] It missed the type of cross-national flow that Al Jazeera English presents, whereby an organization seeks new extra-national audiences. This is a more pronounced encounter than the far more recurrent and ordinary business of foreign affairs reporting.

The historic north–south imbalance in cultural trade echoes in the wall Al Jazeera faces in the United States. Countries where global media companies are headquartered tend to have highly competitive media markets, making them inhospitable to incoming enterprises. Expanding media institutions began seeking export markets after domestic markets were saturated, which meant the business environment had already matured and the profit potential diminished. International markets were a means for ambitious firms to extract further revenues from domestic media products; they presented opportunities to invest surplus capital more profitably.

On the scale of globally competitive media organizations, the largest players are large companies or conglomerates, most of which are based in the United States.[21] As privileged of a position this is to be in, media goliaths like the BBC and CNN, it must be noted, are rarely the top TV news channel in any given foreign market. This is due to the emergence of national news media in almost all mid- and large-sized countries. Global news channels are often relegated to niche audiences, those with specialized backgrounds, cosmopolitan dispositions and specific interests in world news. Al Jazeera's English language channel competed at this strata, a narrow one with well-entrenched powerhouses. What is important to this study is that these companies engaged in international expansion because their domestic markets were already captured—leaving less chance for foreign firms like Al Jazeera to succeed in them.[22] That does not mean such markets, like the United States, are impenetrable fortresses. They are just generally more onerous and risky to enter.

Due to the steepness of the climb into the US media market, AJ's expansion should be gauged skeptically as a potential "contra-flow" going against historically unidirectional movement in media.[23] Naomi Sakr described AJE as "a textbook example" of contra-flow, a channel that speaks back at "the empire."[24] In the ideal of the most optimistic prognostications of the technology-enabled space of flows, traditional geographic skews in news and information are expected to break down, lose their pertinence. Interconnectivity should beckon the free movement of news from sources to audiences, with perpetual, de-centered feedback in a networked fashion. However, we cannot speak of contra-flow without evidence of substantial reversal in traditional patterns. We must ask whether a global south channel actually musters an audience in a population long accustomed to insularity in their news diets. As such, Al Jazeera illuminated the improbability of substantive, foreign-made news landing in the United States.

US–ARAB RELATIONS

Another significant set of obstacles to Al Jazeera's expansion into the United States emanated from the long period of turbulent US–Arab relations. They fluctuated between various degrees of friendship and enmity, collaboration, and exploitation. Since World War II, and more specifically the 1956 Suez crisis, the United States asserted itself as the global power in the Middle East. Its national interests included securing the region's oil for international markets and protecting the region from geopolitical competitors in the Cold War. Naturally, this was marked by decades of conflict, military interventions, arm sales, intrigue, paternalistic aid, resource exploitation, cultural anxieties, and so on—making it a tumultuous interaction. There were several elevated moments of tension, such as the Arab oil boycotts that demanded the United States end its one-sided support for Israel, a relationship that was a primary source of US–Arab distrust. The Arab public at large protested US wars, attacks, or interventions in Libya, Lebanon, Iraq, and Yemen. Deep opposition to US foreign policy found expression among some of the region's regimes and in public opinion, and was adopted among non-state groups of various ideological stripes. Nevertheless, US–Arab relations are not all adversarial. The United States enjoyed relatively stable official alliances with a handful of Arab regimes, namely Jordan, Morocco, Egypt, Kuwait, Saudi Arabia, and, notably, Qatar, AJ's sponsor. There have been carriers of goodwill, including American universities, relief organizations, and groups dedicated to peacemaking, as well as migration to the United States. Still, below the level of official diplomacy, American and Arab public opinion is mutually, deeply distrustful. Much of the enmity is due to the perceived excesses of American power, its unpopular, neo-imperial foreign policies, and the prosecution of destructive wars and policies in the region.[25]

This political context appeared to be an obvious hindrance, but could it be an asset? Given post-9/11 US–Arab relations, some raised the possibility that a transnational media company like AJ could serve as a conciliatory bridge-builder. Perhaps it could expedite intercultural understanding and awareness, as international communication scholars have raised.[26] The basic argument was that AJ can facilitate learning about the other, which could in turn generate empathy and lessen hostility. The temptation was to view AJ as a remedy to the problem of US–Arab antagonism. Yet, the same conflictual politics militated against its distribution and reception—prerequisites to its intercultural impact. A cultural politics of xenophobia scuttled other Arab or Muslim-linked ventures after popular outcry. In the 2006 Dubai Ports World controversy, there was public outrage over a US government's port management contract with a state-owned company from Dubai.[27] Also a sign of the times, widespread protests arose against the construction of mosques and Muslim community centers around the country. The highest profile one was the Park51 center that was planned for lower Manhattan, a block from the World Trade Center; the planners folded the project as a result of the backlash.[28] Al Jazeera's mere presence in the United States was politicized in similarly phobic strains.

While the more current period of popular and official suspicion toward anything Arab or Muslim is the most immediate context, but the longer history of inter-civilizational encounter is also part of the story. The two primary paradigms of US–Arab affairs at the macro-historical level did not portend well for Al Jazeera's US ambitions. The first was set forth in Edward Said's formative book, *Orientalism.*[29] Said linked the West's repertoires of knowing and narrating the East to the long experience of historic imperial conquest, with its corresponding processes of knowledge production and representation about the people and areas it subdued. Contemporary western understandings of the Middle East sustain the tropes generated in the imperial era. The discursive power that empires deployed, their imaginative geographies, proliferated through academic study, art, and literature under the cover, and in the service, of empire-building. Ways of thinking about the Near East as timeless and unchanging, mystical, feminine, irrational, passive, and in need of saving descended from this imperial starting point.

If Orientalism is a component of the ideational terrain AJ must navigate, a mainstream western audience is naturally expected to discount a source from the East, particularly if it is seen as politically oppositional, critical of the United

States. An American audience would fixate on "its Orientalness, so much so that the attribute of being Oriental [overrides] any countervailing instance."[30] The fact of its foreign and, especially, Arab sponsorship would subordinate the qualities of its news for the viewer accustomed to the inherent knowing of the East that Said criticized. Perhaps that explains the common concern about how different AJE was from its Arabic sister channel. Taking Said's formulation as a point of departure, we could ask whether Al Jazeera's derivative channels represent the Orient speaking back to its western authors. If so, the network would have to surmount deep historical-epistemological formations related specifically to its status as an Arab corporation. When historicized via Said's critique of Orientalism, AJ's efforts appear at first glance overambitious. Al Jazeera could only escape this by de-Orientalizing, or over-Americanizing, its US-centered services.

Second, from a very different theoretical standpoint, the political scientist Samuel Huntington's popular and controversial "clash of civilizations" thesis predicted that irreconcilable cultural-religious differences between the West and the Arab-Islamic East would produce conflict.[31] These civilizational blocs are destined to clash for numerous reasons starting with cosmological antagonisms and ending with modern sociocultural oppositions. This simplified yet ominous vision required controversial premises—conceptualizing the small set of civilizations in the were delineated by distinct, essential, and unchanging cultural principles, and presuming they were fated to be incommensurable. Specifically, Huntington predicted that the Judeo-Christian world is doomed to violent confrontation with the Islamic and Sino (Chinese) blocs. Such macro fault lines were expected to define the lines of future conflict. Extrapolating from this framework, Al Jazeera would expectedly be a flashpoint rather than a well-received source of news in the United States. In one sense, those who agree that a clash of civilizations was in fact taking place tend to be suspicious of its channels and interpret their market presence as some sort of "Trojan horse" for communicative war-making. However, Al Jazeera's brand was already perceived by many as hostile to the country, consistent with the narrative of unavoidable clash. The popularity of Huntington's fatalistic prediction reflected in the grim performance of his book as an oft-cited, best-seller. This was itself indicative of a steep sociopolitical hurdle AJ faced.

Samuel Huntington's culturally oriented prediction was steeped in American realist political science. Edward Said's text had a deep influence on critical, postcolonial studies. Despite the vast, almost oppositional, difference between Huntington's and Said's works, they actually converge on this question of Al Jazeera's chances in the United States. The expectations they produce of Al Jazeera's receptivity among Americans are equally pessimistic. As a critical Arab news outlet, it was doomed to be prejudicially opposed as a dramatic threat or disregarded as untrustworthy.

Al Jazeera's corporate identity and branding implicitly addressed the network's movement against the sorts of trajectories that international communication research on historic patterns of media trade and these paradigms of US–Arab relations capture: it is a "global south" network based in the Middle East that seeks to give "voice to the voiceless." It self-identifies as critical of power in the world. These are aspirational mantras of course. Nevertheless, they are meaningful in that they reveal a conscientious positioning against the sorts of ideational, political, and cultural blockages that AJ must maneuver to build global, let alone American, audiences in competition with incumbent news outlets that give predominant representation to the most powerful countries. Many of Al Jazeera's leaders and staff saw the network's purpose as confronting the legacy forces that embolden disregard for and hostility to foreign, especially Middle Eastern, sources of news. However, the pragmatic imperatives of gaining access to the US market led the network to iteratively tailor its style and output to become more appealing to long-formed sensibilities incubated in historic Orientalism, presumptions of civilizational clash, and one-way flows of news and information in the world. These are global and interregional forces. There are further national-level factors that obstruct the network's traction in the space of flows.

National Factors: Political Culture and Political Economy of TV Distribution

The first iteration of AJ's global north expansion, Al Jazeera English, met public resistance and even more widespread indifference in the United States. This meant there was risk as well as a capped upside, two profound reasons that deter commercial satellite and cable operators. These gatekeepers to American viewers were reluctant to take the gamble of carrying a channel like AJE, foreign branded and from a company reputed to be unfairly critical of the country's leadership. Given the political climate after the 9/11 attacks and the Bush administration's pointed criticisms of Al Jazeera, it could hardly be surprising that AJE floundered in the television distribution market.[32] After six years, the channel could only be viewed on a small percentage of American televisions. This section explains how two essential national-level factors constrained AJ's circulation efforts within the space of flows: facets of American political culture manifest in news tastes as well as the political economy of TV distribution industries.

POLITICAL CULTURE

The term political culture refers to durable formations of "relatively coherent clusters of attitudes" that effect political and economic outcomes.[33] This admittedly limited, instrumental conceptualization of political culture—linking it to outcomes—reflects Max Weber's famous emphasis on values as an explanation for economic and political development. Weber attributed the "spirit of capitalism" to a value cluster, the Protestant work ethic. Political cultures pertaining to news have been studied cross-nationally. Hallin and Mancini's work on western media systems linked aspects of media-state systems to their respective political cultures.[34] The deployment of political culture here, however, is a more modest one. This section describes the prevalent attitudinal currents that shape patterns of demand for international news reporting in general, and AJ's in particular, among the US public.

In this analysis, political cultural orientations culminate in various degrees of receptivity toward foreign-produced news. The market potential of Al Jazeera's derivative projects depends, then, on the existence of favorable strains of political culture. In thinking about the role of culture in a question like the circulation of news media, we must investigate how certain attitudinal dispositions engender an open-minded reception. In the first instance, we can conceptualize *news as a cultural form*, so that qualitative differences in news cultures make for differentially resonant publics for AJ's reporting.[35] Second, *public openness to a foreign institution*, particularly one headquartered in the Arab, Muslim Middle East, is essential to an enabling cultural environment for AJ's spread.

News is a cultural form. As Michael Schudson wrote, the genre of news is part of the public's interpretive arsenal, and is therefore associated with patterns of contemplation, deliberation, and/or position-taking on the issues of the day.[36] News is the currency of public life, molding the public's political actions and expectations. Repertoires of news reporting and information presentation reflect the styles and rules of public engagement in the societies in which they are embedded. Schudson's culturological approach to journalism positions it in the larger cultural contexts, the societal fields of action and meaning in which it is undertaken. Despite being a profession, journalism cannot be detached from where its practices are carried out in part because of the cultural dimension of work.[37] A political culture of news informs journalism's role within a given polity, the types of news people rely on most in political life, and how the news they receive and retain translates into social action. A news outlet that does not *fit* with an audience's political culture of news would fail to resonate.

As a *foreign* source of news, Al Jazeera's appeal is contingent on the target market's willingness to experience difference across identity-based lines. Cosmopolitans* are those most welcoming of transnational circuits of

---

* Calhoun noted that "[c]osmopolitanism seems to signal both the identity (and therefore unity) of all human beings despite their differences, and appreciation for and ability to feel at home among the actual differences among people and peoples" (2008, 444). A simple definition is Kant's third definitive article of a perpetual peace. Cosmopolitan hospitality, he wrote, is "the right of a stranger not to be treated with hostility when he arrives on someone else's territory" (1991, 105).

communication by definition; they expose themselves to new ideas and are open-minded about the world.[38] Nationalistic nativists are, by contrast, anti-cosmopolitan. They resolutely prefer the familiar and are predisposed to suspect the foreign. While cosmopolitan political culture facilitates the inflow of sources like Al Jazeera, nativist-nationalist orientations hinder its inward movement.

Despite the self-defined nature of this duality, the relationship between cosmopolitanism and interest in foreign news is not always one-to-one. Although the United States generally ranks high in cosmopolitanism, as measured by its aggregate, attitudinal openness to foreign ideas, products, services, and people, there is not a substantial market for foreign media, from cinema to news, outside of niche ethnic or linguistic immigrant communities.[39] This was consistent with what Arjun Appadurai noted about the disjunctures in the global cultural economy.[40] Countries differ in the degrees, directionalities, and types of flows they permit, seek and send out across unique "scapes," or dimensions of globalized traffic. Money, technology, political ideas, media, and people move in the world on distinct, albeit related, planes. This means that a country like Japan, for instance, might export technology and import ideologies, but resist certain classes of human flows, like migrants. Saudi Arabia, as another example, hosts many migrant laborers and religious travelers, receives foreign media, and actively invests overseas, but rejects outside ideologies and exports its own. This disjuncture explains why an otherwise cosmopolitan country is not an inviting recipient of foreign news media at a systemic level. When it comes to news flows, the US market is more export- than import-oriented.

It is safe to presume that the scale of audience required by traditional media distribution systems like cable television is unlikely due to the rarity of news cosmopolitanism. If demand is too sparse, it will not offset the risk presented by the residual, negative associations of Al Jazeera's brand stemming from the Bush administration. Certain segments of the population do seek out critical and international news reporting. Antiwar protestors on the left, for example, were excited by the presence of oppositional journalism in Afghanistan and Iraq. That President Bush and his cabinet scorned the channel only endeared their critics. Certain immigrant communities, especially those from the Middle East, Africa, and south and southeast Asia, hailed Al Jazeera's first channel as an English language source of news about their home countries. The network further attracted international news junkies, the most enthusiastic viewers. However, outside of highly motivated news-seekers, such as these groups, travelers, or businesspeople conducting overseas trade, Americans generally do not exhibit interest in foreign reporting. It appears immaterial to their lives, may seem complex, and tends to demand preexisting familiarity with issues and regions.[41] The conventional wisdom in traditional US news industries is that Americans in general have little interest in international news outside of conflict, disasters, and stories directly implicating the United States.[42] The domestic appetite for international affairs is diminutive compared with other advanced, industrialized countries.[†] It would therefore be no surprise that Shanto Iyengar and colleagues found that Americans in general score poorly on tests of international affairs knowledge compared with other prosperous, leading societies.[43]

American reliance on foreign sources of news in any medium is minute, even in the age of instant access to news via the communication technologies that constitute the spaces of flow. In terms of market share and the relevance in public debate, there is not a regular or noteworthy foreign news media presence. According to a Pew survey in 2014 (n = 2,901), very few Americans reported getting news from mainstream British news media.[44] Only 3% of Americans said they received any news on government and politics from British publications like *The Economist* and *The Guardian*. Many more, 17%, reported obtaining news from the BBC, though a quarter of the respondents never heard of the famed British broadcaster. This figure of consumption behavior appears inflated given that BBC World News was not widely available on television, nor did it have a regular Internet livestream. The number likely reflects basic familiarity. Only 4% of respondents in that survey reported getting news from AJAM. By contrast, American news outlets like CNN (44%), Fox News (39%), and MSNBC (27%) were more frequently cited by the survey-takers, revealing the wide gap between domestic and imported televisual news.

As opposed to cosmopolitanism and indifference, nativistic brands of nationalism show at the most extreme end xenophobia, or antipathy to the foreign. This deep opposition to people or entities is simply "on the basis of their 'foreignness.'"[45] There is a striking tradition of nativism in US history despite the country's immigrant history.[‡] Inward-looking sociopolitical currents hostile to perceived outsiders intensified in the American public sphere post-9/11. They took shape in expressions of Islamophobia. This active aversion to Islam and Muslims results in patterns of discrimination, furthers misrepresentation, and recycles the exclusionary impulses of yesteryear.[46] Islamophobia does not take Muslim people, concepts, or institutions at face value. It espouses suspicion that "Muslims, even the ones who live here with us, as us, are really them."[47] Such views project Al Jazeera in similar conspiratorial light. Some who objected to the

---

[†] Survey research shows Americans prefer soft news to international and hard news (Bennett 2001); some argue that they still learn from soft news (Baum 2003). In self-report surveys, Americans do say they tune in to foreign affairs news. However, self-reported watching by American survey respondents tends to be inconsistent with their chronically low scores on international affairs knowledge (Tewksbury 2003; Bennett et al. 1996).

[‡] John Higham, a historian whose work on nativism looked at the years between 1860 and 1925, described nativism more broadly as an "anti-foreign spirit" (2002, xi), a deep running "habit of mind" in the American past, one that mirrored our national anxieties and marked out the bounds of our tolerance" (2002, xi).

network being in the country believed it to be a translator of Al Qaeda propaganda that communicated secret signals to operatives, for example.

A full year before Al Jazeera English launched, it was apparent that conservative advocacy groups and a fearful public would campaign against the coming English channel.[48] Hostility to AJE found multiple expressions: pressure on satellite and cable carriers, lawsuits, and petitions. Conservative media watchdog groups held events that framed the news network as a progenitor of terrorism.[49] Cliff Kincaid of the national watchdog group, Accuracy in Media, led the charge. Framing AJE as "terror television," he organized call-ins and letter-writing campaigns to lobby cable companies and contemplated legal strategies to ensure public tax dollars were not spent to carry AJE in the country. The group's website hailed it as an Al Qaeda mouthpiece that incited against Americans and was responsible for the deaths of American soldiers by "radicalizing Muslims abroad to make Americans into terrorist targets."[50] He went on to ask whether "its impact in America itself would be any different?"—meaning AJE will "further stir up and inflame the Arabs and Muslims inside the U.S." Accuracy in Media called attention to AJE's distribution efforts. In materials promoting a 20-minute video about Al Jazeera, it asked rhetorically, "Do you want your cable or satellite subscription dollars to finance terrorist propaganda?" The group posted contact information for the companies and called on them not to "help to provide Al-Jazeera English the audience and the exposure that they seek" because "America is at war with radical Islam." Former AJE news presenter Dave Marash suggested this "right-wing agitation" harmed the channel materially:

> A well-watered "grass-roots campaign" apparently convinced some cable-system operators they would be risking their reputations, not to mention taking on a lot of public criticism, if they offered us to their customers.[51]

This public opposition, he believed, followed cues from the "blatant hostility of the Bush Administration, particularly former Defense Secretary Donald Rumsfeld's incessant attacks."[52]

The political rhetoric and campaigns had an impact. Early on, according to a cable trade publication, "several carriage deals were scuttled" because "special interest groups mobilized protests" based on "misconceptions about the channel, such as that it was an anti-Israel propaganda tool that aired Al Qaeda videos of beheadings."[53] Someone privy to distribution negotiations corroborated that carrier reluctance was due to the fear of protest. An independent specialist in media distribution who worked on behalf of AJE, Cathy Rasenberger, said that cable company decision-makers indicated their fear of controversy presented too much liability. One executive told her: "We personally might watch it, but we can't risk picketers."[54] The combined fear of nativistic and Islamophobic backlash as well as the conventional presumption of Americans as disinterested in international news therefore influenced the availability of AJ on American televisions. These weighed more heavily in carriers' calculus than did public good considerations, such as promoting education and international awareness. This prioritization is the result of the peculiarly commercial political economy of the distribution industry. However, the economic orientation of the network itself was also a factor.

THE POLITICAL ECONOMIES OF AL JAZEERA AND THE AMERICAN TELEVISION DISTRIBUTION INDUSTRY

Examining Al Jazeera's passage into the United States through the lens of political economy reveals a major hurdle to market success—namely the disparate logics of an essentially nonprofit news organization and a highly commercial TV distribution industry. Political economy research on media focuses on "the social relations, particularly the power relations, that mutually constitute the production, distribution, and consumption of ... communication resources."[55] Such an emphasis elucidates the systematic rationales, policies, and resultant criteria that guide allocative decisions by institutions and individuals. This power to allocate resources such as media distribution agreements is simultaneously economic and political, and a demonstration of gatekeeping power.

Al Jazeera: "A Hybrid Private and Commercialized State Enterprise"

In terms of its governance and authorities, Al Jazeera is more like a state, public broadcaster than a private, commercial, profit-maximizing company. The news divisions do not define their advantages or objectives commercially, in terms of advertising, subscriptions, or other revenue streams. Al Jazeera does, however, attempt to generate income outside of government grants and claims it aspires to financial independence; it is what Boyd-Barrett and Xie described as "a hybrid private and commercialized state enterprise."[56] News is a loss-leader for the Media Network, meaning it costs much more money than it makes. The Arabic news channel was originally founded with the Emir Hamad bin Khalifa Al Thani's five-year, $150 million loan under the belief that it would become independently viable by 2001. There was no repayment, making its start-up funding more like a grant than a loan; and subsequent government grants subsidized the network's operations and expansion because it never became profitable. The emir dedicated vast sums of money to building AJ up and out, drawing on the largesse derived from the small country's bountiful supply of energy resources, especially natural gas (Qatar is one of the richest countries in the world on a per capita basis). The network does not have a strong revenue stream from running commercials. For years, advertisers avoided the Arabic channel out of fear of upsetting Saudi Arabia, a regional power that was unhappy with both the coup that put Emir Hamad bin Khalifa Al Thani into power in 1995 and the upstart news channel he founded. It offered the sponsor some value.

The primary purpose of the network was not business, but influence. The news channel helped the new emir assert Qatari autonomy from the Saudi sphere of influence in the Gulf, including its media power.[57] Mohamed Zayani wrote that the small kingdom "was keen on getting out of its shadow" to claim "a somewhat independent voice." While it sought to do this through traditional diplomacy, Al Jazeera gave Qatar a prominence greater than "its size, military power and economic strength" could bestow.[58] The Arabic channel's early coverage of Saudi Arabia led the country to recall its ambassador for several years in the early 2000s, though he returned in 2008.[59]

During the Afghanistan and Iraq wars, the network caused Qatar diplomatic tension with the United States, which considered its vigorous, oppositional reporting biased and damaging. This could be interpreted cynically: perhaps Al Jazeera's oppositional coverage served to buffer Qatar from the popular Arab resentment due to Qatar's hosting of operational sites in the United States' war efforts. The small gulf country hosted the US military's central command (Centcom) forward headquarters at the US military base, Camp As Sayliyah, in Doha (since moved to Al Udeid Air Base); it was one place in which they orchestrated the 2003 Iraq invasion.[60] Al Jazeera was famously critical of the same war. Writing in the early 2000s, Olivier Da Lage considered Al Jazeera not a direct instrument of Qatari foreign policy—its political discourse was not Qatari foreign policy positions, for example—but it seemed part of an overall ambiguous balancing act that matched Qatar's position in the region.[61] Qatar did not take responsibility for AJ's coverage when it caused them issues with other countries. Qatari officials responded that the media network was independent to report as it wished, something the complainers found incredulous because it was a monarchy where formal checks on power are limited.[62]

Qatari sponsorship was indispensable to Al Jazeera's US enterprises. As a well-funded conglomerate, AJ's services enjoyed access to a level of resources that US news media organizations envy. Al Jazeera devoted significant capital to expanding its international reporting network while US companies cut back. Al Jazeera English enjoyed twice as many bureaus as CNN, for example.[63] Due to its funding, many of AJE's reporters could cover the world with their own standards of newsworthiness as a guide, as opposed to chasing the ratings—the standard for its US TV news competitors.

On the other hand, there were disadvantages. Having a state sponsor involves at the very least unspoken pressure to stay in the good graces of funders with well-known interests and sensitivities. Qatar's governance leans more toward Sparks's "authoritarian corporatist" model of state–business relations. In terms of media, it lacks the legal protections and formalized checks inherent to the democratic media model Hallin and Mancini identified.[64] Al Jazeera is not overseen by the domestic, state broadcaster, Qatar General Broadcasting and Television Corporation, and is not subject to the same censorious regime. The network has its own governing board, although some of the members were officials and the founding chair is a member of the ruling family. That does not make it formally independent, even if it was given breathing space to operate relatively freely at given points in its history. Al Jazeera was intended to have a degree of independence to report critically on other countries and thereby compete regionally. That remit was why the Arabic channel could be revolutionary in its range of competing views, giving airtime to dissenters and shattering taboos.[65] It was the first Arabic-language TV news network to really feature opposing viewpoints on political matters that contravened almost every government's positions.

Over time, however, it became more difficult for the Arabic channel to maintain that it was truly independent. Qatari foreign policy appeared to steer coverage, and it selectively lost its boisterous commitment to challenging power. During the Arab Spring coverage, the Arabic newsroom's dynamic ideological diversity dissipated, as staff with secular, leftist leanings departed the channel—the regional divisions echoed in the newsroom. This, critics claimed, left it with a more Islamist bent. Hafez al-Mirazi, the former Washington bureau chief, lamented Al Jazeera's loss of standing in the region as it "no longer represents both sides of the argument in the Arab world."[66]

Even before then, the US government's representatives in Qatar felt that Al Jazeera's reporting was subject to political negotiation. A 2009 State Department cable alleged that Qatar employed AJ coverage as "a bargaining tool to repair relationships with other countries, particularly those soured by al-Jazeera's broadcasts, including the United States."[67] The US ambassador under Obama, Joseph LeBaron, also wrote in a 2010 cable that Qatar's Prime Minister (and Foreign Minister) Hamad bin Jassim Al Thani "offered during his visit to Washington in January to send members of Al Jazeera's board of directors and management to Washington to engage with U.S. officials on Al Jazeera's coverage." What makes this report somewhat credible, as opposed to the Bush administration's protestations, was that he was not necessarily criticizing this. He welcomed it as an opportunity and encouraged making AJ's coverage the topic of bilateral discussion, as it was for other countries.[68] This followed years of American scrutiny on the channel; the State Department and other American officials frequently lobbied the channel about content they found disagreeable or unprofessional.

Did such internal, Qatari pressures come into play with the English channels? Few employees of the English language services cited overt or direct pressure from Qatar's government. The perception of many was that its foreign ministry was far more concerned with the Arabic channel and paid the English services little attention. Reports of such interventions were rare. In 2013, Tony Burman said that in the two years he was AJE's managing director, 2008–2010, "I never sensed any involvement by Qatar's government in our journalism." He said, by contrast, he "found the Canadian government more meddlesome" when he was that head of the national public broadcaster's *CBC News*.[69]

The question of AJE's bias toward Qatar was brought up after the country was controversially awarded the World Cup by FIFA at the end of 2010. This put more scrutiny on Qatar's antiquated, harsh, and widely condemned labor practices. *The Guardian* depicted the guest workers as slaves, for example.[70] Al Jazeera English, by contrast, treaded carefully, covering the labor mistreatment sporadically in small doses, even as the world's attention shifted to this problem in the channel's backyard. Before the World Cup announcement, AJE could have reasonably claimed to have given it more attention than other news channels.

There were multiple published accounts of editorial decisions that hinted at the presence of political considerations. In a case reported by *The Guardian*, AJE's director of news made sure the Qatari emir's UN speech was featured upfront in reporting on the debate over Syria at the international body.[71] There were controversies over website op-eds that were pulled or geo-blocked. One about the shared interests of Zionists and Europe's anti-Semites was removed to avoid controversy in the United States, but then was reposted after a backlash.[72] On another occasion, Saudi Arabia pressed AJ to remove an op-ed from AJAM's website; the network geo-blocked it so it could not be accessed directly outside of the United States.[73] The minefield of the gulf's regional politics did not always preclude Al Jazeera English from hard-hitting, controversial reporting. Its award-winning documentary about the Bahrain uprising in 2011, *Shouting in the Dark*, was the most powerful depiction of the protests and angered the country's monarchy. The journalist who made it, May Ying Welsh, said the network came under "huge pressure" to cancel the program and remove it from the website. Its impact may have been limited as a result. It only broadcast once after the neighboring government formally complained to Qatar, but it is still available online. The program did not air on the Arabic channel. The network responded by inviting Bahrain to respond on other AJE shows.[74]

Al Jazeera English came under criticism by a former reporter for what he alleged was partisan bias and irresponsibility in its conduct. Egypt's prosecution of three AJE journalists for reporting in the country without a license raised several questions about the network's agenda. One of the journalists, Mohamed Fahmy, penned an op-ed in the *New York Times* harshly criticizing AJE and attributing its reporting to Qatari interests:[75]

> The network knowingly antagonized the Egyptian authorities by defy-
> ing a court-ordered ban on its Arabic-language service. Behind that,
> I believe, was the desire of the Qatari royal family to meddle in Egypt's
> internal affairs. While Al Jazeera's Doha executives used the Cairo

bureau of Al Jazeera English to give their scheme a veneer of inter-national respectability, they made us unwitting pawns in Qatar's geopolitical game.

This criticism must be tempered by the fact that he wrote it after a particu-larly aggressive Egyptian prosecution that raised objections from various rights groups. He had been sentenced to three years in prison in June 2014 after a trial that was "widely condemned," according to the BBC.[76]

Fahmy's critique of AJE, however, missed the subtleties of sponsor bias. Believing the network to be hypocritical, he predicted that a Qatari poet's imprisonment would not be "highlighted on Al Jazeera's outlets anytime soon."[77] Mohammed al-Ajami was sentenced to life in prison for criticizing the emir in a poem (he was pardoned in 2016). A search on AJE's website and YouTube page revealed two video reports and an online article in early 2013.[78] They were there, perhaps not "highlighted," and they were relatively tepid, short, and came months after the BBC and CNN covered the case. The bias shows in the restrained tenor of coverage. A much more prevalent issue than outright control from the top is self-censorship to avoid upsetting the heads of the government or Qatari elite. This occurs given the lack of formal protections for the network and its unguaranteed stream of funding. Multiple interviewees from the English-language services felt the need to take extra care with sensi-tive areas relating to Qatari domestic and foreign policy to avoid any potential scrutiny from the state backers.

Furthermore, there is a paradoxical disadvantage of being well funded. While deep pockets were necessary to achieve the level of production quality and reportorial resources to stand out in a crowded field, the luxury of being impervious to market demands for revenue maximization and audience appeal relaxed the pressure on AJE to tailor itself to the tastes of mass audiences. Since its funding was somewhat detached from its performance, it was not essential to compete desperately for audience share. Its wealth gave it the comfort of being uncompromising in its journalism—to cover underreported areas and issues critically—to the point of being anti-commercial. This and the uncertain lines of editorial pressure often meant that AJ's services could not fully compete in the American television market.

More importantly, AJE's mission as a quasi–public service broadcaster made it incompatible with the primary gatekeeping industry of TV and satellite car-riage. Al Anstey, who was managing director at Al Jazeera English before moving to head AJAM, noted, "it's not about revenue for us; it's about getting our jour-nalism to as many people as possible."[79] The largest US cable companies do not intrinsically value that. They calculate distribution decisions based on revenue potential, marketing aims, and public relations outcomes: narrow self-interest.

As an AJE staff member observed, the TV service providers are "commercially obligated to make a profit," but the network "believe[d] that everyone has the right to access information. It shouldn't only be for the elite or people who can afford it. So we will be making our content freely available as much as we can."[80] An AJE executive described this gap as a hurdle in reaching agreements with the distributors. He described their attitude as "Give me a business plan that will make money or I don't want to meet with AJ." This, he felt, was one of "the biggest obstacles" in the US market.[81] The political-economic structure of the television carriage industry was therefore a deterrent to AJ's subsidiaries, but why and how?

The Political Economy of US TV Distribution Industries

When Al Jazeera English entered the United States in 2006, it immediately began competing in two related media markets. The first was for distribution. Cable and satellite carriers select which channels to offer from a wide array of programmers, who in effect compete for this finite resource of carriage since only a set number of channels are available. The second market is for viewers, the audience itself. People have many channels to choose among, yet they only possess limited time and attention. In the traditional television landscape, success in the second market is dependent on success in the first. Of course, distribution is only about availability to the public, but it does not necessarily guarantee anyone will watch. Distribution is necessary but insufficient on its own for drawing a viewership.

Al Jazeera English's first problem was in the distributional market. In the lead-up to the channel's launch in 2006, Comcast, DISH Network, and DirecTV had plans to carry AJE in select markets. They cancelled them unexpectedly for unexplained reasons.[82] No major deals were forthcoming when the channel went live. Due to the lack of agreements with the satellite and cable companies, AJE never had a chance to really compete for mainstream, national TV audiences. Over time, it gained some contracts in small markets like Toledo, OH, and Burlington, VT, and indirectly through two re-transmission arrangements with programmers in major markets like Washington, DC, and New York. Direct agreements with the largest cable companies proved elusive. After six years of AJE's efforts, the network could only claim to be available in 4 to 4.5 million households, or 4% of the country.[83]

Television distribution in the United States is dominated by private companies, Comcast, Time Warner, Charter, Verizon, AT&T, DirecTV, and Dish Network. Cable providers control more than 70% of the television services markets in most local communities.[84] At the national scale, the cable industry can be said to be oligopolistic, meaning a few firms control the largest share of the market.[85] In the early 2000s, concentration among mass media firms, including cable, only increased, thanks in part to governmental deregulation of the cable industry.[86] The four largest multiple system operators (MSOs) served three of every four households and drew in 80% of the revenues.[87] Despite governmental requirements that cable TV carriers offer certain must-carry channels, including local and Public, Educational, and Government (PEG) stations, they enjoy broad discretion over programming. Decision-making criteria for other channels are the companies' prerogatives. As publicly traded companies, they tend to be risk averse, especially when the payout appears limited.

The underlying profit-maximization rationale of American cable distribution can be juxtaposed with systems in other countries that are mandated to promote diversity, education, and the public interest.[88] A team of researchers found that "market-based" systems like the United States' tended to offer less international news than did "public service-oriented" ones.[89] The profit motive incentivizes soft news and entertainment over hard news, especially if it is foreign-produced. Phil Lawrie, AJE's former director of distribution, pointed out that foreign news channels "historically found it difficult to catch the eye of the cable executive" looking for a "hard-core return on investment."[90] In a market-oriented distribution system like the United States', offerings are oriented toward pleasing popular tastes rather than promoting the public good, such as informing citizenry. This explains why AJE gained greater distribution in countries with public service–oriented cable systems, like the United Kingdom, Ireland, and Canada.[91] An early US cable operator that picked up AJE was one of the few municipal publicly funded systems fashioned after the public model: Burlington Telecom in Vermont, which the socialist senator and 2016 presidential hopeful Bernie Sanders worked to establish when he was mayor of the city.[92]

The distribution industry's conventional wisdom was stacked against AJ. Cable and satellite companies generally consider TV news an already saturated market. Slots for new news channels are limited despite the growing total number. Between 1998 and 2008 the average cable household saw a rise from around 60 channels to 130.[93] As Colin Lawrence, BBC World News' commercial director, observed, "with a 200-channel universe and the limited available capacity that brings, not to mention the numerous US news channels, the United States is a particularly tough market."[94] From the perspective of distribution companies, AJE offered niche potential.[95] Such channels are more likely to be relegated to premium subscription packages or to add-on bundles. This in effect limits their potential audience size and decreases the probability that viewers accidentally discover them. Some carriers moved AJE off of basic cable packages to mitigate backlash. Burlington Telecom, for example, transferred AJE from basic cable to a premium package in response to customer complaints and an organized campaign to have the channel taken off air, reducing its maximum number of potential viewers.[96]

The primary US cable networks Fox News, CNN, and MSNBC are basic cable channels and therefore able to attract large audiences. Al Jazeera English wanted to be placed next to these news channels on cable and satellite lineups, to be present among the range of mainstream news providers. To make it economically viable, AJE offered its signal to carriers for free. It granted Time Warner Cable, for example, a "hunting license" that gave TWC the option to carry AJE on any of its local systems without any charges and the right to terminate carriage for any reason.[97] However, carriers see their finite slots as real estate. The scarcity of channels gives them value. Offering AJE entailed the opportunity cost of forgone profit from another, more profitable channel.

The main US TV distributors share a commercial basis with the prevailing cable news programmers, giving the latter a further strategic compatibility AJE lacked. The network did not operate according to the prevailing business logic of the news media industry. This led to tangible incongruences. As an executive producer for AJE and then AJAM Bob Wheelock said: "To broadcast in the United States with the cable distributors, we (AJE) actually have to run commercials."[98] The divergence in missions is so vast that AJE "tried to negotiate down the amount of commercial minutes we have to run," he said. The channel only occasionally ran advertisements and slotted little time for local commercials, one of the revenue sources for local cable franchises. This reduced their incentive to carry AJ's channels. Since AJE was non-commercial and was dedicated to providing one signal for the entire world, it did not accommodate the imperatives of the US TV carriage industry. Furthermore, this disinterest in commercials made AJE appear even less promising to Americans. As one staff member pointed out, "if there are not commercials on your screen you don't look profitable" and will not be taken as credible.[99]

Given the extra risk of carrying Al Jazeera English, the cap on advertising revenue, and the improbability of AJE attracting new subscribers, was there any other way to entice carriage deals? As had been done in the past, a programmer aspiring for distribution could pay carriers to offer them. When Fox News launched in 1996, it spent $300 million dollars in payments to carriers just to be on their channel lineups.[100] From the start, it was available in only 17 million homes, and absent from New York and Los Angeles. Once Fox News garnered impressive ratings, it renegotiated agreements to demand fees from the cable companies. For a controversial company, such payment could be a form of insurance against the risks of backlash from upset subscribers and picketers. Al Jazeera English's executives did not accept that, in the words of a TV executive, "in the U.S. market you have to pay to play."[101] A network chief said in 2011 that AJE was not willing to compensate carriers for beaming the channel.[102] There were some mixed messages about this, however. A few years prior, the director-general of the network, Wadah Khanfar, told the US ambassador to Qatar that they were willing to pay for carriage but that the distributors were still afraid to strike deals due to the risk of public disapproval.[§] It is probable distributors would demand substantial payments. Al Jazeera presented a very different type of liability and much less profit potential than did Fox News. Commercial cable and satellite companies would refuse the hazard of a brand with little economic upside.

In this regard, having a deep-pocketed sponsor like Qatar could be a surprising disadvantage since it would raise distributors' expectations that they could extract exorbitant carriage fees, making them take a more extreme bargaining position. Al Jazeera English, for its part, would want to avoid paying one carrier for distribution since it would encourage others to demand the same if word got out. Al Jazeera English insisted that free re-transmission was its default position. Phil Lawrie, AJE's former distribution head, said in 2009 that AJE would like to reach "a turning point" by going "from being carried for free to securing a fair and reasonable fee," but he added that "our aims are not economic or commercial but securing distribution."[103]

Were carrier anxieties about controversy unfounded? One of the first of the cable companies that offered AJE faced a public backlash—showing how contentious cultural politics alarmed TV distributors. The Toledo-based Buckeye CableSystem serves a northern Ohio customer base that includes 150,000 subscribers.[104] After picking up the channel, it faced angry customers and a campaign calling for AJE's removal. Letters to the editor exhorted Buckeye subscribers to end their patronage in protest.[105] The *Sandusky Register* published complaints about the channel's availability.[106] The national conservative media advocacy group Accuracy in Media (AIM) put out a statement saying the decision showed a "callous disregard for the lives of American citizens during a time of war."[107] The decision to carry may have been good business sense for them given the area's large Arab and Muslim community, but it could be ascribed to the personal predilections of its owner, the local media magnate, Allan Block, who took an interest in world affairs and sought diverse sources of news himself.[108] For good measure, the company's vice president of sales and marketing screened AJE before making it available and found it to be "impartial, independent, and objective," and therefore an "important information source to provide our viewers."[109] Buckeye CableSystem refused to drop the channel. Despite the negative reactions, the cable provider did not appear to suffer greatly as a result. Buckeye's own employees suggested that a year on, many subscribers were happy to have AJE on air.[110] This was an anomaly due to this one operator's peculiar management. The rest of the industry only sees this as a risk, without expecting much financial benefit given the improbability of profitability.[111] The

<hr>

[§] In a 2008 cable, then-US ambassador Joseph LeBaron wrote that "Khanfar shared that AJ was willing to pay for access, but that all the major providers had declined 'for fear of being pursued legally by groups that think we support terrorism'" ("Al Jazeera Tells Glassman . . ." 2008).

commercial logic was therefore a hurdle to the sort of news product and brand AJE represented, thanks both to the minimal demand stemming from popular indifference to international news and the threat of nativistic opposition to the channel.

The Changing Technologies of TV Distribution

This procession of AJ's channels occurred as the mechanism of TV service delivery was transforming technologically. Viewers had been slowly abandoning cable and satellite companies, whose subscription packages were too expensive and inefficient since they included channel bundling. This meant subscribers paid for channels they had no desire to ever watch. Alternatively, Internet platforms like Netflix, Hulu Plus, and Amazon Prime offered access to already-ran programs with lower subscription prices or pay-per-view pricing. Over-the-top (OTT) technologies, such as Roku and Apple TV, were another alternative, and they allowed live and on-demand viewing of individually selected channels offered as applications on these devices. While the OTT carriers could not offer all the programmers because of exclusive deals with the cable and satellite companies, offering channels on an à la carte basis made them an attractive substitute for traditional cable and satellite bundles. These new models of television viewing allow some programmers like HBO to sell direct subscriptions, so they can be accessed via Internet-connected televisions, mobile devices, and personal computers. The traditional TV providers are concerned by programmers and cord-cutters alike leaving them for these new online services. The number of cable and TV subscribers used to go up each year, but now was falling annually.[112] A 2014 survey estimated half of all American households watched video through OTT means.[113] The providers, then, came under pressure to transition from bundled cable and satellite services to more pluralistic, flexible viewing options that give consumers a greater number of choices. The basic model of cable and satellite TV was evolving just as Al Jazeera was determined to gain the antiquated sort of distribution.

Al Jazeera's services in the United States were at both ends of this distributional technology curve. Al Jazeera English's failure to gain cable carriage forced it to adapt to Internet distribution early. As part of its goal of being available to as many people as possible, AJE provided its signal for free via a 24-hour livestream on its website starting in 2009 and as a YouTube channel in 2011. It rolled out mobile and Internet TV apps, and was carried by third-party apps. Instead of continuing to exploit the Internet as its main means of distribution and slowly expanding AJE's reach, the network doubled down on the traditional routes of TV distribution by purchasing Current TV. With Al Jazeera America's launch, the network found a very expensive end-around to the refusal of carriers to offer AJE. The half-a-billion-dollar purchase entitled them to most of Current TV's preexisting distribution deals, putting the new channel in "more than

60 million homes," according to the network. Al Jazeera pulled AJE out of the US news market by geo-blocking its online videos and streams so that US-based viewers could not watch it directly over the Internet. Al Jazeera's cable gambit seemed ill timed; it took place just as the industry's basic distribution model was offering ever more channels to a declining number of subscribers, making the mass audience even more elusive even for those channels that gained wide distribution.** A television news analyst noted the "irony" of the purchase: "the great heyday" of the "cable news operation(s)" had already passed.[114] Amanda Lotz described it as the shift from the "push" era of network era to the "pull" of post-network pluralism. The digitization of TV led to channel proliferation, meaning they had to compete more to entice viewers.[115]

On the other end of the televisual distribution curve, AJ+ embraced distributional technologies. AJ+ published directly through its own app for mobile devices, and via third-party platforms like YouTube, Facebook, Instagram, and Twitter. AJ+ is a digital native creation, rather than being a TV-first operation trying to adapt to the Internet, simply re-editing and packaging broadcast content. AJ+'s formats and videos were created for mobile and social media end-users. It does not broadcast a livestream signal. Instead, it offers on-demand clips targeting globally minded, progressive millennials through the sorts of delivery platforms they use for news and social interaction.

This technological transition in media delivery from traditional cable and satellite carriage to online means suggests a shift in industrial gatekeepers. How does this alter the political economy equation? Platforms like Facebook, Twitter, and YouTube are also profit-seeking. However, advertising revenue is derived differently than with cable and satellite TV companies. Traditional carriers were incentivized to limit the number of channels, giving them greater curatorial power over their real estate, delivering larger audiences to the programmers and therefore growing advertising revenues. However, the tech platforms seek scale, more publishers and users to attract more visits, which increases impression or click-based advertising revenue; they also monetize users differently, providing them free use while collecting their personal data for marketing purposes and exposing them to advertising. The advertising model of tech platforms compels them to maximize programmers/publishers, unlike traditional TV distributors that relied on artificial scarcities to build the most value and keep subscription prices down. Still, the Internet-based platforms are not neutral. Over time, they build in more editorial functions, designing algorithmic means of filtering or ordering content, funneling posts, Tweets, and videos from certain producers to the top of social media users' timelines.

** This should not have been a surprise to channel executives. W. Russell Neuman anticipated the decline of the television mass audience in the late 1980s (1991).

Despite variations in their basic models, all media distributors operate at the "key locus of power and profit."[116] Overall, the tech platforms are more inclusive and friendly to diversity in content than are cable and satellite TV carriers from the perspective of an aspiring market entrant. It is not simply the difference between commercial and non-commercial political economies that matter here; technological capacities, incentives around scarcity, and the advertising models are germane. Al Jazeera's services were more successful deploying online distribution avenues. Since the network's core function was television, however, it emphasized traditional distribution early on to its detriment in the American market. The means of distribution that Al Jazeera sought were crucially important, especially in concert with all the other factors.

Conclusion

Al Jazeera's services had to navigate legacy political and cultural obstacles that made their market entry contested and controversial.[117] These structural impediments varied in terms of their geographic scales. The macro-level theories of international communication were hemispheric in scale, at the grand level of the global north/south. Equally broad, US–Arab relations beckon historic regional blocs, "civilizations" as Huntington called them, or Said's Occident/Orient. Not all the factors obstructing AJ's inflow were supra-national. The political economy of TV distribution varies comparatively at the national scale—thus, the United States differs from other countries—but also within, among cities to some extent (the limited number of municipally owned telecommunication providers for example). Political culture is even more fragmented within nations, even if national differences are broadly identifiable.

The space of flows may architecturally be more open and intense than in any prior era defined by new communication technology, but political bias, economic skews, and the inertia of old habits retain a potency to skew and block informational currency. Although widely championed, its seemingly unlimited capacity is ultimately a potentiality at best; actual flow will not result if audiences foreclose the possibility of reception for prejudicial reasons, if there are gatekeepers to viewing audiences who are inhospitable, and if the source of said flows is not constituted to compete properly in audience markets. As much enthusiasm over globalization as there is, media in motion are still not so ubiquitous as to shatter the traditional hurdles to the integration of distinct informational spheres.

The multilevel obstructions presented in this chapter fit within the book's larger story in this way. They fostered Al Jazeera's eventual locational arrangement with the three enterprises. Without obstacles tied to borders, a corporate strategy of undifferentiated, simple export from news headquarters in Doha would suffice. The persistence of the impediments outlined in this chapter led Al Jazeera, as an aspiring media in motion, to localize and differentiate for the idiosyncrasies of the American news market. This called for situating its services within media capitals—a maneuver that demonstrates the lasting import of the space of places, wherein locationality matters greatly. Surmounting the legacy barriers required the network invest in sophisticated subsidiaries based in cities that offered resources for the channels. The cities, starting with Washington, DC, then New York and San Francisco, were the network's gateways into the United States. The next chapter introduces, justifies, and explicates this *media ports of entry* concept, outlining what they as cities of industrial concentration do for, and to, foreign media setting up in them for entree into a new market.

2

Media Ports of Entry

Port cities often operated in between the grand empires or on
the margins of powerful states. They were places where the
exchange of goods, ideas, and cultural artifacts was the basis of
metropolitan prosperity. As modern publications, movies, and
sound recordings expanded the geographical range of popular
media, these cities were especially well situated to facilitate the
transversal circulation of cultural goods and influences.
—Michael Curtin.[1]

As a paradigm, place is physical, social, and intellectual; it
surrounds constructions like race, gender, or class because
they must stand or transpire somewhere, within a recognizable
place, though that place may range from the dateline of
journalism or the venue of law to the poet's pleasure in setting.
—William Howarth.[2]

Each port is a place.

Let's consider a counter-factual. Imagine that none of the obstacles outlined
in the previous chapter existed. In this scenario, the United States is both a
sender *and* receiver of historically multidirectional information flows. Its prevailing tastes in news media are open, characteristic of a generally cosmopolitan news culture. A robust public sphere demands high-quality international
reporting from foreign sources and seeks out rather than avoids dissonant perspectives. The political economy of the TV distribution industry is such that its
companies prioritize educational matter and diversity that enriches the public
life of the citizenry. If these were true, Al Jazeera would be able to simply export
its news products from Doha and still be relevant to a general audience. This is
the space of flows ideal. Since this is not the case, Al Jazeera had little choice but
to glocalize.

This hypothetical shows why obstacles necessitate a company dedicated to finding success in the US market to locate itself within the country; broadcasting from outside the country inwards is a non-starter. Market
obstructions to straightforward import require foreign firms to pursue diffuse

organizational expansion. This involves heavy in-market capital investiture. Foreign Direct Investment is a mode of market entry that occurs when "a corporation in one country establishes a business operation in another country, through setting up a new wholly-owned affiliate, or acquiring a local company, or forming a joint venture in the host economy."[3] Media companies employing this strategy build or purchase plants within the target markets and variably devolve operational control to in-market facilities. Not all media firms need to pursue an FDI strategy for all target markets. Poorer and smaller countries already tend to rely more on imports and are less likely to produce returns on FDI, for example.[4] If little adaptation of media products is required—for example, in countries with a shared language and culture—FDI is superfluous. *Simple export* would suffice.

Once a firm chooses to pursue a strategy of FDI, there are countless decisions it must make to enhance market accommodation: basic programming, hiring, internal policies, editorial, technological tools, set design, branding, and so on. There is one foundational, though easily overlooked, decision. In entering a large and sophisticated market, a firm must choose *where*, geographically, to position its new operations. Usually there are multiple, competing centers serving the same national or regional market. They are the capitals of politics, culture, television, publishing, technology, and commerce. In smaller countries such industrial centers may all be the same city if they exist at all. In such cases, the locational decision is a simple one. But where there are multiple options, media companies have to weigh numerous factors in a geographic calculus. Cities are of course more than just industrial sites; they are also social, cultural, and political baskets, and this also impacts foreign firms setting up facilities in these distant places. This chapter articulates more clearly this "ports of entry" framework for analyzing AJ's subsidiary operations in Washington, DC, New York City, and San Francisco as instances of glocalization.

The Book's Framework in Summary

This book's framework consists of the following interrelated planks.

- First, media industries tend to cluster in particular cities. Media companies are generally attracted to co-locating in agglomerated *media capitals* due to their economic, cultural, legal, and political advantages.
- Second, globalizing, multinational firms use media capitals as staging grounds through which they can best approach new markets if simple export is implausible. Media capitals are industrially organized to facilitate such in-market movement. In this way, media capitals function as *ports of entry*.

- Third, these media capitals are both *industrial sites* and *anthropological terrains* with unique characters, histories, and social, cultural, and political currents that differentiate them in total from other places.
- Fourth, both industrial logics and the anthropological terrains of media ports of entry inflect their market-entering firms and products. The industrial effect of the port function is to assimilate them to the larger market, while the anthropological terrain encourages the adoption of localized tastes, respectively, toward variegated forms of *domestication*.

This framework guides this study of how the Qatar-based media network came to function out of US cities and to what effect. This chapter proceeds by clarifying and expounding this as a place-centered approach to transnational and global news media.

Industrial Clustering

As counterintuitive as it may seem, companies that compete with each other often cluster.* Economic geography and industrial location theory identify clusters as "geographic concentrations of interconnected companies, specialized suppliers, service providers, firms in related industries, and associated institutions (e.g., universities, standards agencies, trade associations) in a particular field that compete but also cooperate."[5] Industrial clustering in central locations offers various benefits, such as lowered transportation and transaction costs, competition among contracting services, and attracting specialized labor pools. Research on clustering emphasizes the positive economic externalities of physical proximity. Clusters are path dependent since these externalities attract more firms, migration, and investment flows, making them ever more concentrated. Once clusters form and start growing, they tend to expand with greater complexity.[6] Locational clustering may be stronger among media industries, which have been shown to be more robust in measures such as employment growth and international competitiveness, than manufacturing clusters.[7]

Where clusters emerge may make perfect sense, such as being located at a commercial center or a natural seaport, but they could also result from commercial actors' arbitrary decisions, among other factors.[8] Those studying economic clusters, from the 19th-century Scottish business theorist Andrew Ure

---

* Economists from Alfred Marshall (1920) to Paul Krugman (1991, 1998) have studied economic agglomeration, among other geographic facets of economic activity. Marshall wrote about industrial districts and their path-dependencies as places of economic activity, which showed the importance of local economies in stimulating agglomeration.

to Harvard Business School's Michael Porter, identified locational factors such as access to energy resources, a sizable populace, proximity to a shipping infrastructure, storage facilities and markets, and creativity among local businessmen.[9] One media industry example shows how commercial actors' prerogatives can be determinant. The genesis of Hollywood as the center of American cinema exemplifies how the industry's progenitors weighed multiple factors. Michael Curtin explained that Hollywood, America's film industry, emerged in early 20th-century Los Angeles despite its "relative geographical isolation" as a result of other locational draws. The film companies were attracted by: warm but temperate weather, which allowed year-round outdoor shooting; remoteness, which helped studios "sequester and discipline" stars and avoid the social taboos and political distractions of New York; a freer, more libertarian legal regime; and, inexpensive real estate.[10]

One might expect that the rise of digital information and communication technologies (ICT) erodes clustering patterns. In the 1980s and 1990s, scholars and pundits hypothesized advances in technology would entail the "death of distance," the collapse of spatial difference in life and the economy due to intensified global interconnection.[11] This was expected to disentangle clustering, since access to instantaneous communication and the ease of transferring large amounts of data in non-physical formats would essentially diminish the efficiencies of co-location and advantages of proximity in physical collaboration and information-sharing. However, as David Morley observed, even the most networked of sectors in the space of flows, "cyber-industries" defy the hypothesized "de-territorialization of communications." The creators of the space of flows, technology companies, "tend to cluster in very particular places—such as Shoreditch in East London, and the 'CyberSentier' district in Paris."[12] Researchers of innovation and creativity stressed the importance of face-to-face interaction, socializing, and place-based lifestyle aspects like access to bars, coffee shops, and other attributes of cool cities.[13] It is clear that networks of producers are not free-floating in space; each "component in a production network—every firm, every economic function—is, quite literally, 'grounded' in specific locations."[14]

Media Capitals

Clusters of media industry have been studied under the term *media capitals*.[15] They, according to Curtin, are the cities or regions that serve as "powerful geographic centers" concentrating the "human, creative, and financial resources" composing the industrial fabric.[16] Media industry clusters "produce mediated content, such as motion pictures, television programmes/videos, broadcasts, audio recordings, books, newspapers, magazines, games, photography and designs, websites and mobile content for customers that are often based else-where."[17] Media firms that seek national, regional, or global audiences tend to gather in the same cities.[18] Such media capitals boost their resident companies' abilities to carry out their unique work, including originating, producing, and distributing content. They are sites at which firms develop relations with rev-enue sources, such as advertisers and distribution industries.[19]

Curtin discerned three principles to media capitals: First, "the logic of accu-mulation."[20] Firms tend to seek growth, which expands industries, and therefore enlarges media capitals. This can be traced to the capitalist tendency toward expansion. Profit-seeking enterprises seek to make their surplus capital pro-ductive through investment in new markets.[21] Economies of scale incentivize bigness because of realizable efficiencies—for example, larger media libraries that can be repurposed for multiple, new markets.[22] Growing firms also enhance media capitals. A conglomerate may grow its headquarters within a home media capital, while contributing to the buildup of other media capitals through strat-egies of foreign direct investment. Its investitures (capital as resources) gather and affix within these new locations, which further swells them as nodes in cir-cuits of international trade.[23] Like global cities, media capitals are networked.

It is not just a media company's financial resources that are mobile. The human resources of media industries are as well. Second, "trajectories of cre-ative migration" mark out media capitals as destinations for talented and skilled individuals seeking employment in particular media industries.[24] Media work is highly specialized, and firms require a deep pool of talent to draw on for labor. Given that many media companies operate on a project basis, they rely on countless temporary specialists at various phases of a project.[25] Clusters house complementary businesses and freelance hires that staff and support media projects, which then prefer to locate in media clusters.[26] For example, musicians prefer to live near television and film industries because of the opportunities for audio work.[27] Most media professionals prefer to be in media capitals where they have more potential upward mobility.[28]

Researchers have also identified social, cultural, and institutional factors behind the labor migration aspect of media clusters.[29] Creative people do not gather in places only for professional or economic reasons. While firms require "maintaining access to reservoirs of specialized labor," the talent often desire residence in places where creativity is celebrated and fostered.[30] Richard Florida noted that creative workers are drawn to tolerant cities that are diverse, cosmo-politan, and urbane.[31] They seek communities of similarly disposed people. The social factors of cluster economics should not be overlooked.[32] Gina Neff wrote that social relationships are indispensable to industrial inter-workings and that the business-related interactions that matter the most occur "outside of the for-mal boundaries of organizations and inside industrial social settings."[33] Creative labor's gravitation toward industrial sites only perpetuates media capitals' centrality, as firms will seek to locate where the labor pool gathers. Thus, the movement of people could be included as one of what Neff called "the micro-processes of locational logic." This suggests that "individual-level occurrences function to structure industrial location."[34]

Third, even if different media capitals are dominated by the same industries, whether cinema, television, or print, they do not generate homogenized content. As competing centers situated in diverse national and local cultures, they effectively signify variability in the "contours of socio-cultural variation." One could see how cities like "Cairo, Mumbai, Hollywood, and Hong Kong" invigorate different tastes and tendencies even in the same medium.[35] Media capitals help fashion products that are culturally proximate to the markets of audiences they are organized to reach. Cities of vying industries compete to be the primary gatekeepers of a given market and often project their centrality through claims to mastery over an area's target audience. This principle in particular is why the media capitals of Washington, DC, New York City, and San Francisco each sway AJ's three services differently.

Researchers have discerned compelling patterns of geographic centralization in media industries.[36] This growing body of literature catalogs cities and regions that qualify and propose various criteria.[37] Prominent American examples include Hollywood, Silicon Valley, and New York City. Some media capitals are based on a single medium, but often "economies of scope" also drive them to seed related cultural industries that coproduce/collaborate, such as music, television, and film.[38] Furthermore, some media capitals are more transnational than others. Miami emerged as a center for Spanish-language TV, music, and movie production. It houses firms reaching audiences throughout the Americas.[39] There are well-established and aspiring media capitals all around the world. Mumbai is the center of India's leading movie industry, Bollywood.[40] Hong Kong was the historical locus of Chinese cinema.[41] In Germany, Munich supplanted Berlin as the country's TV capital post–World War II.[42] There are countless other examples, such as Dubai, Johannesburg, Mexico City, Lagos, Madrid, and Singapore.

Conceptually, "media capital" productively weaves together "capital," in the sense of resources, "creativity, culture, and polity" through a sociological accounting of their "*spatial* logics."[43] As hubs, media capitals are more than just agglomerations, but are inherently suited to be transmitters of transnationally circulating media. They have pull-and-push leverage for media looking to enter new markets. The magnetism of media capitals is a centripetal force, while the distributional networks that emanate from them are centrifugal.[44] Economic geographers have long noted how "soft transactions or interdependencies" in industrial sites impact their "technological evolution" of local sectors.[45] Thus, particular media capitals attach to types of distributive technologies: network television in New York City, social media platforms in San Francisco, and cinema chains in Los Angeles are a few examples. Thus far, the research and theorizing on media clustering has not given as much attention to what such industrial centers do regarding resident, market-seeking firms.

Ports of Entry

Media capitals should be understood as cities where the space of flows interfaces with the space of places, to apply Castells's conceptual distinction.[46] Curtin wondered whether media scholars should place "more emphasis on the study of port cities, rather than the study of nations."[47] Many media capitals are built-up port cities, after all.[48] Just as a transportation network "is a spatial system of nodes and links over which the movement of cargo and passengers occurs," global media networks connect to target markets through the sorts of cities where production, packaging, and distributional processes take place.[49] Historically, ports were "places where the *exchange* of goods, ideas and cultural artifacts was the basis of metropolitan prosperity," and they expedited the "transversal circulation" of media goods.[50] Ports are both recipients of global processes and originators of productive processes. This book's adaption of "ports of entry" draws from the transportation reference.

The central contribution of this book is to recognize and describe how media capitals function as metaphoric *ports of entry* for multinational media companies seeking new markets. They act as what Aswin Punathambekar called "switching points" or Krätke and Taylor referred to as "local nodes" for media in transit.[51] Given the power of media capitals in respective national or regional markets, market-seeking firms seek them out naturally. As a thoroughfare, a media capital facilitates access to a particular territory of media consumption.[52] Media capitals benefit market entrants because they are organizationally attuned to the "national specificities related to language, consumer taste, and other cultural factors which created national entry barriers."[53] Globalizing media locate within media capitals to improve their chances at capturing shares of target markets. When they open branches, field offices, or production facilities in a foreign city, they are positioned to exploit multiple *port of entry* advantages:

1. *Clustered services.* Alfred Marshall noted in 1890 that service providers often cluster: "subsidiary trades grow up in the neighbourhood, supplying it with implements and materials, organizing its traffic."[54] The media ports bring together constituent firms, specialists, services, and personnel—the advanced producer services (APS) that Sassen recognized.[55] They help the foreign multinational generate, store, transport, translate, advertise, package, and market

media products that head toward the rest of the receiving country.[†] Proximity strengthens "linkages with suppliers, channels, and downstream industries," and due to clustering they tend to be available at lower cost and higher quality.[56]

2. *Hiring and staffing*. As industrial clusters, media ports of entry attract and offer employment prospects to large pools of labor. Staffing new operations with the best talent in media-related trades and professions, including on- and off-camera talent, requires being located where sufficient reservoirs of potential employees are already based, given the difficulties and expenses of moving people.[57] This brings about a constructive interchange within the institutional context: "local teams benefit from the network's global expertise," while "the latter takes advantage of their local knowledge."[58] Having specialists available to render a market legible can boost a firm's appeal.

3. *Learning*. Marshall detailed the ephemeral influence of industrial districts, where the "mysteries of the trade become no mysteries; but are as it were in the air." Even children assimilate the mysteries "unconsciously," he wrote.[59] Information accumulated in clustered industries can be accessed more easily if a firm is in or near the cluster.[60] Industrial conventional wisdoms are generated and fostered through professional face-to-face interactions, giving way to "buzz" about novel strategies.[61] Media capitals foster such exchanges through informal and formal mechanisms, including professional meetings, conventions, happy hours, trade association activity, personal networking, seminars, and continuing education courses.[62] Also, emulation of competitors, a form of learning, is augmented by co-location due to informal trade in secrets, casual discussion, rumors, and other face-to-face communications. Scott observed that "[p]lace-based communities" are both "foci of cultural labor" and "active hubs of social reproduction in which crucial cultural competencies are maintained and circulated."[63]

4. *Collaborations and partnerships*. Co-location enhances the opportunities to collaborate with other firms and organizations, and improves access to resources that can finance cooperative ventures.[†] Being in the same place as potential collaborators heightens the chance of cooperation. Such serendipity is structural. Whyte claims the city as the place that has the greatest "likelihood of *un*planned, informal encounters."[64] However, media ports are also arenas of deliberate, strategic relations, and host venues for industrial interactions, from conferences to happy hours.

[†] Mazzarella's (2003) work on the role of Indian advertising firms helping global companies customize and make more appealing their products for the growing Indian consumer base offers an example of native interlocutors. Even the most powerful western media companies rely on an array of local interlocutors to perform well in overseas markets.

[‡] Industrial concentration in a place encourages "recurrent collaboration and mutual interdependence of money and ideas" (Powell et al. 2002, 303).

5. *Competition.* A cluster intensifies competitive pressures from other firms. Staff feel "pride and the desire to look good" vis-à-vis their colleagues at other firms.[65] Competition may enhance peer effects, such as groupthink, but also encourages strategic differentiation—either way, firms actively adjust in response to competitors. Being co-located with rivals allows strategic mastery of the target market, facilitates talent poaching and raises the incentives to emulate and innovate.

6. *Sociopolitical acculturation.* Outside of commercial advantages, media capitals, particularly those located in political centers, help acclimate global media to the sociopolitical climates of the countries they enter. Government policies play a role in media capital formation, after all.[66] Political elite historically hold great sway over news media and governance.[67] A port of entry where political life is centered will find willing translators to help foreign firms adapt the local political grammars and mixes of ideological currents. Such capitals heighten firm awareness and accounting of the predominant politics of a market, lessening the risk of a firm violating its tenets or being marginalized within the range of political discourses.

7. *Legal-regulatory regimes.* Ports of entry are subject to legal and regulatory regimes, marked by both formal features and informal attributes (such as corruption or general litigiousness). Some media ports of entry operate with more/less strict intellectual property standards, press laws, or are subject to protectionist measures in trade that weaken the potential expansion through them. This presents firms with a calculus of opportunities and potential costs. Expert services in the media ports of entry help companies comply with the rules governing market access.

A port of entry is not just a culturally neutral gateway that benefits a resident media firm. As a theater of industrial dynamics, it assimilates foreign clients, modifying them. A port of entry possesses an industrial might that makes resident firms conform, reconstituting them according to the norms and conventions of industrial standards. Each of the industrial benefits listed above simultaneously exacts heterogeneous pressures of market assimilation. To provide examples: *Access to services* can create dependencies on native services, like contractors, which gives them outsized leverage. If the foreign form lacks the localized knowledge the contractor possesses, it hazards an asymmetric relationship. Locating near *large labor pools* improves staffing but also moves the character of the firm closer to that of a domestic equivalent. *Learning, collaboration, competition,* and *acculturation* all entail by definition assimilation effects. Falling under the jurisdictions of new *legal-regulatory regimes* can incur legal vulnerabilities and responsibilities that pressure the firm to conform to local standards. Ports of entry therefore domesticate media moving through them in their own ways—one of the primary points of this book.

The Domesticating Power of Media Ports of Entry

Ports of entry are by definition imbued with transnational connectivity, as places of encounter between foreign firms, domestic industries, and migrant laborers/media workers, including "expatriate" executives among others. Just like transportation ports, they are contact zones, where foreign and local cultures meet, undergo "friction," and produce the multifaceted "coproductions" that typify glocalization.[68] As global nexuses of industrial, institutional, and creative action, these cities are "multidimensional, intersecting, conflictual"—thus they may evade simple place classification or predictability.[69] Since such motion in people, goods, and services may be related to the commercial or industrial draw of the city, it necessarily alters the underlying character of the place, to the extent that such a reduction is even defensible. This complicates the secondary effect of place proposed by the media ports of entry framework, that a place has distinct characteristics that influence its residents.

The hyper-mobility of capital, cultures, and goods into and through cities expectedly compromises the distinction of their characters. Zygmunt Bauman characterized the fluid movement of everything in modern life as giving way to a "liquid modernity" where traditional structures and institutions break down.[70] Rapid flows have also seemingly reconstituted cities, or parts of them, as transnational, so that they exhibit qualities of being blandly cosmopolitan, marked by the generic template of corporate logos indicating safe familiarity. For the most connected classes, the globalized elite, their neighborhoods appear interchangeable, with the same types of stores, architecture, urban design, and, concomitantly, lifestyles.

Is the placeness of a city sacrificed by this fluidity? Doreen Massey constructively challenged the view that places are statically defined by essential characteristics. She argued places are inherently "extroverted." The "specificity" of place is not discoverable from "some long internalised history," but is composed by "a particular constellation of social relations, meeting and weaving together at a particular locus."[71] These inter-relations also occur over distances. From the perspective of a satellite in the sky, she wrote, cities are meeting places where social contacts, communication flows, and mobilities in the world come together. These currents are so substantial they can appear to overwhelm "what we happen to define for that moment as the place itself."[72] However, place is recoverable as a meaningful geographic category of social life, she argues. The following sections further defend the notion that media ports of entry are their own places in the anthropological sense, and that this further intersects with news media practices both pragmatically and subjectively to show how the locational choices of news agencies like Al Jazeera's are consequential.

ANTHROPOLOGICAL TERRAINS

A port of entry is a *lived place* in the anthropological sense. There are socio-cultural dimensions to cities that exist beyond the industrial milieu—sources of the variation Curtin raised.[73] Both the industrial and the larger social, cultural, and political tenors of ports of entry act upon and deeply guide foreign firms present in them. As Massey observed, "the global" is "locally produced," and global products such as media "are just as material, and real, as is the local embeddedness" that produces them.[74] We can identify in each of the cities a placeness that cannot simply be reduced to their industrial cores. This is captured by detecting anthropological characteristics of each city.

Beyond their industrial dimensions, then, media ports of entry are cities defined by distinct social, cultural, and political traits. The metropolitan cities that are media capitals have their own histories, local identities, and characterizable attributes—the sorts of factors that define them as *anthropological terrains*. While cities "are effectively nourished by strong electronic links to a wider world" through the space of flows, they "prize their differences from other places" and celebrate their own "local institutions . . . unique ambiences and customs."[75] They have their own intelligible social, cultural, and political topologies, even if they do not always come together as some simple, coherent whole. Cities, of course, always have more than one character. Anthropological fieldwork in the ethnographic tradition calls attention to the multiplicities within places as lived micro-terrains.[76] This sort of research empowered place by highlighting its inherent "multivocality," or diverse mix of voices shared by no other places.[77] For example, Bauman observed that parts of cities include places of exclusion for the poorest and minority communities (such as ghettoes), whereas other sections demand utter assimilationism (namely consumerist areas). Cities contain, as well, the sort of non-places that are transient, like hotels and airports, and "empty spaces," the marginal leftovers of the city as it was planned by those in power, the overlooked zones.[78] This book's presumption on place touching media firms is not a denial of this heterodoxy.

Media workers might be from or already integrated within the locality. They reveal their fit within a place through their evolving individual social practices, identities, and views. Environmental psychologists thought of place as a bundle of stimuli giving rise to an ecologically informed notion of self. Thus, "[p]hysical space" is more than essential to social practice, it is essential to self-identification.[79] Place is where socialization happens. Place-identity was initially understood a sort of medley of personal experiences, remembrances, sentiments, and sensibilities derived from place[80]—but it became more sophisticated over time, integrating concepts from other subfields, including cognitive psychology and taking on difficult questions like human agency over place.

How people come to know things about their world is deeply tied to place. As Raymond Williams wrote in the early 1960s, "[i]t is only in our own time and place that we can expect to know, in any substantial way, the general organization" of life.[81] Epistemologically, our deepest knowledge of a society is formed where we are now. Direct experience is emplaced. While we can seek knowledge of other times and places, these will always be abstraction absent "irrecoverable" elements.[82] Presence in a place is certainly not the only way to learn about it, but it provides a qualitatively different and arguably richer way of learning than through secondary sources, or what we encounter through screens from a distance.

Places signify political distinctions, as well. In the American context, we speak of the New England town hall tradition of direct democracy in small cities and towns. The notation of red state/blue state indicates partisan voting preferences; local districts have become more politically homogenous through gerrymandering, in which political parties redraw the borders of representative areas. Some cities are also known by their political orientations. Just as Dallas, TX, is associated with conservatism, Berkeley, CA, is renowned for left-wing politics. It could be that such places attract respective partisans, but they also reproduce similarly oriented denizens. A political sociology approach to place holds it out as a geographic unit where spatial processes (like general ideologies) meet individual and collective agency, producing an empirical, geographical variation in critical facets of political life analyzable from a place perspective.[83]

Places are of course not fixed or unchanging.[84] Asserting an essential, timeless character to a place is unsustainable. Furthermore, in describing the politics of a place, one must not be ensnared in exclusionary "localism" or mistake place as unitary in identity. Massey wanted the question "what does this place stand for?" to be one people have stake in answering, making it necessarily up for contention as a community should struggle to define itself.[85] Larger spatial processes are not determinant but are "coeval" in places—touching down in local sites.[86] The saying "all politics is local" captures this notion that macro-level phenomena are most perceptible in the immediate space of one's life. In the era of globalization, place has become an even more important arena for political life.[87] To the extent unique sociopolitical styles distinguish the cities that host media capitals, they constitute one basis for the peculiar place effects that differentiate media ports of entry.

Places are not just formative for cognition and politics. Tuan argued that there needed to be systematic inquiry on how human "affective ties" take form within material settings and local milieus.[88] Centrally concerned with the emotionality of place, he saw how feelings and sentiments bonded people to the immediate surroundings of their quotidian lives. Places cyclically "incarnate the experience and aspirations of people" while a place's residents embody aspects of where they live or are from.[89] Thus, attachment to place strengthens as people stay longer. Tuan's work inspired a humanistic geography that subordinated spatial processes to place as the primary container of social life, culture, and subjectivity. This view fell out of favor as the globalization paradigm entailed a greater emphasis on transnationalism, mobility, and distanciated relations. Henning explained that the proliferation of mediation in social relations has made possible a geography of life in which "people who feel a sense of belonging can live far away from each other, and people sharing the same neighborhood may not even talk to one another."[90] The central position of the space of flows in media studies has made this a common focus. However, the pendulum has swung too far in the direction of spatiality, as we have lost an appreciation for how face-to-face interactions and co-presence are still powerful shapers of who we are and what we do; and how media-making institutions work in place.

We can talk about places having characteristics distinct from their industrial components, while accepting them as diverse, multifaceted, and somewhat transnational themselves. These place attributes do unquestionably also touch on industrial practices, however. Applying the ports of entry framework to AJ's services is an assertion that anthropological place impacts media work. For news media, place matters because it shapes the pragmatic work of news reporting and production as well as subjectivity, or how its workers perceive the world around them.

LOCATION AND THE PRAGMATIC WORK OF NEWS

The decipherable symbols, signs, and resultant expressions that comprise news flows are the outcomes of productive practices by individuals and firms. The authors and editors are always set somewhere. This section zooms in on how place pragmatically renders resources that story origination, newsgathering, and production call upon. Many journalistic practices are situated locationally and therefore vary across places, reflecting their idiosyncratic attributes. As a disclaimer, it must be emphasized that placeness is not the sole defining factor of journalism. There are multiple journalistic contexts that matter, including group solidarity, standards and processes, the norms and identities of professional journalism, news agendas, demand-side characteristics, individual information producers' views, and organizational mandates, among others.[91] Not all of these vary greatly by place.

From a phenomenological perspective, the practices of journalism are emplaced. The professional resources journalists draw upon are very often artifacts of locationality. Heidegger saw "place-as-pragmatic"; it is the immediate "realm of worked-on things."[92] Television news programs and packages are such worked-on things. Place is "transformational" because it houses what is available "at hand" for those engaged in the work of media creation.[93] Journalism is essentially a pragmatic craft. It is action that relies upon, and is constrained by, the availability of limited resources, raw materials, to produce a timely product, a story.[94] Places differ in what original journalistic resources are available. Location thus shapes the practical work of reporters even if the advanced communication technologies have diminished the urgency of proximity. Informational work in general is bound within "space, time and social relations," thus putting information "into circulation" through the space of flows; but it begins with the meeting point of the three in local place.[95]

First, the most immediate context of where space, time, and social relations meet to touch journalism is in material edifices, the offices and buildings that house people at work. Rather than being annihilated by telework, these sites of production still matter for carrying out work flows, enforcing hierarchical positions and the normative order, and facilitating transparency and accountability.[96] Buildings both situate actual work, and are themselves communicative. They project images about their tenants, as prestigious and established, upstart or scrappy, or on the edge of failure if dilapidated, for example.[97] By housing and structuring work patterns, they influence organizational culture. Furthermore, buildings are apposite here because they most immediately emplace the work of journalists within a creative milieu and city at large.

Second, pools of ready-to-quote, "credible" sources tend to concentrate spatially in places.[98] Source relations are best maintained through personal, social interactions, and the trust it takes is sometimes best fostered through face-to-face exchange.[99] Sustained relationships between reporters and their sources are often premised on some sort of tacit quid pro quo, which takes an iterative series of interactions to manifest. Such access is crucial to gaining exclusive information. Proximity is not requisite, but makes more likely the emergence and maintenance of such a mutual, working interconnection. By the same token, distance could entail greater reliance on publicly available official sources. Those reporting from a different place often have to rely on a smaller range of nonexclusive official sources and could become even more dependent on them.[100]

The local fluctuation in source-journalist relations between provincial capitals can be seen in the variability of news access to public officials. Sub-national governmental organization, policies, and political culture vary in such ways that impact official–journalist relations. In China, for example, two investigative newspapers in Zhengzhou and Guangzhou diverged in how they developed in part because one of them was subject to greater local "bureaucratic centricity"; it therefore had to worry more about pleasing local authorities than did the other.[101] In some places, reporter–official relations relatively favor the news media.§ In the United States, media access to local and state governments varies

---

§ Tong (2013) also identified local market conditions as a factor. The more robust investigative newspaper he studied was subject to greater competition, which pushed it to be more adversarial with local government. Furthermore, social context, including cultural notions of authority, was a factor.

because the rules and customs of transparency do as well. Place matters for news media since how source and government relations are nurtured vary.

Third, the availability of a reporter's raw materials often varies locally. Governmental bodies and agencies, for example, routinely produce information useful to journalists, both through documents and press events.[102] Access to records collections, archives, libraries, and other holders of primary sources differ at the local level, especially because many still require on-location access. Despite efforts to enhance the provision of digital records, maintaining digital repositories is costly and labor-intensive.[103] Securing court documents is smoother and more simple in person at courts than from court websites, even those that do offer access to electronic records.

Fourth, for television news gatherers, access to visuals is essential. Brooker-Gross described how television news' "organizational imperative for visually attractive information" is a factor in where a station seeks to locate "headquarters, studios, news bureaus."[104] Presence makes it easier to secure original on-location footage, which is a premium for television. While cheapened air flight lowered the costs of deploying reporters, travel takes time and presents a competitive disadvantage next to those already on news scenes. Those working in a place furthermore know the locations better, which can qualitatively change how they cover the story and depict the settings. As an AJE executive producer noted, "there's agencies that will provide you the picture, but not the context, not the actual reporting" that can be best obtained from the ground.[105] One can tell when news organizations simply acquire visuals and then "voice it over in London, so it appears international."[106] There is no substitute for physical presence in, and familiarity with, a place.

Similarly, with guest booking in broadcasting, it is better for experts, authorities, and others who appear on air to be in the studio. When remote guests appear from a distant studio, they are not easily interwoven into the discussion. They have to stare into the camera rather than talk to a fellow human being, making the exchange between the host and the guest less fluid and more unnatural. Also, from a technical and logistical standpoint, "multisource newscast is more challenging" than in-studio newscasts.[107] Being more complex, technical errors are more likely. Thus, being in a place where such guests are concentrated is advantageous for the quality of television production.

Lastly, reporters' beats differentially avail themselves across cities. Beats are routinely reported topics or areas. Central sites of interest for news will offer unique beats that cannot be covered with appropriate quality or depth from a distance. For instance, covering the State Department can only happen in Washington, DC. Being a national security reporter would make more sense in Washington, DC than in Omaha. Reporting on the technology industry may not require a presence in northern California, but it is the largest and most concentrated location, even with other tech hubs in New York, Austin, TX, and Seattle.

Financial reporting still concentrates in New York, where the industry and the largest stock exchange are based. With beats, as Mark Fishman observed decades ago, "the world is bureaucratically organized for journalists."[108] Particular media ports of entry house idiosyncratic arrays of these pragmatic routines that journalism is structured around. Thus, location shapes professional practices and therefore impacts the substance of their production.

Technology and how people adapt it may alter these in such a way that place matters less, but they have not yet rendered these factors obsolete. Place is one container of the at-hand resources of journalism. Technological advances inspired dramatic and yet-unrealized prognostications that a new era of untethered telework was upon us. Nicholas Negroponte, for example, predicted that by "the year 2020, the largest employer in the developed world will be 'self'."[109] Reporters deploy technology to facilitate their objectives and enhance previous practices, making it unlikely to totally displace the preference for interpersonal, direct interaction in specialized work like journalism.[110] Non-mediated access or physical "co-presence" entails much richer reporting.[111] Co-presence allows for more holistic and efficient communication, facilitates trust-building and is therefore likely to withstand technological inducements to "organizational, temporal, and spatial reshaping."[112] Given the resource and time demands of co-presence in reporting, journalists must often make do with their second-order channel of communication, speaking or listening in via phone.[113] Proximity is preferable even if not always feasible. Fishman noted that "good news practices entail going out into the world," while culling information secondhand or only through devices is cheaper reporting.[114] It is inferior epistemologically, as a way of knowing what is happening. This is also the journalistic profession's conventional wisdom, despite the incentives and pressures demanding timeliness and cost saving that hinder such direct observation.

PLACE AND SUBJECTIVITY

More than just the pragmatic dynamics of location for journalism, place is formative for people's subjectivity and experience, both of which color how they construe the world. This further broadens the variability of media ports of entry.

The inner sense one has toward the world is shaped by place. Place-based resources are offered up within distinct fields of meaning—as marked by catalogs of "instrumental actions, signs and references."[115] Thus, the "'ready-to-hand'" resources of symbolically rich work like journalism are linked to interpretive action, schemas or how the world appears: a person's subjectivity. The interaction of subjectivities between the Self and the Other can fall along a range. At minimum one is "aware of the presence of an Other." At the highest degree, "one actively works at making sure that the Other and the Self are perceptually, conceptually, and practically coordinated around a particular task" such as the joint production of meaning through shared expressions, dialogic exchange, and symbolic interaction.[116] Co-presence of multiple people in a place more powerfully facilitates intersubjective involvements between them. Intersubjectivity is maintained through communication principally, which is most powerful in the immediate confines of being in the same place.

Philosophers emphasizing the body related it to the subjectivities of place. For Whitehead, the body is "the most intimately relevant part of the antecedently settled world." Merleau-Ponty proclaimed that a person's place in the world exists before the person does.[117] One's body, where it is located, orients one's experience to the world. The places where people meet then are sites of "intersubjectivity."[118]

The positionality of the body in relation to place and subjectivity was at the crux of critiques raised against the embedding program for war reporters. The US military assigned journalists to units of the allied forces that invaded Afghanistan and Iraq. Their bodies were among the soldiers'. The concern was that they would grow to sympathize with or feel pressure from the troops with whom they were placed. The embed program appeared to be "too cozy" a relationship between the press and the government.[119] Had a reporter been based out of a Kabul bureau when the Afghanistan bombing campaign commenced, as Al Jazeera was, the filed reporting would have differed. War reporting is an extreme case, but it demonstrates how one's body vis-à-vis an unfolding story structures how it is told, putting perspective into news.

This notion of the emplacement of subjectivity is not just theoretical. It is at the core of the practical concerns of editors and managers who work in the news industry. A consideration about the link between place and outlook manifests in the editors' conventional wisdom that basing journalists in one foreign beat for too long compromises their professional distance from where and whom they cover—known pejoratively as "going native." Editors try to moderate this kind of over-domestication by revolving correspondents and making sure they return to headquarters regularly. A foreign editor at the *New York Times*, for example, stated they rotated foreign correspondents every four to five years because they "have a tendency to go native."[120] This is not at all unique to the *Times*.** The fear is that reporters in foreign places assimilate aspects of the interpretive communities so that they adopt new perspectives, ways of knowing and seeing the world, from the people around them.

There is an inverse epistemic problem related to the subjectivities of location. The critique of "parachute journalism" is that a reporter flown in to cover an

---

** Newspapers in the United Kingdom won't allow correspondents to remain in Brussels covering the European Union for more than four or five years so that they can maintain a critical distance. Editors try to mitigate against this by bringing correspondents back occasionally so they can reconnect with the audience (Hamilton 2009, 111). The *Chicago Tribune* paid for its correspondents to return for a week every two years (Barker 2012, 210). Outside of this industrial conventional wisdom, empirical evidence of such influence is lacking.

unfamiliar place will offer shallow, uninformed reportage due to their distance from the place of focus.[121] Some, however, defend it as a professional practice.[††] Both this critique and "going native" indicate an industrial common sense that one's accommodation to, or lack of familiarity in, a place shapes perspectivality on news. The concern is that this proximity will show itself in content quality. This was something AJE's first managing director Nigel Parsons sought to minimize through the initial four broadcasting center model—the positioning of productive facilities and editorial functions in different cities and regions would:

> allow people to see events from the eyes of the people of that region, rather than through foreign eyes, which has tended to be the case in the past. And that's a benefit to both, the viewer inside of the region and the viewer outside of the region. People are tired of seeing themselves through foreign eyes. We want Africans to tell us about Africa. We want Arabs to tell us about the Middle East and Asians to tell us about Asia.[122]

The planners conceived such a decentered structure as a means of building a truly global operation, resulting in authentic, multi-perspectival reporting that would appeal to broad international audiences. This was designed so that AJE did not simply represent Doha's outlook. If it were to be such, Parsons quipped, "[w]e'd just do it out of Doha."[123]

The proposition that reporters are shaped by their locales contradicts the principles of journalistic professionalism. Professional modes of expertise, or standardized trades, rely on "locationless logics" in order to facilitate the movement of practitioners between contexts.[124] Journalistic professionalism's orthodox formulation hinges on the adoption of agreed-upon and institutionalized norms that transcend rootedness in place, including the intentional minimization of subjectivity in reporting. Certain facets of journalism practice are indeed universal. As Silvio Waisbord explained, newsroom understandings around "newsworthiness and quality work ... do not seem considerably different from Mumbai to Mexico."[125] Yet, many of the foundational principles of professional models of journalism simply do not travel well. For example, "public service,

---

[††] In a defense of parachute journalism that presented the economic necessity and the reality that most foreign correspondents cover a region rather than one place, Ericson and Hamilton (2009, 143) relayed a tale that demonstrates place's impact on perspective. When the *Minnesota Tribune* deployed its own reporter to cover the formation of the United Nations, rather than depending on "Washington or overseas-based correspondents" it boosted Minnesotan support for the UN because the reporters could more easily relate the issues to the readers, whom they "lived and worked among" (Bailey 1990, 185).

objectivity/neutrality, and fairness" are "weakly institutionalized" in some places.[126] The tolerance for overt subjectivity in reporting varies greatly.

Journalistic norms are themselves geographically bound. The globalization of journalism as a profession is inevitably about hybridity, convergence, and mixing with "local conditions." For example, Waisbord noted that in Brazil western-style journalism was melded within the country's peculiar conditions that distinguish it from the countries where the Anglo-American and French traditions of journalism emerged.[127] Global notions of journalism have moved in the world, to be sure. But their process of assimilation resembles glocalization more than standardization.[128] It is therefore plausible to accept place-based variation in what it means to be a professional journalist.

Emplaced subjectivity among news professionals is not just the concern of editors. Policymakers have problematized the link between place in media production and the perspective of news organizations. For instance, British officials opposed London's centrality in the TV industry. The 1951 Beveridge Committee referred to the "dangers of Londonisation"—the growing social and cultural influence of London over the United Kingdom. To better reflect national diversity, the BBC relocated facilities to Manchester and Salford Quays. A more inclusive, regionalized media required moving beyond the capital city—introducing inefficiencies and a host of other problems stemming from exiting a media capital.[129] The British authorities understand the tacit power of place to inflect media and try to legislate against locational skews in national media that are supposed to be representative of the country's diversity.

Conclusion

The media port of entry concept highlights the nodal, reconstructive power of media capitals for media moving in the space of flows. Ports are useful for globalizing media firms that seek entry into target markets but face obstacles to simple export. These sorts of cities are more than (re-)transmission points or stopping points; their power makes the first-order question of where to locate "a matter of significant strategic concern."[130] Globalizing media firms seek to use such places to *reroute* to target markets, but they find that must realize that the sorts of supports that enable their movement beyond the ports exercise a reflexive touch. The cities bring to bear unique influences on media production and distribution processes; they are sites of coloration, such that they influence media firms in unanticipated ways. Different media ports of entry produce their own versions of domestication because their dominant industries imagine national audiences uniquely and deploy distinct technologies of distribution to reach them. As complex and variable permutations of industrial sites and anthropological places, these ports are ultimately varied, contributing to the "complicated global terrain" of media in movement.[131] This emphasis on urban centers presents a quite different understanding of Al Jazeera in the United States than would a lens of the geopolitics of news, or assessing AJ as a Qatari contra-flow, both of which emphasize the national scale as the primary level of action.

What sorts of expectations for each of Al Jazeera's channels can we derive from an emphasis on the domesticating power of the three cities in which they were based?

- Al Jazeera English positioned one of its broadcasting centers in the political capital of Washington, DC. It would adapt to the sort of *media-politics rationale* of Beltway journalism over time and seek legitimation among US political elite.
- Given Al Jazeera America's placement in the capital of US television news, New York City, it would expectedly come to resemble *traditional, American TV news* outlets it competes against—CNN, MSNBC, and PBS.
- Finally, the San Francisco–based digital news outfit AJ+ would adopt the identity and appearance of a tech company start-up, rather than a purely journalistic enterprise—reflecting the emergent template for *new media* operations in the Bay Area.

There are a few qualifications about media port of entry effects. The linkage between place and subjectivity suggests why the port of entry chosen by an expanding media organization is important, but it could also insinuate that their effects are in total homogenizing. However, local industrial milieus and anthropological terrains are just two forces among many others. This multiplicity is why all news media operating in the same place are not exactly the same.

To go back to the difference between the industrial and anthropological contexts, they are not always complementary. There is a possibility that intense industrial clustering could actually insulate media workers and institutions from larger places of work. Terzis observed that in some highly clustered news beats, such as the European Union's headquarters in Brussels, foreign correspondents live in metaphorically gated communities, among expatriates, effectively isolated from the larger city.[132] As one UK-based reporter said, reporters covering the European Union are part of a "cocooned media operation" that effectively works to inculcate pro-European Union sensibilities.[133] They are more influenced by the media-politics of the European Union rather than Brussels or Belgium per se. In other words, if news media are too enclosed within an attached industry, it could affect media work while dimming the influences of the anthropological landscape.

The most important qualification is that media ports of entry effects are gradated and highly contingent on the derivative entities having functional independence from parent companies. The more autonomous a branch office, bureau, or subsidiary, the more freedom it has to assimilate within its new surrounds. Thus, the institutional context mitigates locational assimilation. A tightly controlled branch is less free to strategically integrate, accentuating its foreignness. Thus, certain organizational structures of multinational enterprises (MNEs) can determine how they navigate the liabilities of foreignness.[134] Horizontally organized MNEs are those where the sub-units in various countries all function in standardized fashion, offering the least capacity for differentiation. Due to their inflexibility, they are not well positioned to confront the liabilities of foreignness. The same goes for firms that do not invest in customizing their offerings for the particularities of divergent audiences; they try to provide different markets with the same product. Vertically organized firms, however, do not require sub-unit replication. Having the capacity for high adaptability and variation lets them take measures to diminish the liabilities of foreignness. To be successful in a market, they need the freedom to operate optimally within their local places. Most media companies are vertically organized, but their sub-units' abilities to adapt within target markets are constrained by budgetary limits, insufficient competencies, tight mandates, and bureaucratic controls. Al Jazeera's organization vis-à-vis the United States shifted over time, from being more horizontal with AJE, to more vertical with AJAM and most vertical with AJ+ —meaning the latter two were better equipped to adapt within their ports of entry and become more domesticated.

The following chapters examine the emplacement of the executive, marketing, and productive work of AJE, AJAM, and AJ+ in their respective media capitals. The chapters reveal how the cities shaped the media enterprises' practices, values, and identities through various kinds of ecological influences, while taking into consideration the institutional context in the form of Doha's administrative authority. The chapters also raise how the various distributional mechanisms wielded their own power. Presenting three cases of institutionally related but editorially distinct AJ channels brings to the surface the variability of the disparate media ports of entry for this controversial news media conglomerate desiring a share of the US news market, against the odds.

3

In the Beltway Before the Spring

The Rise of Al Jazeera English, Except in America

> In a sense, this is the place where politics and policy meet, so when Al Jazeera will be viewed in Washington, the cable networks in the US will conclude that it's worth it to carry Al Jazeera.
> —Marwan Bishara, *Al Jazeera English* host in 2009.[1]

> As a longtime Washington journalist, I know that there is a tendency to become part of whom you cover a little much. So, we find it refreshing to have the foot a little bit outside.
> —Bob Wheelock, AJ's executive producer for the Americas, 2013.[2]

Introduction: The Story of AJE in Washington, DC, Told Through Office Space

When AJE launched, its DC broadcasting center was placed in the same building as the Arabic channel's bureau. The leased office space was in a nondescript commercial building at 1627 K Street NW. K Street is recognizable as a synecdoche for the private industries of "influence-peddling" that cropped up around the government to effectuate policy change. Lobbying firms became "industrialized as K Street commercialized in the 1970s and early '80s."[3] K Street has taken on an iconic status as a symbol of Washington, DC's media-politics industry. Al Jazeera English's location there symbolized what it would go on to do, seek visibility and political affirmation as an institution operating in Washington, DC. Its precise location was an accident. The story of its office location reveals how post-9/11 politics bore directly and materially on the channel's being-in-place, through the material manifestation of its facilities.

Initially, the network faced trouble securing a DC location. Just before the 9/11 attacks, Al Jazeera's Arabic channel was set to open a new bureau in the offices of the Freedom Forum, a press organization that advances journalism and administers the Newseum, the Washington, DC-based museum dedicated to news media. The Forum agreed to lease office space in its Virginia building to the Middle Eastern broadcaster. After the 9/11 attacks, the Forum rescinded the offer, telling AJA's bureau chief Hafez al-Mirazi they were "worried about some of the other tenants" being displeased with the channel.[4] Al Jazeera was forced to stay in its cramped National Press Building office.

Two years after failing to get the lease from the Freedom Forum, AJ made another bid for office space with a requisite TV studio. In 2003, the network attempted to rent a 17,000-square-foot space from Conus, a TV production company at 1825 K Street NW. The building's landlord, Cafritz Co., denied the agreement because, as they wrote in a letter to the production company, they saw AJ as "potentially being a target for people who do not understand or do not agree with its business principles and philosophies of those of its ownership."[5] This brought about a lawsuit between the two, as the tenant company Conus argued the denial was unreasonable. Until the case was resolved, AJ worked out of Conus's office "as a client," not a tenant. Al Jazeera staff accused Cafritz Co. of interfering with its work, alleging they prevented Verizon technicians from setting up high-speed Internet access. The bureau chief declared that they meddled in "al-Jazeera's ability to conduct its business."[6]

Al Jazeera finally—in its third attempt—rented the office building at 1627 K Street NW. The landlord, however, forbade the appearance of the name and logo on the front door. Instead, it read "Peninsula Productions."[7] In 2013, executive producer Bob Wheelock observed that even when they had 150 people working there, "you walk into this building and you have no idea where you are."[8] This was a telling sign of the struggle for visibility that the network waged in Washington, DC. Al Jazeera could be in the city formally, physically, but had to cloak its visibility as a result of the politics of post-9/11 Washington, DC.

These impediments to finding space to work out of did not deter the network. Over the next several years, the DC operations upgraded substantially, as its staffing numbers blossomed. Before 2001, the Arabic channel's bureau employed four people in Washington, DC. By 2005, it was 20. At that time, they expected AJE would add another 50—making its DC center the largest outside of Doha.[9] By 2009, AJE had 137 permanent staff. This came at a time when incumbent news organizations were decreasing their DC bureaus.[10]

They quickly outgrew the skinny and ill-fitting 1627 K Street NW building. Spatially, AJE's facilities were laid out vertically within the office building such that the organizational division of labor overlapped with the allocation of floors. The ground floor had a small studio shared by both the Arabic and English channels. The fourth floor was also shared. Al Jazeera English housed its engineers, creative personnel, and camera crew there. The equipment and servers were kept there, making it the floor for technical expertise. Al Jazeera English's main news set, tech operations, and gallery were on the seventh floor: the central stage for production. On the eighth floor, AJE put program staff, planners, guest bookers, as well as the anchors' and correspondents' offices. It was the editorial floor. Al Jazeera English's bureau chief, as well as human resources, finance, administration, and programming staff, were placed on the eleventh, the administrative floor. This sort of ordering in such a narrow building structurally constrained its growth. One program, *The Stream*, was based at the Newseum due to the shortage in space. The building was also somewhat dilapidated, which did not convey a positive image. With rickety elevators and narrow stairs, movement between the floors was bottlenecked. The network badly needed new office space. This time around, the search went much more smoothly.

In 2014, AJ moved to a new building at 1200 New Hampshire Avenue, NW. The 46,000-square-foot facilities housed three studios and control rooms. It contracted the design with the Lawson & Associates, Architects firm, locally based in Bethesda, MD. Lawson planned the CNN and CCTV broadcast facilities in Washington, DC, building operating spaces of similar size and functions—an example of a port service facilitating industrial emulation. Rather than being vertically stacked over four or five floors, the new DC facilities were horizontally spread out on two floors connected by stairs, rather than just a slow and cumbersome elevator. On the first floor, there were two broadcast studios and an insert studio, as well as control rooms. Studio A was dedicated to the daily program, *The Stream*, which integrated online communities and social media conversations in shows that addressed a wide variety of social, cultural, and political topics. The other main studio was designed for multiple English and Arabic shows and news bulletins. At the middle was a circular anchor desk, the traditional centerpiece of news studios. Upstairs, there was a more open floor plan, with office spaces, edit suites and another studio. The DC control room, which connected to Doha, was there as well.

Unlike past years, there was no controversy over its latest office space move. Nor was the network required to hide its signage. By the time of that office space search, AJE was no longer taboo in the city—a dramatic shift. This material history of the soft infrastructure of AJE's DC office spaces portrays a channel that moved from being *medium non grata* to being acceptably present, no longer ostracized, and finally free to publicly display its logo. Between the frustrated search for office space and the seamless construction of shiny new studios, AJE's position and stature according to the city's prevailing media-politics rationale, transformed.

This chapter and the next present how the channel took advantage of Washington, DC, as a media port of entry to seek political rehabilitation that coincided with larger political events, from the symbolic post-9/11 cleansing that Barack Obama's presidency signaled to the sensational reception of the so-called Arab Spring in its earliest, heady days. What follows is an overview of the DC center's fit within the network's four-broadcasting-centers model, an account of its infrastructure of production, and an assessment of how the DC center's relative degree of autonomy structured its ability to integrate within the larger media-politics industry. The remainder of the chapter hones in on AJE's integration within the media-politics rationale of Washington, DC, before the series of Arab uprisings in 2011 (when chapter 4 picks up).

Al Jazeera English's Four-Broadcasting-Centers Model

The necessary starting point is a reminder that autonomy is essential for a subsidiary to freely navigate a media port of entry. The DC broadcasting center was *not* the channel's headquarters. It was part of a larger multinational organization based in Doha. Al Jazeera English's editorial functions were divided between four centers—Doha, Kuala Lumpur, London, and Washington, DC. This model was a novel attempt at decentered news production, as each branch functioned as an editorial hub to which regional bureaus and dispersed field correspondents connected. However, Doha's center became the central command over time. This limited the DC center's editorial autonomy as a site of news production. Yet, due to the market's importance, Washington, DC, took greater responsibility over marketing and publicity functions, essential port of entry activities.

The channel's planned decentralization was intended to prevent it from being too embedded in one place—an intention relating back to the point about the subjectivities of place. Al Jazeera English's planners expressly did not want the channel to be construed as Middle Eastern in the way the BBC was seen as British. The channel's first managing director, Nigel Parsons, asserted that western global news outlets "coming out of these powerful countries" will "absolutely naturally reflect the agendas of those countries."[11] By contrast, locating its productive functions in one city would make it more likely to adopt the epistemic orientations of place.

The four-centers model ensured that AJE had its own identity as the sum of the geographically dispersed components and not simply be a version of the flagship Arabic channel. Riz Khan, an early AJE host, attributed its alterity to it offering "international, 24-hour, global news that's not out of a Western center." A former AJE manager in Washington, DC, specified that according to this vision, Doha "wasn't a mothership," but was on equal editorial footing with the Kuala Lumpur, London, and DC centers.[12] This reflected then "multiple perspectives," and give a more prominent place for "global south" reporting than did other global news enterprises, namely the BBC and CNN International, he claimed.

Many of AJE's early employees found this vision refreshing. For Dave Marash, an AJE anchor who left a long career as an ABC correspondent to join, "the original concept" of four centers "was literally cosmopolitan—the whole world covered from many points of view representing the whole world."[13] With each being "autonomous," the centers would "initiate their own assignment decisions and lineup priorities," he noted. The end result, a channel rotating its central production facilities, offered "a truly cosmopolitan, multipolar gloss on the world."

This cosmopolitanism was, however, funneled into AJE's single, undifferentiated global broadcast signal. When AJE launched, each broadcasting center took turns generating AJE's singular output. The centers were equipped, staffed, and funded to generate the content to fill their segment of the daily broadcast schedule. Each center had a studio with an anchor's desk, high-level editorial staff, producers, and control room(s), making each an independent station. They could handle lengthy injects if there was "a big breaking story." For example, with "the US elections," AJE "could then just stay with DC for six hours, eight hours as need be," a senior manager explained.[14] Being regionally situated, they were able to report on each region from within it, authentically representing places and issues.

How much could this be adapted to particular audiences? Al Jazeera English tried to structure the broadcast schedule such that each center's slots in the 24-hour cycle overlapped with the range of prime-time viewing hours in their respective regions. Implementing this proved more difficult than one might expect, as the centers are not equidistant and prime-time viewing hours differ everywhere in the world. The planners did achieve some, but incomplete, overlap. Starting at 4 PM Eastern Standard Time, Washington, DC's center broadcasted for four hours. It would sign off even though it was 8 PM in Washington, DC, and 5 PM on the west coast (9 AM for the Kuala Lumpur center to sign on). This missed when Americans are most settled in for TV viewing: the prime-time hours of 8 PM to 11 PM on most days. Over the years, AJE's staff was always "juggling" the schedule and "trying to go around the world" so that Asia "gets a more Asia-centric show" and "by the time we head over to London it's very European-centric."[15] They never tried differentiating the signal by region through technical means, which would provide more customization. This was a de facto rejection of glocalization's principles. It aspired to be one global voice in a sense, yet over time it became a more Doha-centric operation.

DOHA'S CENTRALITY?

Despite framing the four hubs as equal, Doha effectively emerged as the main "center," and it became more apparent over the first few years of AJE's life. This slow centralization was natural given it was the largest hub, and proximate to corporate headquarters. It showed in the allocation of broadcasting hours. Doha was responsible for a disproportionate number of the day's hours. The bulk of the day's programming and news content, 11 hours, was out of Doha by 2010.

This clustering of authority in Doha had a corollary in the material, technical infrastructure connecting the centers. As dispersed as the hubs were geographically, they were linked infrastructurally via a large fiber network through the master control room (MCR) in the Doha headquarters. The MCR is located on the ground floor next to the rows of producers, bookers, and news desks that surround the anchors' desk. If the news presenters' desk with the screen backdrop was AJE's face, the MCR was its central nervous system. The MCR was where technicians control the "ad hoc, occasional and recurring satellite, fiber, and broadband global area network (BGAN) ftp feeds" from the centers, bureaus, other contracted studios, and vans and devices for on-location shots.[16] The MCR personnel tracked editorial requests for live feeds from the other centers' studios and producers, or correspondents in the field. They also channeled feeds to and from the studios' control rooms in each of the centers. The MCR collected "rushes," or raw footage clips, and placed them in the video library for producers and others to access. The direct production of news took place at those studios. Their control rooms switched between live coverage, presenters reading the news and the airing of packages. They sent out the completed signal, sans graphic overlays, back to the MCR, which added the top-level graphics, such as the logo, and lower-third graphics, and routed the final signal out to the satellites and the Internet for endpoint distribution. From the standpoint of the technical architecture, the location of the MCR enabled Doha's emergence as the central hub and authority over the final output. This may have been more logistical than editorial, but the internal infrastructure put central administrative weight on the Doha center, where after all, the top executives were located and final decisions were made. Despite being a "material support" for a space of flows, as Castells described, there was a built-in technical centricity that structured in Doha's control. An emphasis on the four-broadcasting-centers model disguised its role.

Under the operating guidelines and the distribution of editorial discretion, however, each broadcasting center initially enjoyed some level of autonomy, consistent with the original intent of the model. This led to unforeseen consequences. Inconsistencies in coverage and internal conflicts emerged as the centers covered the same stories differently or intruded on each other's territory.[17] Doha-based staff were often at tension with "producers and technicians" at the centers, while some of those who worked at AJE complained that Doha was "exerting greater editorial control over its output."[18]

For example, there was one publicized occasion of Doha overstepping the DC center to report on American stories in ways that the US-based staff found disagreeable. After Dave Marash resigned from AJE less than two years after it launched, he claimed it was because of the DC center's loss in editorial freedom, which he felt led to instances of superficial, simplistic reporting.* He relayed an anecdote about a moment of editorial tension between Doha and the DC center:

> There was a series entitled "Poverty in America" which, in the first place, was done in a way that illustrates some of the infrastructural problems that disturbed me greatly. The idea of a series about poverty in America was broached by the planning desk in Doha. The specifics of the plan were so stereotypical and shallow that the planning desk in Washington said that we think this is a very bad idea and recommend against it and won't do it. And so the planning desk in Doha literally sneaked a production team into the United States without letting anyone in the American news desk know, and they went off and shot a four-part series that was execrable.[19]

Marash claimed that AJE diminished the DC center's autonomy and abandoned "multipolar transparency." This anecdote indicates the DC center's autonomy was constrained by the organizational design, which could not maintain the equal allocation of editorial authority it initially vowed. Driven by further imperatives of efficiency and editorial discipline, AJE modified the model starting in 2009 with "The Next Frontier" initiative, when it began a restructuring process that formally altered the DC center's weight within the channel.

THE NEXT FRONTIER

Although it was a monumental effort at a diffused TV news operation, the fragmentation of editorial authority and production between the four centers proved inefficient and unwieldy to manage. Citing a budget review, AJE found that excessive resources went into redundant processes between the centers, from hardware acquisition to transmission costs. It was maintaining four competing news stations in effect. Just the real estate for each location was expensive. Editorially, there were coordination problems and ambiguities over editorial chain of command that resulted in different centers covering the same stories and sending reporters to story locations. An AJE manager in Doha said about coordinating the channel's output: "it's so much easier just doing it here at the end of the day."[20] It also improved editorial discipline.

Al Jazeera English's second managing director, former Canadian Broadcasting Corporation (CBC) editor-in-chief and executive Tony Burman, wrote that these

---

* His resignation came after he was informed that he was being moved from news anchor to correspondent, which would give him less leverage editorially, he explained (Cunningham 2008).

inefficiencies raised costs, and came at the expense of funding for on-the-ground newsgathering at the bureau level. To address these, Burman initiated the "Next Frontier" restructuring initiative. As an allusion to territoriality, it was the perfect title for what was in essence about the geographic distribution of the channel's work-flow and organizational responsibilities. It was intended to diminish the editorial independence of the centers, but it also redistributed more resources to building out smaller bureaus. In a February 2009 email published by *The Guardian*, Burman said the "gradual reshaping of our regional broadcast centres" would overall expand its newsgathering.[21] Shifting the locational spread of its facilities was intended to improve its newsgathering.

The broadcasting centers were overbuilt. An AJE manager in Doha echoed this, noting that the 150 staffers in Washington, DC, were "too many to be in that one place" and that "[w]e actually need to get out" to better cover the rest of the country.[22] The Washington, DC, center, however, remained at its capacity, continuing to produce programs, news bulletins, and injects when needed. That it survived showed the value of the US market to the network and the importance of AJE having a visible presence in Washington, DC. By contrast, the network phased out the Kuala Lumpur center and downsized the London center considerably, moving staff members to Doha. This recentered editorial processes in its Doha headquarters.

A former AJE manager corroborated this account, saying the recentralization dated back to the appointment of Tony Burman as the managing director. The ex-manager, however, took the stated financial reasons with "a pinch of salt," given the largesse of the Qatari government in subsidizing AJ. He believed it was ultimately about giving Doha more control over the satellite offices that sought editorial autonomy.[23] Others at AJE, including DC-based correspondent Alan Fisher, felt the restructuring was a better rationalization of resources that allowed coverage of the United States to improve and increase.[24] This suggested the DC center would have less internal influence as well as freedom to integrate into Washington, DC, as a port of entry. However, this was primarily about editorial control. The DC center became more important as the network's principal interface within the media port of entry.

Al Jazeera English's Turn to Washington, DC

While the organization scaled back its four-centers model, it began putting a premium on Washington, DC, as an avenue into the US market. A channel executive saw the United States as "an important market for us" due to country's preeminence in world affairs.[25] The network director-general who oversaw much of AJ's growth, Wadah Khanfar, said the American market was pivotal for them because the country was the most powerful in the world.[26] An AJE promo for its 2008 US presidential elections coverage implied as much, calling the US presidency "the most important job in the world . . . it impacts on the lives of billions." Al Jazeera English saw being in the United States as the chance to affect a center of global power. This was essential to both Qatar's aspirations for enhanced visibility, as well as the desire of journalists and producers to have a policy impact with their reporting. Yet AJE's interest in the United States had critical underpinnings as well; its basic mantras of giving "voice to the voiceless" and covering the "global south" were implicit critiques of western media power in the context of global news. This made AJE's fit within the national market tenuous.

The channel "fought for years" to gain TV distribution in the United States.[27] When it struggled early on, some in the network attributed it to strictly political causes—a reasonable presumption given the Bush administration's record of public hostility. In 2007, AJ sent a delegation of executives and staff to the United States to meet with Congress, grassroots organizations, and cable companies to gauge support for and opposition to the channel, and to build relations with influential figures and institutions. One of their principal concerns was that there was official opposition to AJE. A participant of that delegation provided details: they met with seven or eight members of Congress, both Republicans and Democrats.[28] The message the members gave was that "it was really a commercial issue . . . not a political issue." By "political," he meant in the sense of formal governance, of regulations and the authorities of elected officials. Those they met with assured them there was no such cause. After the trip, they were no longer convinced that officials demanded that distributors exclude AJE. They believed it was due to the discretion of the carriers. The commercial calculus, of course, reflected both a particular political economy that avoids unprofitable controversy and the larger post-9/11 atmosphere that was highly polarized around political and cultural issues. The "negative stereotype about Al Jazeera" as Osama bin Laden's mouthpiece made cable companies reluctant because carrying AJE might cause them to lose subscriptions, the staff member said.[29]

For unclear reasons, AJE did not launch in the United States with a major marketing campaign in late 2006. Cathy Rasenberger, who managed AJE's distribution efforts independently, asked the network to expend resources on marketing and efforts to gain distribution, but said her requests "fell on deaf ears."[30] It seemed they knew they had to play the long game. Nigel Parsons, the first managing director, said in 2008 that "[w]e never thought the USA would be an easy market, nor do we think the answer to breaking into it is to throw money at it unnecessarily." He was optimistic that eventually American demand would grow and distributors would pick up the channel. Other executives insinuated that they wanted to perfect the product first.

Over time, AJE came to adopt Washington, DC, as its entree point, not just an integral place to report the news from. Two main developments in 2008–9 facilitated this. First, with Barack Obama assuming the presidency, a former AJE manager noted, "things changed."[31] Al Jazeera began to experience a warming of relations with the United States government, just as Obama's rhetoric toward Arab and Muslim countries showed signs of rapprochement after the end of the Bush administration. An overt sign came when the network's Director-General Wadah Khanfar finally got a visa to enter the United States. It was never guaranteed that he would receive permission to travel inside the country under the Bush administration. He said that given the "accusations by Mr. Rumsfeld, Mr. Wolfowitz and others, who saw in Al Jazeera a threat to the American presence in the region," it was very "difficult for me to come and speak."[32] Khanfar was not going to find out if he would be denied entry by hazarding a trip. During Khanfar's 2009 trip to the United States, he met with senior officials and advisers at the White House, State Department, and Pentagon, and spoke at established think tanks and foundations in Washington, DC, and New York. This was one impetus for making the District of Columbia a bridge and not just a large bureau.

Second, Washington, DC, became the first major city where AJE could be viewed on a significant number of American television sets. Cable systems serving Congress, the Department of Defense, and the State Department were among the first to offer AJE. Then, it had a major breakthrough in 2009 when the DC-based educational programmer MHz carried the channel on one of its over-the-air sub-channels and through one of its slots with cable carriers in the area.[33] This put AJE on Washington, DC's radar. In 2010, AJ's Director-General Wadah Khanfar claimed that AJ's "theory of reporting news" won many fans in the political capital: whomever he "met in Washington, he loves Al Jazeera. From politicians to think tanks to ordinary people, people love Al Jazeera."[34]

As a result, AJE invested more resources to promote itself in the United States, most of its outreach and publicity not originating in Doha was handled by the DC center. Its primary arena was the political capital in which it was co-located. The presumption, according to an AJE marketer, was that "if we can get people in DC to like us and we're accepted by this political class, we'll go further" in garnering interest from the rest of the country.[35] A network executive noted that being in "DC was very important" because it allowed the channel "to reach some opinion formers and opinion makers."[36] Washington, DC, was a natural jumping-off point. Channels' heads recognized this and deliberately sought to conceive of ways to better utilize the DC center.

THE AMERICAS PROJECT

Al Jazeera English convened a select group of employees to contribute ideas for improving AJE's performance in America. In 2009, AJE initiated a "U.S. & The Americas Project." The "Notes From Kickoff Meeting" illustrated how AJE staffers envisioned the DC center as a mechanism for advancing AJE. The meeting drew staff from all over the network into various teams, but it began with a presentation that expressed in several bullet points the factors in the turn to Washington, DC, as a gateway:

• We have a unique opportunity to make a breakthrough in the US and the rest of the Americas.
• Momentum is on our side in terms of audience potential, media and political environment, etc.
• But we won't have a second chance.

This "opportunity" was a reference to the changed environment after President Obama's election and to AJE's first major distribution deal on July 1, 2009.[37] The channel gained access to the DC market through the sublease agreement with the MHz network.[†] Washington, DC's status as both a place of production and as the first major distribution market, a foothold, intensified AJE's reliance on it as a port of entry.

The brainstorming session began with a discussion of the staff's visions and ideas for how to implement them. As indicative of a media-politics rationale, meeting attendees proposed AJE should be "[p]erceived as bold, but not necessarily anti-establishment or anti-American," because it might alienate Americans. It could be valuable as an "outsider observing 'the Empire'" but relevant to DC insiders as the "TV of Record for the internationally minded." This reflected AJE's desire to achieve critical insider status, a style of presence in Washington, DC, as an oppositional source yet one that is accepted, valued, and given access.

In discussing short-term tactics, the staff saw the DC center as ideal for both "Communications/Marketing/Outreach" and "Distribution/Carriage." The meeting's attendees urged greater utilization of Washington, DC, as a media port of entry, as a locale from which to get AJE into the national market. Suggestions included building relations with other news media in Washington, DC, reviving the dormant "I Want AJE" push, launching a "DC marketing campaign" and "building branding in DC." Such relational and advocacy approaches epitomized the media-politics logic. For the distribution team, the top ideas were to improve "DC-based web resources," organize a "letter-writing campaign," and "[g]enerate and promote an intensive series of DC stories to drive DC viewing and thus prove the impact of our carriage here." The meeting notes, which reported vote

---

[†] MHz started as a public alternative to PBS affiliation that promoted world news and views in Washington, DC. The MHz deal put AJE on Comcast, Cox cable, and Verizon FiOS in Washington, DC, as well as terrestrially in parts of northern Virginia, DC, and Maryland. It was initially on mid-sized, multi-market cable provider RCN as channel 34, but was replaced by Ethiopian TV without public explanation.

counts for each idea, showed these were much more popular ideas than commercial tactics like, for example, paying for slots on cable TV. This standard practice garnered just three votes (out of 49).

The following February, the Americas Project teams submitted a memo to AJ executives outlining a plan. To succeed in the American market, AJE would have to address its "poor brand identity." Since there were few viewers being exposed to the channel and the network did not undertake "proactive brand-building" activities, the public's "negative misperceptions have been allowed to persist." One of the memo's "essential" recommendations along with a "branding review" was "the engagement of a full-time, permanent Communications team for the Americas, based in DC, to oversee all these activities."[38] Until that point, marketing and PR directed at the Americas was directed from Doha with assistance from a London-based firm, though it had at various times staff working in the DC center.[‡] Though Tony Burman, who led the memo's drafting, said the network leadership rejected the three-year plan, some of the elements were adopted piecemeal over the next several years. Al Jazeera English boosted its communications and marketing staff in Washington, DC, and became more active fostering relations there.

Al Jazeera English in Washington, DC's Media-Politics Logic

Although the DC center operated within a larger organization, it simultaneously worked within a local milieu, that of Washington, DC. The institutional context was formative, but the locale of action was the city, a gateway to a larger market. Washington, DC is a national, political capital with a significant presence of news media, as well as civil society organizations, private sector associations representing business and industrial interests, and government agencies. As Burman observed, Washington is "a city of news addicts, a city that probably per capita has more people globally engaged and interested than perhaps a lot of other places in America."[39] The city's dominant industry is government and the affixed nexus of media, advocacy, and contracting firms, and is personified by "Washington political insiders—politicians, consultants, lobbyists, journalists, political analysts, high-level civil servants."[40] For any national or international

---

[‡] Its marketing and communication work was managed at the executive level from Doha, and it farmed out its media relations and PR to Brown Lloyd James, whose New York, Washington, DC, and London staff oversaw the account. The firm previously represented the BBC in the United States (Black 2005).

organization, having a presence in the city is essential to the "DC factor," a relevance to political life that boosts one's role in the national public sphere.[41]

To speak of *media-politics* is to recognize that the degree of differentiation between the media and political fields, drawing on Bourdieu's field theory, is rather weak.[42] In their cross-national comparative work, Hallin and Mancini outlined different measures with which one could gauge media-politics: political parallelization, or the proximity between press and electoral parties, and the ratio of independent professionalized journalism to that which is instrumentalized by power-seekers.[43] Timothy Cook saw a near absolute convergence between these fields in the United States; he considered news media a political institution. News media and politicians are mutually interdependent because they rely on each other while engaging in "the negotiation of newsworthiness."[44] Media and politics meet most distinctively in political capitals like Washington. Cook contended that mainstream news media were political institutions themselves. Even news media that are not close to the establishment measure success by their political import. Such relevance is "in the air" in Washington, DC, to borrow Marshall's description of learning in industrial districts.[45]

The industrial confluence of media and politics in Washington, DC is a component of what the area's nickname, "the beltway," represents. A reference to the circular shape of the highway that encircles the city and its immediate suburbs, this commonly known phrase drawn from the physical transportation infrastructure is a shorthand for the sociopolitical milieu around government-centered industry. Many of the organizations and jobs that relate to federal governance are located within the metro area. As a placial marker, "the beltway" is often deployed as a demarcation of insider/outside status in relation to the larger business of government. "Inside the beltway" refers to the work and larger culture of supplementary and associated activities in policy, advocacy, contracting, and civic-related institutions. Being inside the beltway is to be "in the know" when it comes to public affairs. Those "outside the beltway," or everyone else, are presumed to have a weaker understanding of what actually happens in the center of US politics. Using Washington, DC, as a media port of entry to be "inside" the beltway while maintaining its institutional editorial identity meant that AJE aspired for a sort of critical insider position.

The great multitude of institutions functioning within the beltway, tied to media and the processes of government collectively, shows the characteristics of an industry, with their own mores, matrices of insider information, rotating doors, and networked relations. Media wanting to report on the US government must have a presence in Washington, DC, to gain proximity to the raw materials of officialdom, enjoy access to elite sources deemed credible in the news sphere, and be able to cover national issues credibly.[46] Being part of the media-politics industry therefore requires presence in Washington, DC. Al Jazeera English's placement of its US center inclined it to pursue DC-style relations and validation as the means to building a wider American audience. As a former manager at AJE expressed, being in the "middle of the global power" helped it in "addressing the US's political elite."[47] This is a fundamentally different context of production, marketing, and promotion than New York City, Chicago, or Los Angeles, for example.

All news media rely on relationships with governmental actors to obtain access and exploit the advantages of exclusivity—which have their own politics. In Washington, DC, the most beneficial relations are primarily with prominent political actors, the chief news-making stars of the political capital, and, just as important, their staffs. However, political actors have advocacy agendas and see media as instruments in their own efforts. They weigh news media relationships according to their own estimations of utility, against, especially in Al Jazeera's case, the liabilities of any affiliation, including mere appearance as an on-air guest. A great deal of their assessment will hinge on what their peers or constituents say about a certain channel, and what they hear about its reach, credibility, or influence—the informal reputation management of industrial behavior. Al Jazeera English's executives were well aware it confronted preconceived notions in Washington, DC, since it carried the parent company brand, "Al Jazeera," in its name and because it was headquartered in the Middle East.[48] They recognized that it had to alter AJE's reputation in Washington, DC, in order to shift the media-politics calculus, to be able to book the city's newsmakers as guests and to win access to them as sources. This was challenging after years of the Bush administration's vilification.

Al Jazeera English's fit in place was primarily context-dependent. After the election of President Barack Obama, AJE hoped he would embrace the channel. This would facilitate the brand's refurbishment. Then–managing director Tony Burman said that while the "brand is hugely respected in most parts of the world," the US market was "a problem" and a "challenge." He admitted that AJE was "seen by some people as being a network that is sympathetic to interests that are hostile to the US." "But," he thought, "it will change as the administration changes."[49] The presumption was that there would be greater receptivity to AJE as a news medium as Washington, DC's political atmosphere became more hospitable. If well-known government officials, elected representatives, and Pentagon figures appeared on AJE, it would demonstrate that the channel was not compulsively anti-American, that it was on par with the US news networks.[§]

[§] Ambinder (2009) described General Stanley McChrystal's 2009 appearance on AJE as an example of the changing tenor toward AJE after President Obama took office. Host Riz Khan bragged to Ambinder about his elite guests and how they vouch for AJE's reporting. For example, Bill Caldwell, a major general in Afghanistan, "told me that had he forced all new recruits to watch Al Jazeera because that's the way they can watch international perspective." Khan told Ambinder that after Caldwell appeared, Secretary of State Hillary Clinton's office called to book her.

Political approval and access were thought to be avenues to legitimation and therefore crucial to finding an equitable position among TV news peers in this market of top priority. This was the perfect expression of the media-politics logic defining Washington, DC, as a port of entry.

Building a DC Presence

Al Jazeera English's DC center engaged in multifaceted outreach to make the most of Washington, DC's media port of entry qualities. A former AJE employee who helped build external relations said they focused on the government, think tanks, policy-makers, journalists, and students. While they conducted some marketing in other places such as New York City, "DC was a priority" because it was where they were based and they had TV carriage locally. Furthermore, it was small city where influencers, those who shape broader attitudes, are highly concentrated and therefore efficient to reach.[50] The channel relied both on mediated promotion, from local media advertising to bus stop and metro subway billboards, to events, including holiday dinners, talks, and documentary showings. Al Jazeera English reporters also frequently appeared at DC events sponsored by NGOs and other institutions—including the various correspondents' annual dinners where the city's journalists hear from leading politicians and celebrities.

Al Jazeera English sought to build its local stature through audience tapings, showings, panels, and speaking tours. In November, 2010, the program *Fault Lines* held a televised town hall debate on the 2010 midterm elections at the Newseum, a frequent site of AJE-sponsored events. The panel included a broad array of speakers, including a Tea Party spokesman, to show its desire to present a broad spectrum of American political views—reflecting sociopolitical acculturation to the US political spectrum at the time. Al Jazeera English also set up talks for two of its Middle East correspondents, Ayman Mohyeldin and Sherine Tadros, who covered Israel's 2008–9 Gaza war. They spoke at Georgetown University and the University of Maryland in order to generate more interest among students. With these events, AJE emphasized its credibility as an authentic source of international news that reported directly from the ground. It was a source of news Americans needed to understand the world.

Al Jazeera English also collaborated with advocacy organizations to raise awareness about various topics and to promote the channel among the DC NGO community, a natural audience. One event at a local DC restaurant, Busboys & Poets, featured a showing of a program on the murder of Brazilian rain forest preservation activists. A panel afterward included representatives of international organizations, such as AmazonWatch, Greenpeace, and Amnesty

International, as well as the AJE correspondent who put together the report. Another event in Washington, DC, showed a program that covered the famine in Somalia; the discussion afterward featured Somali-American activists. Al Jazeera English also took part in events organized by other groups. On the two-year anniversary of the devastating Haitian earthquake, two organizations, TransAfrica and Let Haiti Live, showed an AJE program, *Haiti: After the Quake*, and had the reporter Sebastian Walker speak on a panel. In 2013, an NGO that builds schools in Somalia held an event and showed an AJE documentary about their work. In these public events, AJE collaborated with DC advocacy groups and NGOs.

To advertise these kinds of events and to share videos and articles locally, AJE's DC outreach staff established an email listserv. In July, 2010, it contained nearly 451 work email accounts. An analysis of the accounts revealed the primary targets of AJE's email campaign at that time (Table 3.1). Of the types of contacts AJE's DC office made, 30% were media workers and another 30% were staff and managers of advocacy groups, NGOs, and research institutes. Nearly one-fifth were students or faculty at universities and colleges. The fourth most common email analyzed was for a government employee or official, domestic and foreign (mainly embassy staff). The remaining types garnered no more than 2% each.

The media AJE reached out to were a mix of national and local media. National media located in Washington, DC, frequently appeared on the list. Ten NPR

Table 3.1 **Washington, DC Center Email Listserv Members, 2010**

Advocacy, NGOs, & Think Tanks	139	30.8%
Media	136	30.2%
Educational Institutions	86	19.1%
Government	34	7.5%
Businesses	23	5.1%
Intra-Governmental Organizations	9	2.0%
Miscellaneous	7	1.6%
Lobbyists & Lawyers	6	1.3%
Tech Companies	6	1.3%
Religious	5	1.1%
TOTAL	451	

employees, and another five from a local NPR affiliate, WAMU, made the public broadcaster the most frequently targeted institution. The list included many mainstays of American press: seven *Washington Post* and four *New York Times* reporters. Al Jazeera English sent emails to magazine writers from *Harpers, The Atlantic, The Nation,* and so on. All the major TV news giants, with the exception of Fox News, were included. New media were represented on the list as well. Eight *Huffington Post,* five *Politico,* and four *Foreign Policy* editorial staff members were on the list. The latter two were mainstays of Washington, DC's new media scene.

Washington, DC-based civil society made up the largest group of the email announcement: staff at a diverse multitude of think tanks, research institutes, nonprofit charities, and advocacy groups. Among the listed think tanks were the New America Foundation, the Brookings Institution, and the Center for Strategic and International Studies (CSIS). Emails also reached research centers, like Gallup, Pew, and the Wilson Center, as well as policy-oriented entities, such as the Council on Foreign Relations and the International Crisis Group. Advocacy groups Human Rights Watch, Free Press, Media Matters, the NAACP, and others were also contacted. Many of the DC civil society groups have international programs and amplified AJE's coverage on their own news roundups and social media accounts.

Due to resource constraints and other practical considerations, AJE's marketing efforts and advertising tended to focus on Washington, DC. The channel purchased web banner advertisements in the *Washington Post, Foreign Policy,* and *Salon* websites with high traffic from Washington, DC. Al Jazeera English preferred to advertise in Washington, DC, according to an executive "because we can't afford to blow so much money nationally," but in Washington, DC, "I know they can watch a sneak peek."[51] Also, however, advertising and marketing dollars go further in Washington, DC, because of the ease of reaching national and international media workers, think tanks, advocacy groups, and others likely to recirculate AJE's content further. This was part and parcel of the strategy of winning political clearance in Washington, DC.

Interview Booking

One way Washington, DC's value as a media port of entry was apparent in newsgathering and in marketing and outreach was through the practice of interview booking—featuring outside guests for taped or live news bulletins, news packages, or programs. In its first several years, AJE's DC center had trouble booking a diverse array of guests. This was a barometer of the liability it presented in media-politics terms. An AJE program host, Avi Lewis, spoke to the difficulty in getting Washington, DC, elite to appear on the channel in

2008: "we find, when we're trying to book guests for Al Jazeera English, that [we're] treated as a quasi-terrorist organization, which is shocking as a serious news organization," and this was not limited to Republicans only; it went "completely across the political spectrum."[52] This reflected one of the prevailing logics of Washington, DC's media-politics industry, the framing of issues through the lens of the partisan binary.

Emblematic anecdotes portrayed this bipartisan discomfort with AJE. At the 2008 Democratic National Convention, the party chairman Howard Dean was making the rounds to appear on various media. Steve Clemons, a political observer and later editor at *The Atlantic*, relayed that Dean walked into AJE's booth, which the network shared with Fox, but "[w]hen he realized it was Al Jazeera, he reeled out of there and fairly rudely."[53] Al Jazeera English's attempt to get on air a conservative candidate for Congress, Allen West, was a particularly extreme example of the rampant suspicion toward the network. While booking West, the AJE interview producer asked for the candidate's address to send a car to take him to the studio—a standard practice for TV news channels. West, a veteran of the wars in Afghanistan and Iraq, panicked. He told the *New York Daily News*, "my b.s. flag really went up."[54] He suspected "it was a kidnapping attempt" and preferred to play it safe: "I am not going to entrust Al Jazeera with my life." Furthermore, his campaign manager notified the FBI, which according to the manager, said was the right thing to do, thereby only affirming their paranoia. Al Jazeera English denied trying to kidnap West. The spokeswoman at the time, Molly Conroy, told the newspaper that booking him was part of AJE's efforts to get on air a multitude of voices from across the US political map. It wanted to avoid being pegged as partisan by US standards. To correct perceptions of liberal bias, AJE made special efforts to woo Republican lawmakers and officials. A *Politico* story noted that the hiring of a Republican-run lobbying firm that worked to advance Qatar and Al Jazeera's standing with the party may have paid off.[55] It quoted Suhail Khan, a Republican who was in the White House Office of Public Liaison during the George W. Bush administration. Khan saw the "PR campaign" as a success because AJE "just began booking Republican guests."

Similarly, Pentagon officials were often reluctant to appear. An Army public affairs officer wrote that although Al Jazeera English enjoyed "growing credibility and popularity among service members, DOD leaders seem to remain averse to engaging Al Jazeera in on-camera interviews or private meetings."[56] Al Jazeera English reporters at the DC bureau in Washington, DC, spoke of the difficulty in getting access to the Pentagon. This showed in its content. In the officer's analysis of AJE's coverage, he observed that "current or former DOD senior leaders have been, for the most part, few and far between."[57] In his assessment, this was not for a lack of AJE's efforts.

When government officials did appear, AJE made sure to advertise it beyond the normal pre-program promos. It frequently listed in marketing materials its "past guests" to signal that AJE was a politically safe news source. For example, the channel highlighted that Republican Senator John McCain, the undersecretary of state for public diplomacy under Bush, Karen Hughes, and Bush's secretary of homeland security, Michael Chertoff—all Republicans— appeared. When Al Jazeera sought to book guests, it listed previous guests to allay fears. Wikileaks published hacked emails from the publisher and global intelligence company, Stratfor; one revealed a 2009 interview request for a program in the DC bureau.[58] The email listed "Previous guests on the show," and went on to name 16 prominent officials, starting with: Secretary of State Hillary Clinton, Secretary of Defense Robert Gates, and Chairman of the Joint Chiefs of Staff Admiral Mike Mullen. It used its booking record to assuage anxieties about the channel. Relations with high-profile guests were a media-politics asset.

Booking high-level officials represented for AJE's larger approach of political validation a means to attracting viewers. A senior marketing staff member was perplexed there were popular suspicions of AJE when so many of the "guests that appear on our screen are Americans."[59] He was confused why more Americans were "not watching the channel" when the guests included "leading Americans . . . not just the underdogs." His example was "Hillary Clinton," who "did a special session" on AJE. This exemplified the media-politics logic: embracing and being embraced by the DC political elite seemed an intuitive step to wider market access.

This distinct politics of legitimation around TV appearance showed how the elite were part of the channel's at-hand resources in Washington, DC, yet could influence its coverage through simple decisions around appearance and display. In a short write-up, Clemons commented that it was "interesting to watch Al Jazeera gain prominence in Washington over recent years—with the likes of Hillary Clinton, David Petraeus, Stanley McChrystal, Leon Panetta, Susan Rice and others appearing on Al Jazeera and Al Jazeera English."[60] Booking these top officials in the Obama administration was tantamount to prominence. What AJE gained through high-profile-guest booking could be attributed to the DC broadcasting center's location in Washington, DC. Clemons wrote that "[m]any of these high level political interviews might not have been secured if Al Jazeera had not had the robust array of DC-based news products in house at the time."[61] He warned that diminishing the capacity of the DC center—as was announced with the Next Frontier project—would lessen the network's presence in the political capital, effectively limiting its ability to navigate the media-politics dynamics of Washington, DC, that guest booking represented.

Conclusion

Being in Washington, DC structured AJE's broadcasting center's at-hand resources for reporting, which influenced the perspective through which the United States was covered. Its location and early sublease carriage through MHz meant the territorial reach of its marketing was primarily local. Over time, the DC center carried out more of the external relations work that showed in how the channel interacted within the peculiar media-politics atmosphere. It became more deeply emplaced in the city where media and politics most prominently converge. Al Jazeera English's onetime Managing Director Tony Burman referred to the need to exploit Washington, DC as "a political and kind of media capital."[62]

The political elite's reception of AJE was central to its market expansion playbook. Burman offered as proof of its growing prominence the fact that members of Congress and "important people in the administration" had AJE as their first choice in international news. Affirmation from the country's governing elite, he thought, would translate into greater demand nationally. Al Jazeera English's "goal," Burman said, was "to convince Americans to tell their cable and satellite companies that, you know, what is available in Washington . . . should really be available nationwide in the United States."[63] AJE presumed that political affirmation would bolster its marketability in the rest of the country—a simple reversal of its perception that the Bush administration's hostility doomed its brand in the United States. The tactics of advancing this included holding public events with NGO partners, building a communication target list of the politically engaged and other media workers, and booking political elite guests, among other things.

By the start of 2011, Washington, DC was yet to deliver on its port of entry potential. The channel had not found the requisite political validation that would underscore its value to the American public, nor had it gained adequate distribution on cable and satellite systems. Al Jazeera English was still far from the mainstream position it desired, both in Washington, DC, and nationally, where it was available in a minute number of US homes. As we will see in the next chapter, AJE finally underwent a profound political reincarnation during the series of Arab uprisings in 2011, taking it from the margins to center stage among the DC elite.

4

Al Jazeera English's "Moment" in the Media-Politics Capital, Washington, DC

> Al Jazeera is no longer on the fringe. It is now mainstream
> and accepted by the very likes of even Secretary of State
> Hillary Clinton who testified to Congress that Al Jazeera is
> one of the best news out there.
> —Josh Rushing, AJE journalist and program host, 2011.

In early 2010, Secretary of State Hillary Clinton stopped in Qatar during a tour of the region. She appeared on a televised AJE town hall meeting at the Qatar Foundation in Doha. Longtime DC bureau chief for the Arabic channel Abderrahim Foukara hosted the event. The network announced that the secretary of state met with Wadah Khanfar "and the network's senior editorial staff for a meeting to further dialogue with Al Jazeera." A network employee said that Al Jazeera managers "put their frustrations on the table," but that "the meeting was very positive."[1] The message was that network executives "seek a more stable working relationship with the United States," after the adversarial years of the Bush administration. This warming of relations further opened Washington, DC up as a media port of entry—as a site of legitimation. However, it was not until the following year, 2011, that AJE's ascension in the United States appeared imminent. Al Jazeera English's coverage of momentous popular uprisings in the Arab world elevated its visibility in Washington, DC. The network tried to leverage the newfound fandom to grow its distributional footprint and draw a larger audience in the country.

The Arab Spring Rehabilitates Al Jazeera's Image in America

Al Jazeera English's coverage of the series of uprisings called "the Arab Spring" was a powerful on-the-ground presentation that piqued America's, and especially Washington, DC's, interest. The Tunisian uprising began in December

2010 and ended January 14 with the resignation of longtime dictator Zine El Abidine Ben Ali. Al Jazeera English was slow to report it since it had been banned from the country, but it began putting together reports based on social media content and phone interviews with Tunisian activists. After Ben Ali was toppled, AJE was primed to broadcast the subsequent Egyptian rebellion that kicked off 11 days later. The network dedicated extensive resources to following and documenting the mass protests that gripped the world's attention. As Egyptians gathered in Cairo's Tahrir Square to call for President Hosni Mubarak's ouster, many Americans tuned in to AJE for some of the most in-depth on-the-ground reporting in English-language news. Some who held neg-ative, prejudicial views began to see the channel in a whole new light, as a force for reform and freedom. Increasingly, political elite, media figures, and public intellectuals publicly declared their adoration, endorsing the previously contro-versial channel.

The Arab Spring and American reliance on the channel appeared to some at the network as the event that finally hastened AJE's arrival in the United States. Tony Burman, by then AJE's chief strategic adviser for the Americas, said that the Egypt story "did in 18 days what I thought it would take two years to do," referring to AJE's springing prominence. He noted that the "impact and impor-tance of Al-Jazeera seems to be visible to all, particularly people in Washington."[2] The city as the central place for political redemption was exemplified by the excitement over reports that AJE had a fan at the highest level: President Barack Obama. The head of state and his staffers kept up on news in Egypt, in part, by watching AJE. Elsewhere, it was reported that in candid remarks to political donors, Obama said he told Qatar's emir that the country and the network were a force for democracy in the region. "Reform, reform, reform—you're seeing it on Al Jazeera," he declared.[3] This was a stunning reversal from the vilification by the nation's previous leader.

The most noteworthy approval from a high official came during a taped US Senate committee meeting on American foreign policy priorities and budgeting in early March 2011. Then–Secretary of State Hillary Clinton handed the network a major public relations victory. She praised AJE, giving it an unprecedented, public, emphatic endorsement from a top US official. She said it was gaining an online audience in the United States because it was "real news." Secretary Clinton asserted, "Al Jazeera has been the leader in that they are literally changing peo-ple's minds and attitudes. And like it or hate it, it is really effective."[4] The network replayed the clip of her comments in its promos. Her remarks were framed as proof of the channel's political recognition in official Washington. Little of the coverage of her remarks, however, acknowledged the overt motive in the state-ment. The secretary was seeking more funding for America's own informational activities, namely its international broadcasting programs aimed at the rest of the world—which compete with Al Jazeera. She used the term "information war" to describe indirectly the state of competition between her government and the young news network. Thus, embedded within this praise was a quintessentially bureaucratic, media-politics objective, obtaining further government funding from Congress. That did not stop the network from quoting the secretary in its promotional materials. Her affirmation of the channel's value revealed the promise, peril, and the nuance of reliance on Washington, DC as a port of entry for its market entry. Utilization of a political capital as a media port of entry risks the reverse: of being utilized strategically by power brokers.

Al Jazeera English's immersion into the political capital produced rather confused moments of television where the tension with over-assimilation to Washington, DC's media-politics surfaced. In one illustrious example, AJ's most vigorous elite critic during the Bush years, the former Secretary of Defense Donald Rumsfeld, appeared on AJE's program *Frost Over the World* in October 2011. This was a coup given the past hostilities. Rumsfeld surprised all further when he told the since-deceased news legend Sir David Frost, "I am delighted you are doing what you are doing." By "you," he meant the network. He added to the on-air praise, noting that the network's "audience has grown." This gave it the potential, he celebrated, to be "an important means of communication in the world."[5] Such an endorsement from a provocative figure was not universally welcome at the network. The former secretary's connection with US policies and actions, such as the invasion of Iraq and the arrest, detention, and other punishment of AJ personnel, actually caused ire among employees and risked the network's larger credibility with audiences that recall the secretary unfavorably. This gave rise to internal controversy and external criticism that Al Jazeera sold out. To make matters worse, Frost's interview was on the whole uncritical, even fawning at points. Other media reported this odd endorsement.

The need for damage control appeared to motivate a second interview with Rumsfeld just days later. This time, the influential bureau chief and network veteran Abderrahim Foukara questioned the former secretary of defense. The follow-up was a testy exchange. In a drawn-out question, Foukara asked him in leading fashion whether the former official's decisions "absolve[d]" him of "the responsibility of tens, maybe hundreds of thousands of innocent Iraqis killed." The ex-official did not entertain this question in the slightest. He grew agitated, countering instead, "now you gonna stop?" Rumsfeld accused Foukara of "haranguing" and said, "this is worthless, this is not an interview." Rumsfeld may have been correct; the confrontation appeared to be a strategic communication itself, as the network sought to distance itself from his controversial seal of approval on Frost's program. For one thing, his praise could affirm perceptions that the network was in the service of US foreign policy with its Arab uprising coverage—an accusation made by Mubarak's government and regime loyalists, among others. Al Jazeera English posted the testy interview to YouTube with a title highlighting its contentious nature: "Rumsfeld in heated conversation with Al Jazeera."[6]

The network had reasons to be confident. Al Jazeera English gained a great deal of praise from influential public and media figures. Lee Bollinger, the president of Columbia University, penned an op-ed calling for AJE's distribution in the United States. The channel, he argued, was a public service that educated Americans about international affairs.[7] Well-known figures in American media, such as MSNBC program host Rachel Maddow, former *New York Times* columnist Frank Rich, and Sam Donaldson of *ABC News* also spoke highly of the channel for its coverage. *NBC News* chief foreign affairs correspondent Andrea Mitchell was glowing, calling the channel "indispensable." Aware of the baggage of proclaiming the brand, she added "[t]here's a big difference between Al-Jazeera overseas and Al-Jazeera English." Nevertheless, the network was important for her work, the Washington-based reporter admitted, and she stressed that the State Department relied on Al Jazeera as well.[8] As it did with then-Secretary Clinton's remarks, AJE promoted these as endorsements that signaled to the American public and distributors that it was no longer a political taboo, but was valuable to the informed citizen.

Advertising Its Moment

Such a move from the media margins to the center of a major news story inspired speculation that it was finally "AJE's moment."[9] A "moment" in this sense is temporal, but it is also a reference to a landmark news event, an occasion that drastically improves a news network's stature. It was due to the channel's strikingly in-depth and persistent coverage of an event that captured the world's attention. This use of "moment" was reminiscent of the speculation around CNN's arrival during the 1990–91 Gulf War when the then-decade-old channel's 24-hour news coverage and potent visuals advanced it to a leading position in international news. No longer was it to be lampooned as the "Chicken Noodle Network." CNN rose to become a global news giant. Tony Burman referred to this as a model. He was "hopeful" that the Arab uprisings were "a turning point" and "perhaps this will be to Al Jazeera English in the United States what the First Gulf War was to CNN in the early '90s."[10]

Al Jazeera English sought to take advantage of this "moment" by publicizing it as such; an attempt at a self-fulfilling prophecy. The network accelerated advertising during and after the Egyptian uprising, placing advertisements in the *New York Times*, *Foreign Policy*, and the *Washington Post*, as well as on foreign policy blogs. The print ad (Figure 4.1) featured the list of endorsements—from Rachel Maddow, *The Nation*, and Sam Donaldson—as well as a quotation from *Business Insider* reporting that President Barack Obama watched AJE. At the top of the ad was the line "It is **Al Jazeera's Moment**," which was attributed to the *Times*. The ad directed readers to watch the channel online. The *Washington Post*

Figure 4.1 Al Jazeera English print newspaper ad that ran in the *New York Times* in February 2011.

website banner (Figure 4.2), which sat just below the site's header, featured a quotation: "Even the President of the United States Is Watching Al Jazeera." The overt message in this ad is one of endorsement—that AJE is being relied upon by leading figures in media-politics. Even the head of the country thinks it a crucial source. In short, AJE was validated politically.

The hope that this positive reception would translate to cable and satellite carriage came up in an unlikely TV show. In March 2011, just weeks after the collapse of the Mubarak regime, AJE's Egypt correspondent Ayman Mohyeldin appeared on Comedy Central's popular satirical news talk program, *The Colbert Report*.[11] Mohyeldin won accolades and fame for his thorough and insightful reports from revolutionary Egypt. Besides being a sign of the times—the

Figure 4.2 Al Jazeera English web banner ad that ran in the *Washington Post* in February 2011.

changing receptivity to the channel post–Arab Spring—his appearance is worth recounting because the issue of AJE's entry into the US distribution market was broached. Stephen Colbert, who satirically played a pompous yet down-home, conservative, populist television host, asked his guest in his typically ambiguous, layered, tongue-in-cheek manner: "We've got like 17 Showtimes and a channel for pets, how come, if you guys aren't dangerous, you're not on any of our channels here?" Mohyeldin's response was consistent with the view of many at the company: "People come to Al Jazeera because they get good international news." The US-raised reporter added that the cable companies "not carrying Al Jazeera, are sadly helping contribute to the misinformation that is happening in this country." Al Jazeera English sought to persuade distribution companies that its "moment" justified wider carriage—a rhetorical linkage between its legitimation in Washington, DC's media-politics industry and the prerequisite to building a substantial American viewership.

THE "DEMAND AL JAZEERA" CAMPAIGN

In the midst of this spiked attention, AJE revived efforts to drum up organized support among the public. It finally followed up on one of the ideas from the Americas Project. The DC bureau worked with Doha to push online viewers to request that AJE be made available by their local cable companies, so they and others in their communities could watch it on television. Drawing on a great tradition of Washington, DC, advocacy organizations, AJE established its own astroturf-like campaign.* As popularity for AJE accelerated in the midst of the Egyptian uprising, the channel shifted its somewhat idle web-based campaign, "I Want AJE," to the more urgent "Demand Al Jazeera"; and it added new online functions, such as a video upload page to solicit users' video-recorded endorsements. It also hosted a letter-writing form for people to contact cable companies.

---

* Astroturf groups are "fake grassroots organizations that may look and feel like they are community based, but which are created to manufacture the illusion of public or scientific scepticism or support for government or corporate policies and practices" (Greenberg et al. 2011, 70).

The DC office marketed it through the website, social media, and on its listserv. More than 100,000 Americans wrote letters to their cable providers requesting the channel. For one of the meetings with Comcast after the Egyptian uprising, AJE printed out 13,000 letters. The network claimed another 40,000 emails went to the largest cable company. Al Jazeera English supporters held a handful of meetings in different cities around the country, which they advertised on meetup.com, a group activity–planning website. Al Jazeera English publicized these sessions, which aimed to devise local campaigns to promote TV carriage. A former organizer of the campaign with AJE said that most of the signatures came from the large cities on the coasts. Al Jazeera English studied where the letter-signers were based in order to target the major cable companies in those areas.[12] They tried to strategically parlay this mobilized expression of popular demand into television carriage through a traditional advocacy campaign executed from their DC offices.

The Al Jazeera US Forum, 2011

If there was a pinnacle of Al Jazeera's use of Washington, DC as a media port of entry, it was the inaugural Al Jazeera US Forum held in mid-May, 2011. It took place in the months after its "moment," when Americans took notice of its leading coverage of the popular uprisings in Tunisia, Egypt, Libya, and elsewhere in the region. The two-day gathering was held at the Newseum on Pennsylvania Avenue. Located half way between Capitol Hill and the White House, the newly built museum, the news media industry's shrine to itself, served as the staging ground for an event intended to project the network's post–Arab Spring message: Al Jazeera was doing vital journalism and it was finally publicly recognized by the American political elite. The event was an enactment of the media-politics logic that media success is interrelated with access and the political elite's embrace.

The Forum's program had two parts. The evening of May 16, 2011, AJ held an invitation-only banquet. The next day's talks and panels were publicly promoted. On the morning of May 17, AJE program host Josh Rushing expressed the significance of the redemption of AJ's reputation. Rushing suggested that AJE occupied a new position in the American news spectrum, as "mainstream," because it was praised by "the very likes of even Secretary of State Hillary Clinton." He made the point of elite approval by spotlighting prominent guests, such as former national security adviser and staple of the foreign policy community, Dr. Zbigniew Brzezinski, and the famed *Post* reporter, Bob Woodward. Their presence symbolized the channel's welcome among Washington, DC's political elite. The Forum was a declaration in the media-politics grammar of Washington, DC that the era of stigmatization was over. The brand was fully rehabilitated.

LEGISLATIVE LEADERS SING THEIR PRAISES

During his opening remarks, Rushing emphasized the channel's new elite credentials by referring to the private, invitation-only banquet the prior evening:

> Senator John McCain with Representative Nancy Pelosi, both praised
> Al Jazeera at its news coverage and its efforts in spreading democracy
> across the Middle East, words that would have been stunning to hear
> from them five or six years ago.

Having congressional leaders in their respective chambers and from different parties appearing together at the Al Jazeera function was a momentous occasion. Representative Pelosi acknowledged the novelty and joked that it was not without risk. She was relieved to see Senator McCain there "because I was preparing for the onslaught of criticism I was going to receive … but now I'm covered right?" Looking at the senator, she said, "You cover me, I cover you." This was tongue-in-cheek but not necessarily an exaggeration given the past hostility to the network. Their appearance alone—going back to Washington, DC's politics of association—gave AJE a bipartisan boost. It was just the sort of performance that resonated in the beltway's symbolic economy.

Both politicos depicted Al Jazeera as essential to the cascading reform and revolutionary movements that spread in the region. Pelosi went so far as to congratulate Al Jazeera. She said that the network publicized the Tunisian revolution to the rest of the world. This, she claimed, inspired Egyptians to mobilize against their longstanding president, Hosni Mubarak. McCain echoed this by saying that "al Jazeera has played a key and leading role" in the "seismic events (of) the Arab Spring." He assigned to Al Jazeera an outsized influence over the protests:

> I'm very proud of the role that Al Jazeera has played … when that
> young man who was humiliated by the police in front of his friends
> and contemporaries and family in Tunisia decided to burn himself to
> death, that would have been confined in earlier years to a single iso-
> lated incident and it was al Jazeera, it was al Jazeera that spread that
> story time and time again so that it penetrated the conscience of not
> only the people of Libya, of Tunisia but countries all over the Arab
> world so I congratulate you, I congratulate you.

Among the perceived causes of the Arab Spring, Al Jazeera was the crucial communicative bridge between protests and mobilizations in Tunisia and elsewhere in the Congresswoman's telling.

Senator McCain was a leading legislator, especially influential in foreign affairs. He was keen to link Al Jazeera's acceptance in Washington, DC with its overseas impact, even framing it with US foreign policy keywords, freedom and democracy. Al Jazeera championed this association. When the Arabic channel's DC bureau chief Abderrahim Foukara introduced McCain, he told the senator that he recalled his "concession speech" after losing the 2008 presidential election as a robust "message about democracy." Foukara tied it to his identity, personifying the Arab Spring, when he noted "the fact that I as an Arab can still remember that two years on is testament to how powerful it was." The feelings were requited. McCain claimed he was "proud" to be "the first United States Senator to visit the headquarters (in Doha) and to give interviews" to Al Jazeera. He also paid lip service to the network's role in spreading information integral to the Arab Spring.

As McCain closed his speech, however, he disclosed indirectly the terms of his embrace. Senator McCain referred in his speech to Libya's rebels, saying they deserved everyone's support. Pushing for the United States to back Libyan rebels against the dictator Colonel Moammar Qaddafi, the Libyan dictator who rankled a long sequence of American presidents, was the focus of his foreign policy agenda at the time. The Senator told an especially evocative story about his recent visit to Libya. McCain stopped at a Libyan hospital where rebel fighters lay dying. There, he recalled, a "young man whose face literally burned off said 'thank you for your support Senator McCain.'" He claimed that encounter "puts into perspective how little we really actually have done for the cause of democracy and freedom." He exhorted the gathered crowd, "I urge you to redouble your efforts." It was unclear whom he was enlisting in this rebellion, exactly—Al Jazeera or the attendees that evening. As he continued, it seemed he addressed the network: the "employees and people who have worked to bring information and knowledge." The implicit conditionality of McCain's alliance was that Al Jazeera's coverage of the Libyan uprising dovetailed closely with the senator's agenda—generating a political marriage of convenience. It was not, therefore, that AJ was depoliticized and seen as some purely journalistic operation agnostically delivering high value news, but that its politicization was in the correct direction from a member of the US political elite's perspective. Part of this moment for McCain was an opportunity to pursue the potential congruency between his preferred foreign policy and the tenor of AJE's reporting in Libya, which like its reporting on other countries, covered oppositional movements closely and sympathetically. This hints at the possibility that the reincarnation of the Qatari network vis-à-vis the DC-based power structure reflected a media-politics calculus institutionalized in the nation's capital.

REPRESENTATIVE NANCY PELOSI ON THE NEWSEUM

Showing her own appreciation for the communicative value of material culture, Representative Pelosi made reference to the edifice in which the Forum's attendees gathered. She connected the event and the building to highlight the value of news media, saying the setting in the Newseum was "especially appropriate." During the museum's opening, the representative recollected, she was a speaker and discussed the freedom of the press as a paramount right, central to the democratic political system. Later in her Forum speech, she observed, "we are in Washington DC in a building that has the Bill of Rights and the First Amendment written on the wall of the building." The structure directly and materially encodes the basic formal principles of news media in this polity, which are often construed as exemplifying American exceptionalism. In her closing, she said the "most fundamental political belief that we have" is "in democracy." Then she continued, "so I thank you Al Jazeera for your contribution to democracy in the world." The setting of the Newseum, as Pelosi insinuated, enshrined America's basic values like freedom of the press, materialized them. So she blessed Al Jazeera by noting the fit, baptizing it into the American press tradition. The network was now accepted as a force for democracy—which is also a staple rhetorical feature of US foreign policy, the primary frame through which the politicos approached the channel despite its desire for political domestication. Nevertheless, Washington DC's nearly ritualized acceptance of the network was embodied through the precise edifice of the Newseum, which, along with the National Press Club, is an architectural incarnation of the news industry: American journalism's tribute to itself.

The Newseum signified AJE's emergence in another, less obvious way, one the participants would not have realized. The museum was founded and principally funded by the Freedom Forum, the same group that reneged its offer of office space to Al Jazeera's Arabic channel in 2001 because of the risks it presented. A full decade later, its building would host the event marking AJE's ascension in Washington, DC's media-politics. This coincidence underscored just how much the company's image was resuscitated in Washington.

AL JAZEERA ENGLISH'S PROGRESS IN WASHINGTON, DC, PERSONIFIED BY FOUR SPEAKERS

The channel's transformation in the political capital is captured by the biographies of four figures at the Forum. When AJE's Josh Rushing spoke in the morning and described the channel's transformation to the mainstream, he was an appropriate messenger—Rushing himself embodied the network's hopes for the American market. Before Rushing joined Al Jazeera, he was an officer with the US Marine Corps, and during the Iraq War worked as a spokesman for General

Tommy Franks. He was a subject in Jehane Noujaim's 2004 documentary about Al Jazeera's reporting on the Iraq War, *Control Room*. It captured the budding relationship between Rushing and Hassan Ibrahim, an Al Jazeera reporter in the military's Central Command (CENTCOM) media center in Qatar.[†] Through their exchanges about the war and broader themes of US–Arab relations, Rushing's views evolved over the course of the film. It was an evolution that continued after the period covered by the documentary ended. The military was not pleased with some of his comments and ordered him to keep silent about the film. He resigned from the Marine Corps after serving nearly fifteen years. Less than a year later, he joined the network, helped with AJE's launch, and was deployed as AJE's American spokesman. He also worked as an international correspondent and cohosted the *Fault Lines* program, AJE's investigative documentary series. Having gone from a military spokesman to an Al Jazeera reporter, Rushing was a symbol of the potency of the network's mission and the potential of American minds to transform. For years, channel executives displayed a faith that only if Americans gave AJE a chance, they would see it as quality news and overcome inhibitions echoing from the Bush administration's antagonism. Rushing personified this hope.

At the Forum, Rushing introduced Al Jazeera's director-general, Wadah Khanfar, who was widely respected as a journalist and political observer. The same week as the Forum, the US magazine *Fast Company* named Khanfar as number one on their list of the world's most creative thinkers. Al Jazeera English's "moment" could be seen through the drastic change in Khanfar's status with the United States. It was only in 2009 that he anticipated he would be able to get a visa to enter the United States. Two years later, he was an honored guest in the nation's capital. This was an outgrowth of the fanfare during the Arab Spring. He was enthusiastic about its facilitating role in the protests. Khanfar, for example, claimed AJE's live reporting was not just crucial to the flow of information but to physically protecting the protestors:

> When at Tahrir Square we had our cameras there reporting live from secret places, because the government banned us. [The] images were not only politically important, but it was also a matter of life and death for those who are protesting in the Tahrir Square because the camera gave to them protection [from security forces] reluctant to attack and to kill when they know that their images are screened live on Al Jazeera.

[†] *Control Room* (2004) was noteworthy for showing how the channel operated in the context of a US-led war where the Pentagon sought to shape news reporting to control the narrative, in the parlance of strategic communication.

While he championed the citizen as the most important reporter, he qualified that news organizations like Al Jazeera were still necessary; "professional journalists" still "have a task to investigate." Reporters best advance "transparency," work to "understand what's happening," and they "have a great responsibility to guard the truth." Al Jazeera still had a special role even in this new age of distributed journalism. That comes with great risk, he admitted. Some of their journalists had to report "undercover" and were pursued and expelled by "intelligence agencies." They were empowered, he said, by being the "voice of the voiceless." This concept of news media as giving voice echoed Representative Pelosi's statements the evening before, where she depicted as central to democracy the press's role of amplifying the public's concerns. Khanfar positioned AJE within the heralded free press tradition to which Pelosi considered the Newseum a shrine.

Following his opening statement, Khanfar turned to introduce the newest network executive, Amjad Atallah. Khanfar announced that he "will be with you here in Washington," as his newest emissary to the city. Atallah, the new AJE bureau chief for the Americas, spoke very briefly, acknowledging that he was joining the network at a "real high point." Atallah's hiring was notable because he was not a seasoned journalist, but was "a well-connected player in the Washington foreign policy community," according to *Politico's* write-up of his appointment.[13] Previously, he comanaged the "Middle East Task Force" at the DC-based think tank, New America Foundation. He had worked as a peace negotiations adviser with the Palestine Liberation Organization in the early 2000s, then with the Public International Law & Policy Group and the Save Darfur Coalition in policy advising and advocacy roles. *Politico* reported that his employment was "part of a series of staffing shifts within Al Jazeera English to beef up its coverage of Washington." A former AJE staffer said that under Atallah, AJE emphasized "public relations and outreach" even more, and that he accelerated local meetings to boost AJE's visibility in Washington, DC. By the time of the Forum, he was just two weeks into the job. His hiring overlapped with the post–Arab Spring push to elevate the operation's presence in the beltway. The Forum launched him as the network's representative for Washington, DC. His hiring fed into the "buzz" of the local media-politics industry.

Next, the famed *Washington Post* reporter and editor Bob Woodward spoke. Rushing's introduction included the telling comment that Woodward was "a guy who literally brought down a presidency and yet still gets invited back into the White House." He stood for what Al Jazeera aspired to enjoy, the simultaneous, paradoxical mix of both high-level access and license to challenge American power. Few journalists could accomplish this *critical insider* positioning that Rushing spoke about. None of them have been foreign or nearly as controversial as AJ was. The desire to be oppositional, while having access and being part of the conversation in Washington, was an unlikely balance.

Through this event the network performed the media-politics presumption that acceptance in Washington would get them a larger audience. It seemed obvious given that the demonization and politicization of AJ began in Washington, DC. From the network's perspective, Washington, DC would be the place of its rejuvenation as its central hub of North America operations. The warm embrace by the national political elite after the Tunisian and Egyptian uprisings seemed to commence the fulfillment of that promise, but there was a hidden cost to the palatability in Washington, DC's media-politics terms.

The Conditionality of the Al Jazeera Moment

Beneath much of the celebration about AJE's "moment," there was a tacit recognition of the contingency of the media-politics rationale that instrumentalizes news media. This was recognizable in Senator McCain's comments during the Forum. The bargain implicit to the "moment" for some politicos was unintentionally revealed by a spokeswoman for Representative Paul Broun (R-GA). She articulated the conditionality of the channel's new popularity: "If Al Jazeera English hopes to establish itself more so on American soil, it must prove to the United States that their intentions are primarily improving our relations with the Middle East—rather than promoting anti-American rhetoric." In other words, AJE was welcome so long as its reporting would be to America's advantage, avoiding criticism of the United States or its foreign policy. Al Jazeera English's approval among the political elite, then, was tenuous because it was based on its alignment within a particular political constellation at a given time. This point about AJE's political utility is at the heart of the larger media-politics of Washington, DC. The lesson is that the most powerful institutions and individuals in political capitals will submit foreign firms to their own aims when it is beneficial.

Washington, DC's media-politics logic was also exercised in Doha as an expression of US foreign policy. The United States, with its imperial reach, tried to discipline and assimilate Al Jazeera well before AJE was established because of the US interest in advancing its image in the region. The State Department cables Wikileaks published are an archive of various meetings between US ambassadors to Qatar or their diplomatic staffs, and network officials. One ambassador, Chase Untermeyer, relayed in a 2006 cable that those working at AJ "know they are under the microscope," being monitored and held to account for coverage the State Department finds disagreeable.[14] Part of his job became generating flak, or registering "negative responses to a media statement or program" with the company. As Herman and Chomsky found, the efficacy of such feedback reflects the power of the flak producer to inflict costly threats.[15] These protestations found expression in multiple venues from Doha to the public statements of Bush administration officials.

Some US policymakers welcomed AJE as an opportunity to further discipline the network. Ambassador Untermeyer, writing before AJE's launch, predicted that the network's "globalization will only increase the pressure upon them to adhere to international standards of journalism and result in an organization that can be dealt with upon familiar ground, and within a framework already established by the mainstream media."[16] This observation would prove prescient. Its efforts to get into the US market created new sorts of vulnerabilities to the forces of political assimilation. This was not the channel's immediate concern, however. It was driven to pursue a wider presence on American televisions.

Toward Legitimation

The sudden gains of US validation during the Arab Spring showed hints of concretization months later when Americans turned to AJE's coverage of a subsequent, breaking international story. After United States Special Forces raided Osama bin Laden's compound in Pakistan and killed him in May 2011, media and government officials relied on AJE as a source. Joe Scarborough of MSNBC interviewed an AJ correspondent on *Morning Joe*, a weekday morning TV talk show, the morning of May 3, 2011. Scarborough even referred to the interviewee as "our friend from Al Jazeera"—a chumminess that would have been difficult to imagine during the Bush administration years. In a White House press conference later that day, John Brennan, the deputy national security adviser for homeland security and counterterrorism, responded to a reporter's question by citing what he watched on AJE. The press conference was aired live on several news networks. He spoke from the same podium where officials of the previous administration condemned Al Jazeera.

This legitimation was also evident among members of the general public. When news of the bin Laden assassination began breaking roughly before midnight on May 2, 2011, web traffic to AJE's site increased tremendously, showing the largest bump since the news of Hosni Mubarak's resignation. The vast majority of the web traffic came from the United States. Stories of ordinary Americans viewers tuning into AJE for news about bin Laden's killing hinted at the political normalization of the moment. In a Sierra Madre, CA, bar, everyday Americans, military veterans among them, requested the bartender turn the TV to AJE—and that was the patrons' "consensus" choice.[17] A New York City high school student who participated in a class discussion about bin Laden mentioned to the reporter that he watched AJE "all night."[18] Such stories paint a mundane acceptance, and they illuminate by contrast how far AJ came as a brand since

2004, when President Bush called the channel "hateful propaganda" in the most significant speech of the year.

It was fitting that the death of bin Laden symbolized the reformation of the Al Jazeera brand in the United States. The Bush administration previously used AJ's airing of bin Laden's videotapes to paint the networks as sympathetic to America's enemies. In 2009, Burman quipped to a reporter that "Osama bin Laden does not have a weekly interview show" on the channel, in reference to persistent myths he had to address in the United States.[19] The two were often linked in public commentary, showing an association engraved in the popular imagination. The assassination of the Al Qaeda figurehead, then, correlated with the redemptive turn in AJE's status in the United States, as it outgrew the lingering antagonism of the war on terror era.

The Continued Struggle for Distribution

Despite this heightened interest during the "moment" of the Arab Spring, AJE failed to procure the cable and satellite distribution deals requisite to its mainstreaming. Past negotiations with the largest carriers failed to produce results. In the midst of its "moment," AJE reentered talks in late February 2011, carrying the momentum of publicity, newfound public fandom, and the testimonies of the media-politics elite. Its executives met with the nation's largest cable operator, Comcast, among others.[20] Despite carrying with them boxes of letters from subscribers calling for AJE, no deal came through. Comcast revealed to an opponent of AJE carriage that no agreement was reached, and it appeared unlikely since the country's largest carrier "is not currently in active talks to complete such an agreement." Al Jazeera English did sign smaller deals with local, independent operators in Rhode Island and Massachusetts by late April 2011, but these did not add substantially to its paltry numbers of TV households.

The most promising advance was a momentous sublease agreement in New York City. The channel signed an indirect, third-party retransmission deal with a local broadcaster. This was not the result of a change of heart by the companies, but due to the preference of the station's proprietor. On August 1, 2011, the independent station WRNN-TV began airing AJE 23 hours a day on a digital sub-channel (48.2) and showed its own staple program for one hour, an FCC condition for being made available on cable and satellite as a "must-carry" broadcast channel—this was one of the few regulations kept in place, interestingly, to protect localism and prevent small stations from annihilation by cable TV carriers more interested in profitable content providers. This regulatory vestige then offered AJE a foothold opportunity to build an audience in the nation's largest media market, but it was an anomalous arrangement, not the kind of direct carriage agreement AJE expected after its sudden rise.

There were several plausible explanations for satellite and cable's continued reluctance even after the Al Jazeera "moment." An industry source suggested the cable industry's leader, Comcast, wanted to see if the interest in AJE lasted beyond the Arab uprisings and to better estimate its prospective audience size.[21] Other industry insiders speculated the threat of pressure and risk stemming from the small minority of American conservative activists opposed to the channel being available had an effect: "Some people would attack some of the distributors like Comcast and others who would carry it for being un-American for carrying Al-Jazeera," said Jeff Zucker, the ex-CEO of NBC who would later head CNN. He added that news sources like Fox News "would go after some of those distributors if they were to put Al-Jazeera on."[22] This suggested the persistence of deeper political culture, a nativistic nationalism unswayed by the channel's political revitalization in Washington, DC.

American Demand for AJE after the Egyptian Uprising

Did the distribution industry's obduracy simply reflect public opinion, namely low demand for AJE? The author and a colleague conducted an online survey to gauge the public's attitudes toward AJE and whether it should be made available on American televisions (Appendix A). Participants completed the study online between February 23 and March 5, 2011, two to four weeks after Hosni Mubarak stepped down, during the exuberant response to AJE in US media and among the political elite. Survey respondents were asked, "If your local cable company was considering carrying Al Jazeera English, would you have a preference or try to influence its decision?" The same question was asked about CNN International, to give a point of comparison.[‡]

In general, people preferred cable companies carry CNNI to AJE, but that is not the main interest here.[§] When the answers are broken out, as Chart 4.1 indicates, we learn more about their views. The first obvious insight is that the most frequent response to each was indifference. The clearest

---

[‡] The participants had five options ranging from "I would directly pressure the company in support of carrying Al Jazeera English (CNN International)" to "I would directly pressure the company against carrying Al Jazeera English (CNN International). They could also answer if they had just a preference for or against, or if they were indifferent.

[§] The general mean responses for AJE (m = 2.99) and CNNI (m = 2.58) were statistically different (t = 6.70, α < .001).

disparity lay in the number of people who said they oppose, in view or action, the cable companies offering AJE as compared with CNNI. While 7% reported they would actively oppose AJE, not one respondent said the same for CNN International. There was much more opposition to AJE than CNN International. An optimist working for AJE could stress that 30% of the respondents preferred AJE be made available, a substantial proportion of the population that could make for a gigantic audience if their responses actually translated into TV viewing habits. Unfortunately for AJE, roughly the same were against. This stalemate was likely an improvement for them compared with prior years, but it revealed that the cable companies' anxieties about protest were well founded.

What can we say about the people who opposed AJE? We found that they tended to identify as politically conservative, and they scored high in questions gauging anti-Arab prejudice, suggesting that opposition to AJE rested within a particular ideological disposition consistent with nativist nationalism and anti-Arab xenophobia (Appendix A). These views were robust, impervious to the glowing praise during AJE's "moment."

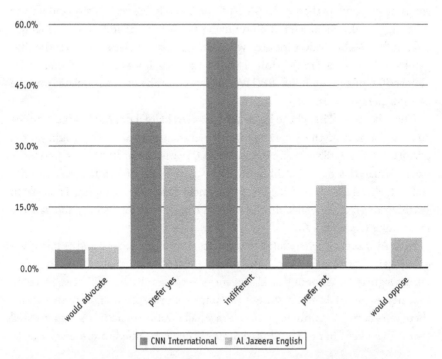

Chart 4.1 Want this channel carried on cable? Survey conducted by author via Amazon Mechanical Turk, February 23–March 4–5, 2011. n = 179 US adults (Appendix A).

WEBSITE PERFORMANCE

Besides the letter campaign, AJE presented its website's boost in US visits as evidence that Americans wanted the channel. Al Jazeera English was available free online, providing a livestream and bountiful videos on demand. The year 2011 brought a surge of Internet traffic to the site. The channel announced a 2500% increase in website traffic during the Egyptian revolution, with more than half the traffic from the United States. Data from Google Trends corroborated the claimed increase.[**] There was a significant rise in daily visits during the Egyptian revolution, surpassing 500,000 daily visits, compared to less than 100,000 daily hits previously.

Did this make AJE a player in global news, and therefore a requisite addition for TV distributors claiming channel scarcity? One question is how its website fared against alternatives. By 2012, its traffic plateaued at about 250,000 visits daily, more than its pre-Egypt 100,000 but less than its peak 500,000 numbers; about half of the visits came from the United States. These were impressive increases, yet were minuscule by major news website standards. Compared to the BBC's and CNN's websites, AJE's website was still very far behind in 2012 in worldwide and US traffic, the last year AJE was actively seeking a market share in the United States. In the United States, the BBC's website was many times more popular than AJE's website. BBC World News, website and survey data suggested, was much more promising as a potential addition. Although it did not fare well in New York City, where it was tested a decade before, the BBC gained wider carriage in the United States. By 2014, it was in 30 million homes, almost 30% of the country.[23] BBC World News was ahead of the queue from the carriers' perspectives.

There is a useful insight to be gleaned from website data. AJE's largest online audience came from the same city that served as its port of entry. Looking at the performance of AJE's website in its top 20 US cities according to the network's Google Analytics data, Washington, DC was the site of the heaviest website traffic (Table 4.1). It rated highest in the most sessions per capita. Those from Washington, DC, were also on the website the longest on average and saw the most pages (Appendix A).

Still, Al Jazeera English failed to translate its political capital and online viewership gains into further cable and satellite distribution deals. What the 2011 Forum signaled, the coming of Al Jazeera as a regular player in US news and politics, never materialized. Despite AJE's improved reception among Americans, there were some remaining opponents, a small number of activists who insisted that AJE be kept out of the United States. They continued to present a risk to

---

[**] Google phased out Google Trends for websites, "which allowed people to compare traffic to and audiences of different websites," in September 2012 (Matias 2012).

Table 4.1 **AJE Website Traffic per US City, July 1, 2008–September 1, 2014**

City	Sessions	Pages/ Session	Avg. Session (seconds)	2010 census	Per capita sessions
Washington, DC	7,191,855	3.06	656.10	601,723	11.95
Seattle	4,986,077	2.83	523.26	608,660	8.19
Minneapolis	2,97,0186	2.96	508.92	382,578	7.76
San Francisco	6,011,871	2.75	524.11	805,235	7.47
Portland	3,05,7901	2.88	558.08	583,776	5.24
Atlanta	2,121,537	2.52	419.77	420,003	5.05
Denver	2,525,758	2.73	520.53	600,158	4.21
Boston	2,425,022	2.59	459.27	617,594	3.93
Austin	2,40,3676	2.76	519.73	790,390	3.04
New York	18,929,305	2.74	523.17	8,175,133	2.32
Chicago	5,845,583	2.62	461.20	2,695,598	2.17
San Diego	2,804,470	2.76	510.25	1,307,402	2.15
Columbus	1,49,0893	2.74	439.22	787,033	1.89
Los Angeles	7,110,616	2.56	446.74	3,792,621	1.87
San Jose	1,674,781	2.83	548.75	945,942	1.77
Houston	3,591,925	2.70	457.10	2,099,451	1.71
Philadelphia	2,412,909	2.74	497.23	1,526,006	1.58
Dallas	1,886,575	2.53	430.95	1,197,816	1.58
Phoenix	1,433,616	2.73	489.82	1,445,632	0.99

Source: Google Analytics data, provided by AJE staff.

cable operators, making the channel even more of a "commercial liability," as an AJE executive called it.[24] Cable companies considered the network "radioactive," according to a former AJE manager.[25] He also noted they were concerned about "losing subscribers." However, the companies told AJE at the start of its distribution efforts that "space is limited" on their systems and they "could not afford to give up valuable bandwidth." A senior AJE official said that the "MTV's and the sports channels and the stuff that's going to make revenue is all upfront" in the triage for channel slots. Plus, an international news channel is not going to bring the carriers equitable revenue. Had AJE actually attracted an overwhelming number of people, the commercial case likely would have overtaken this risk in the distributors' calculus. The political economy of the TV distribution industry is an unavoidable factor.

The Institutional Context as a Check on Media Port of Entry Effects

As much as AJE sought to fit in place in Washington, DC, it was limited by the institutional context, an important check on assimilationist pressures at the port of entry. Bureaucratic independence matters because it grants a subsidiary more latitude to accommodate a target market through enhanced differentiation. While Doha allowed the Washington, DC center some autonomy, it initially oversaw limited marketing and outreach functions. Overall, the institutional structure meant that AJE's DC center could not completely immerse into the DC brand of media-politics. Al Jazeera English refused the normal strategies of market entry such as catering its product for a particularly American audience. This manifested in technical aspects, namely how its broadcast signal was structured as a singular, continuous output. There was no uniquely American news or version of AJE for Americans. The most customization was in it partially timing regional coverage to overlap with regional prime-time viewing hours; but there was only some coincidence. Americans would view programming produced out of the other broadcasting centers or Doha during part of the prime-time hours. This one signal for one world fit with the claim to be delivering, as a result, truly international news. But it also delimited how much time could be given over to the DC center. Thus, the localized pressures stemming from Washington, DC, to be more politically expedient to the United States was less likely to influence the organization as a whole.

Al Jazeera English in effect rejected a differentiation strategy that had become an orthodoxy of media glocalization. BBC, for example, launched BBC America, a special channel that featured more entertainment than news, just to break into American televisions.[26] In 1997, CNN International "separated its broadcast into four regional signals, or feeds—Asia-Pacific, Latin America, Europe and the United States"—with each having customized programming and scheduling adapted to local time zones.[27] Russia Today, also by contrast, explicitly aimed at gaining a US audience through launching RT America and by adopting a goal of maximizing its YouTube video views vis-à-vis its competitors. The willingness to differentiate requires devolution of powers to those in-market operations that are positioned to take advantage of ports of entry resources that facilitate the inflow of market entrants.

The lack of willingness to compromise AJE completely for the United States showed in the decision to keep "Al Jazeera" in the brand. Russia Today's strategic adoption of "RT America" highlights one move AJE did not take. It did not modify its name, for example, which may have disguised it to avoid phobic responses rooted in American political culture or distrust of the network.

Onetime managing director Tony Burman said many apply "the political stigma that's been attached to Al-Jazeera Arabic" to AJE, which sets back its distribution aims.[28] The Americas Project suggested reconsidering the branding, but network heads rejected the recommendation.

There was another institutional limitation on AJE's ability to take advantage of Washington, DC as a media port of entry. The DC office had a very small staff for marketing and promotions, of roughly three to five, aided by interns, during the 2011 push for carriage.[††] Often, the team was led by or included personnel from an outside public relations firm headquartered in London and with a small office in Washington, DC—rather than a DC-rooted shop. The DC marketing team, which was under Doha's command, was formally assigned to cover all of the Americas, even though they expended most of their efforts on Washington, DC, out of practical necessity. As Riz Khan observed, this lack of marketing initiative was tied to its political economy: "We're not a commercial channel so we don't go out and sell ourselves the way we should."[29]

Finally, another constraint was that not everyone in the organization thought gaining a sizable market share in the United States was even feasible. According to Lindsay Oliver, the former commercial director, "[w]e'd love to have cable distribution, but it's not going to kill us if we don't."[30] Staff debated, behind the scenes, whether investing significant resources was worthwhile. The onetime managing director Parsons rationalized its lack of success, saying the US market was famously tricky for foreign media companies and therefore not worth significant investment.[31] As for making itself more appealing for Americans, an executive urged they did not entertain compromising the integrity of their news product; AJE was "not really necessarily interested in the lowest common denominator" audience.[32] The variable assessments of AJE's potential by those in Doha explained why it limited its options in entering the US market. Given the network's politicization under the Bush administration, its presumed, de facto mode of entry was one of political legitimation, and it imagined no other route in. Furthermore, AJE's US presence was concentrated in the place where such a media-politics logic prevails, making it a natural fit.

[††] By contrast, the marketing and distribution staff working to promote the BBC in the United States was much larger in size and presumably better resourced since it was handled by Discovery Communications, Inc., the parent company of the Discovery Channel ("BBC and Discovery ..." 2002). When BBC World News wanted to enter Asia, albeit a many times larger market, it employed 30 personnel for marketing alone (Shrikhande 2001, 157). With CNN's expansion to Asia, as part of its "regionalization" project, it hired 36 personnel and spent $5 million annually to attract Asian audiences (Coleman 1997).

The Next Frontier Completes

It was not until 2012, three years after it was announced, that the Americas leg of the Next Frontier restructuring concluded, under Al Anstey's directorship. Anstey sent an email to staff in late March 2012 announcing completion of "the 'next frontier' project to restructure our broadcast model for News contribution from America."[33] He explained that AJE "will no longer be opting-in with presentation from the DC Centre into news bulletins." Instead, there would be "more live contribution from the field from stories we are covering across the USA." The program *Inside Story* was still produced in Washington, DC daily, but the show "Empire" was moved to New York, "a natural base given its global make up and its global influence." Anstey emphasized that downscaling the DC center was intended to devote more resources to the field. He cited new bureaus in Chicago, Los Angeles, and Miami as building on their "existing presence and strength in Washington DC, and New York, and our bureaux across Latin America." At that time, according to a former AJE staffer who worked in Washington, DC, "the Washington bureau lost a lot of its autonomy, so for example, decision-making on what the US-based correspondents would cover, instead of being made in Washington, was being made in Doha, and they were commissioning less."[34] A former AJE manager said that the DC broadcasting center did have a skew toward covering the city, and national politics there, "because we were all there."[35] However, the DC center's declining power within AJE's output was a blow for a well-staffed operation at "the center of political power" in the world, according to a former AJE manager.[36] This was the first sign of them succumbing to the realization that if AJE could not gain wide distribution via cable and satellite carriers in the United States after the Arab Spring, it probably never would.

Conclusion

The network's fandom in the beltway post-Arab Spring was based on the political ramifications of its news coverage. This was inadequate for success in a TV distribution market defined by commercialism. Washington, DC's embrace was at best a form of clearance, but it did not involve decisive pressure on the carriage industry. The commercial political economy was generally a buttress against the "moment" taking sway over distributors. The companies were concerned about the bottom-line, firstly, and had to fear negative publicity as a severe downside that required considerable demand for which to compensate. Furthermore, they considered the US TV news market saturated—as they did for decades, even before Fox News launched—and relied on their conventional wisdom that Americans had insubstantial interest in international news. The exuberance of Washington, DC made them appear only slightly more open, but it proved insufficient to convince them otherwise.

This ingress through Washington, DC revealed the tendency of actors in the political center to instrumentalize news media, to strategically utilize media firms for their own ends, or at least when they find it beneficial. As Curtin noted, "political capitals tend not to emerge as media capitals" because governments and advocates impulsively work to submit media to their interests.[37] This is the domestication pressure of a port of entry when its underlying industrial logic is political. Working in Washington, DC, AJE was subject to the paradox that access to officials was both necessary to be part of the national public sphere, but also made them more vulnerable to flak—or critical pressure. Being able to book elite guests could be an incentive for altering content and tonality, and could also provide the powerful a means to discipline the foreign media firm for overly critical reporting. The more AJE wanted Washington, DC's affirmation, the more susceptible it was to the political conditionality of its acceptance. This was somewhat checked by Al Jazeera's institutional controls, even though the US government had mechanisms of pressure on Doha as well. Since AJE was multi-sited and transnational, the maneuvers from Washington, DC were only one of the channel's fronts. The DC center was not totally autonomous from the headquarters.

Al Jazeera English was not able to really achieve the *critical insider* status it desired. After all, its "moment" was the result of a peculiar alignment in a transnational media-politics constellation during the first year of the Arab Spring: AJE's coverage and editorial vantage points, Qatari foreign policy and US interests, foreign policy and sympathies. This more than anything else was the basis for much of the newfound adoration in Washington, DC, which suggests it was a tenuous, fragile, fleeting "moment." With some foresight, indexing AJE's fate to its DC value should have raised the question of what would happen to such sentiments with the next US-led war in the region. Would the channel's goodwill and influence among the politicos evaporate? Would it be back to 2004 demonization all over again? As the onetime ambassador to Qatar suggested, Al Jazeera's attempted globalization increased US influence over the network. It is not clear that anyone at the channel was looking that far ahead. The immediate goal of just getting on air was far more pressing. This is a reminder that media ports of entry exact costs of assimilation, not just the benefits of being gateways. There is a toll.

The network eventually surrendered the aim of delivering AJE to a substantial portion of the United States when it purchased Current TV in 2013. It established AJAM and AJ+ as wholly American subsidiaries, and geo-blocked AJE in the United States so that Americans could no longer directly access its content online. By trying to create more Americanized channels, the network succumbed to the glocalization imperative that gave India's McDonald's McCurry and created dozens of national versions of the Colombian telenovela, *Ugly Betty*. The subsequent channels were more clearly differentiated for the idiosyncrasies of American news tastes. They did not solicit Washington, DC's validation.

5

Al Jazeera America

The Defunct New York City Broadcast Channel

Our headquarters are in New York. We're an American company
that is part of a global media network. Our management is best
in class, from top networks in the United States.
—Mary Caraccioli, AJAM executive producer, 2014.[1]

Al Jazeera seems to be making compromises, probably to
placate the cable and satellite companies.
—Tony Burman, former AJE executive, 2013.[2]

Introduction: The Story of AJAM in New York Told Through Office Space

In early 2016, the *Commercial Observer*, a real estate industry website, reported Al Jazeera America (AJAM) paid Boston Properties $45 million to break an office space lease in a midtown Manhattan skyscraper, 250 West 55th Street.[3] The lease was for 85K square feet on three floors in the 38-story building: 11K square feet on the ground floor; 50K square feet on the second floor, which had the ultra-high ceilings needed for a broadcast studio, and; 24K square feet near the top of the building on the 36th floor. The first year of its lease was spent on designing and constructing the office space. There were setbacks. For example, the construction company moved a load-bearing column, only to position it in the wrong place. Fixing it cost millions of dollars, an AJAM staff member said.[4]

This office space was to be a real home where AJAM comes into formation. When AJAM was looking for office and studio space in early 2013, months before it launched, it considered multiple sites in the city—including the former, iconic building that housed the *New York Times* (229 W. 43rd St.)—until 2004, before it moved to its towering citadel.[5] The AJAM representatives looking at the building were attracted to its preexisting wiring "for digital media distribution," but they were worried that excessive columns obstructed the open floor needed for television studios.[6] In lieu of an impressive headquarters, AJAM operated out of a patchwork of offices in multiple buildings scattered around lower Manhattan. Its main location at 305 West 34th Street was temporary. It rented studio space in the Manhattan Center at 311 West 34th Street. The digital team and corporate offices were more than two miles away at 435 Hudson Street. This was a dysfunctional arrangement, as physically fragmented as its inner workings were. Al Jazeera America never moved into its new premises.

The channel terminated the agreement for the West 55th Street space because it was closing down after less than three years of operation. No one at the channel saw the closure coming. It signed a 20-year lease. Instead, the unoccupied, partially built offices and studios in the gleaming Manhattan tower were testament to the channel's unmet potential. The costly penalty for exiting the lease was a relatively paltry amount for what proved to be an exorbitantly expensive endeavor just to create AJE's Americanized replacement for the United States; the first CEO described it as "an American news channel that broadcasts news of interest and importance to its American audience."[7] By entering the US market via New York City, AJAM came to resemble a traditional, American commercial television news broadcaster—a model that was past its prime.

Al Jazeera America's Origins and Development

Former US Vice President Albert Gore and media entrepreneur Joel Hyatt cofounded the news channel Current TV in 2005. Based in San Francisco, it was intended to be an "independent, non-partisan voice" for young Americans. Reaching 60 million TV households, its TV distribution and advertising fees brought the company $100 million annually. However, by early 2012, Current TV was struggling with marginal audiences and strained relations with cable and satellite companies disappointed that it fell short of viewership goals. Hyatt and Gore wanted to sell. They searched for potential buyers. In September 2012, The Raine Group accumulated a list of 100 possible purchasers, including Al Jazeera. In a September 18, 2012, email to Gore, Hyatt referred to AJ's aspirations to break into the United States and its improved reputation.[8] He also estimated the deep-pocketed company would pay "a billion dollars."[9] Al Jazeera's heads showed interest. Hyatt traveled to Qatar to negotiate, reaching agreement on December 6, 2012. The network spent $500 million on the acquisition. The deal closed January 2, 2013.

Al Jazeera acquired Current TV as a means to penetrate the US TV market after years of failure with AJE. It had to race to transition from Current TV to AJAM quickly, as carriage agreements were due to expire in a few short years.

It needed a sound footing to boost its position for renegotiations. Failure to show high ratings risked loss of the carriage deals. The company could not afford to spend years preparing, as did the English channel. As for its location, the network had the choice to headquarter it in San Francisco or New York City. Al Jazeera America inherited leases in both cities. Although Current's headquarters and main studios were in San Francisco, New York City made more sense for assembling a new channel on short notice and for the larger goal of becoming more commercially vibrant. New York offered the largest pool of potential employees, complementary services and was a chief gateway to the larger market. Compared with San Francisco, New York City is closer to more of the country's population and thus locations of news stories, news-making figures, and potential expert guests. The channel went live eight months after the purchase.

How did this new channel identify itself? Al Jazeera America's first CEO, Ehab Al Shihabi, an architect and custodian of its rapid launch, sent an email to all staff on the first-year anniversary of its launch spelling out how he saw AJAM as adapting the network's "uncompromising journalistic ideals" for the United States while fulfilling the country's desire for "unbiased, fact-based, in-depth coverage of domestic and international news, without the punditry, opinion and 'infotainment' seen elsewhere." Core to the company's brand, he wrote, was a "courageous and provocative" commitment to covering "under-reported stories" that centered on ordinary people. In other emails, he made sure to reference AJ's mantras of "giving voice to the voiceless" and "the opinion and the other opinion."

Distance from Doha

Al Jazeera America's independence from the network's headquarters evolved over time. At the start, AJAM programs and news were editorially autonomous, planned internally with little oversight from corporate headquarters. During planning, there was little input from seasoned AJE personnel. Some in Doha protested that AJAM departed from the network's standards. Influential AJ persona and one-time program host Marwan Bishara wrote an 1800-word internal email dated July 10, 2013, that was leaked, published online, and reported in various outlets. His missive raised alarms that AJAM was deviating from the AJ mission. Bishara wrote that "[t]he new effort in America benefits from and builds on our brand, journalism and credibility," yet it was attempting "to distance" itself. That AJAM was being planned and built without input from those at AJE who understood the United States raised the prospects that AJAM was going to fail to live up to the network's mission. He rejected the built "firewall" between AJAM and the network. Al Jazeera America was intended to be independent in order to freely compete in the US market.

This autonomy ultimately became unsustainable as major editorial differences emerged with AJE and the protests from Doha became louder. Coordination between them deepened. Al Jazeera English's head of output, for example, issued messages on editorial guidance; AJAM had web teams in Doha handing off with New York and vice versa; the network tried to shuttle people between New York and Doha for short stints to encourage better acclimation to the network within the institutional context. Later on, especially as the channel floundered in the US market, AJE's managing director and head of news-gathering moved to AJAM. Al Jazeera America became more integrated with AJE and the Doha headquarters.

Not everyone was happy with this evolution. Former AJAM employees protested that Doha's control became overwrought. Some contended that Doha "vetted" daily tasks, bogging down their ability to work efficiently.[10] In a lawsuit against AJAM, a former senior vice president stated that network management in Doha was "dictating the coverage of [this] supposedly independent subsidiary."[11] A confidential source told the *Financial Times*, "[i]t's clear they are running it from Doha."[12] Executives in Doha were emboldened by the channels' lackluster showing. But the interventions came after it was independent enough to immerse within New York, the country's TV capital.

New York as a Port of Entry

Mayor Michael Bloomberg called New York "the media capital of the world."[13] As the most important media city in the most powerful media-producing country, it plays a leading role on the world stage. It would seem a likely port of entry. New York City more than any other city embodied Castells's "space of flows," a reference to its nodal power in the international circulation of media, people, capital, and goods.[14] Moreover, the city was a "birthplace of the most important media technologies and industries" in modern times, from publishing to advertising, radio, and television.[15] After the city's establishment in the early 17th century, it became an early center for printing. Later, 19th-century "penny presses" blossomed in New York, producing a rich array of competing newspapers, newsletters, journals, and magazines for a growing city and country. Advances in film, photography, radio, and, then, television concretized its centrality within the national media sphere. New York's status as a TV capital was an outgrowth of its importance in radio. The main commercial radio corporations, NBC, CBS, and ABC, became the first television broadcasters.

New York City was an engine of America's international media and economic power. Like London and Amsterdam before it, the city powered an empire.[16] New York's media industry was integral to American television becoming a lucrative cultural export. Likewise, New York City hosted the prisms through which Americans understood the world, for example, news magazines like *Time*, *Life*, and *Look*. International news wire services, the Associated Press, and United Press, provided news copy for media around the country.[17] New York was also a primary location for foreign media bureaus, which "covered the entire nation and hemisphere 'from the vantage point' of New York City."[18] It was a site of incoming and outgoing media about the world.

The more than 300,000 individuals working in 10,000 media companies exemplify New York's stature as a media capital. They generated half of the country's revenue in publishing and broadcast television, and one-fourth of newspapers' and cable programmers'.[19] To further its growth, a local economic center proposed the city build on its function as a "media gateway." In a 2009 report, it stated that "NYC should seek to be . . . the US entry point for foreign companies"—in other words, a port of entry.[20] Pointing to the city's preexisting assets, utility as an travel hub, and identity as a common site for media industry events and conventions, the report said the city government should actively lure foreign media companies to set up North American headquarters.[21]

New York City emerged from the paradoxical coincidence of the free flow of information, capital, goods, and people along with the massified centralization of commercial power. Jan Morris's eloquent tribute to the city described it as a "landing-stage, a conduit, a place of movement." What passes are not "just fissile" objects, but includes "people, ideas, philosophies," the main objects of currency in this port city.[22] Internally, the city was a bastion of robust speech and press at the same time corporations based in the city fought to establish monopolies to dominate the production and distribution of information.[23] Thus, the largest and most centralized TV news companies were headquartered in New York: the traditional broadcasters and cable news outlets, Fox News, MSNBC, Bloomberg News, and upstart Vice News. Even Atlanta-based CNN had been shifting more of its operations there gradually.[24] New York was a natural stopping point for a news media channel on the move into the United States, and it would be pressured to adopt traits of other US TV news organizations. Flows and agglomeration are, after all, mutual and complementary.

COMMERCIALISM

When Current TV went up for sale, Michael Wolff wrote that digital media could use it as "a bridge back to business logic and plausible mogul dreams."[25] He was referring to the conundrum that online sources faced. *The Huffington Post*, for example, grabbed 35 million monthly visitors and generated $60 million a year. On the other hand, Wolff noted, Current TV reached far fewer people, tens of thousands daily, yet grossed $101 million. In other words, "failure in the cable business" was more lucrative than Internet success. Al Jazeera chose the more commercially advantageous path, although its raison d'être as a Qatari project was actually to expand its reach. A large audience was much more valuable to the network and its sponsor than revenues—reflecting the incongruence in the political economies of the state-funded network and the US TV industry. It is not clear those at AJ who engineered the Current TV purchase understood this dilemma fully.

Al Jazeera America was planned to infuse a commercial imperative into the network's aspirations of quality journalism. This led it to identify and pursue an audience while claiming to advance a modified, domestic version of AJ's given mission of principled, critical journalism. Al Jazeera America anchor-man John Seigenthaler defined AJAM's market as Americans who are "tired of the yelling and screaming on MSNBC and Fox, tired of the stories on CNN, and looking for real news, serious news, in-depth, fact-based news."[26] This was a marketing gambit. Al Jazeera America bet that demand for such TV news existed and calculated its reporting resources gave it an advantageous position over the opinion-dominated shows and perpetually "breaking" live coverage on the cable news outlets. Still, the audience AJAM presumed was largely imagined. It was a *Field of Dreams* plan: "if they build that channel, Americans will come."[27]

Al Jazeera America's commercialism was apparent in its allotment of advertising time, which Bob Wheelock said was something AJE always tried to negotiate down.[28] Al Jazeera America offered six minutes per hour of commercial time, which was more than AJE's, but minor next to domestic channels' 15 to 17 minutes.[29] Al Jazeera America was initially reluctant to chase advertising, avoiding industry events and missing the upfront ad sales market. An *Advertising Age* report noted the channel "pulled out of the Television Critics Association press tour" and "declined to take questions."[30] A media-buying agency executive noted that AJAM was still risky for advertisers. The network maintained that it was taking its time in order to generate substantial ratings first and that the channel could rely on the "scatter market" to find its advertisers.[31] By 2015, it adopted "programmatic TV sales" that automatically paired an advertiser with the channel based on viewer demographics. A former AJAM staff member recalled that the channel attracted an older, mostly male audience.[32] That was consistent with AJAM's frequent placement in higher cost cable packages. Ads for companies like Gilette and AIG aired on AJAM. Other ads were for obscure products. An ex-AJAM employee joked that it ran commercials for survivalist bunkers, "sex toys," and "giant teddy bears."[33] Its advertising revenue was meager. According to SNL Kagan, AJAM generated a mere $7 million in advertising in 2014.[34]

Al Jazeera America's market research spun out generic categorizations of demographic/psychographic audiences. In its materials for advertisers, AJAM's identified three "powerful and diverse audience segments."[35] First, the "News Enthusiasts" were diverse, upscale, early adopters who possessed significant purchasing power. Second, "Modern Activators," the "youngest segment," were heavy users of technology, upwardly mobile, and had influential social circles. Finally, the "Curious & Informed" broadly valued information and entertainment, were career driven and family oriented, and valued convenience. Along with these barely descriptive designations, AJAM provided demographic statistics about its TV and digital audiences to advertisers. This pseudoscientific analysis was in the language of the channel's drift toward proto-commercialism.

Though the channel was more commercially oriented than AJE, it was nowhere near generating break-even income and ending reliance on Qatar's largesse. Nevertheless, its executives repeatedly told journalists that it sought long-term commercial viability.[36] Al Jazeera America's plans to become profitable inspired occasional bouts of aggressive cost-cutting, including laying off between 60 and 100 staff and reducing programming in order to trim the bloated budget in 2014. The channel's president stated in a memo the layoffs were consistent "with our long-range plan as per our original business case."[37]

FORMATS AND DISTRIBUTION

By inheriting Current TV's distribution footprint, AJAM locked on to the track of traditional TV carriage. As such, it had to abandon AJE's goal to reach as many people as possible without concern for revenues. The value of Current TV was in the instant access to tens of millions of US homes, but it came at the expense of having to play by the carriers' rules, which proved constrictive and expensive. Al Jazeera America spent even more money to keep the carriage agreements in force, and they limited its range of options for content delivery, as well as program formats.

In the weeks before the deal was finalized, AJ requested that Hyatt obtain pledges from carriers to honor the sale. This was wise given that many carriage agreements feature "change of control" and other exit clauses that made them potentially nontransferable. In mid-December, Hyatt met with DirecTV, and ultimately offered them $10 million to strike a "key man" clause that allowed the carrier to terminate the contract if a certain individual (Gore) was no longer involved. Comcast consented on December 20, 2012. AT&T, however, was concerned that customers would object to the channel. Hyatt discouraged them to base the "decision on any form of ignorance or bias." AT&T consented soon after. Time Warner Cable (TWC) was the only carrier that refused its consent. The larger cable company claimed it already enjoyed an option to carry AJE for free due to a preexisting February 2012 "hunting" agreement with the network.[38] Under Current TV's carriage deals, it received 12 cents a sub-scriber.[39] Time Warner Cable was reluctant to pay for AJAM since it had free rights to AJE.

Still, after the sale, several companies sought release from the contract, bet-ter terms, and/or payment. In March 2013, AT&T sent AJAM a letter of termi-nation based on contractual issues discovered in a review. DirecTV also sought exit. Before AJAM even launched, the footprint they expected diminished from Current TV's 60 million households—two-thirds of the country's cable/TV households—to 35 million.* The Current TV purchase was "48 hours old" and AJ found "itself in a vicious battle to retain distribution rights."[40] Eventually, Al Jazeera would expend even more resources to firm up the deals with TWC, DirecTV, AT&T, and Verizon. By late 2014 AJAM could claim to return to Current TV's presale 60 million households at significant surplus cost. The desire of sim-ple presence on US televisions proved costly. Distributors exacted even more concessions, compromising AJAM's content.

DOMESTICATION BY DISTRIBUTION

The imperative of market success built into cable and satellite distribution domesticated AJAM independent of the integration into New York. This made it, in one former AJAM employee's words, a "conventional media company" by American standards.[41] First, and existentially, AJ tailored its content to US audi-ences by launching AJAM. It was bound to offer a majority original content, meaning it could only somewhat leverage the strength of its preexisting interna-tional news apparatus. The promise of a new channel was needed to get carrier consent to transfer the deals; many had already rejected AJE. In Doha, there was a perception that AJ was contractually obligated to launch a new channel. Bishara asked in his email, "Have we signed a deal where AJAM program/con-tent must be substantially different from AJE?" Bishara warned this meant AJ sacrificed its "accents" to speak like an American channel.

Second, Current TV's contracts included content-based conditions. DirecTV stipulated that Current TV offer lighter fare, like shows by Google, user-gen-erated videos, *Trivia* and *Current Hottie*.[42] Al Jazeera America eventually paid DirecTV $75 million for a new contract. Employees believed that cable and sat-ellite agreements restricted AJAM from airing programs in Arabic with English subtitles or those produced by Al Jazeera Arabic and Al Jazeera English, accord-ing to former Senior Vice President Shannon High-Bassalik.[43] She asserted that programming that put forward "Arabic viewpoints over all others" violated its cable and satellite contracts, "which required Al Jazeera to remain neutral in all positions."[44]

---

* Current TV's availability in 2012 was 52%, or around 59 million homes (Hagey 2014).

Third, AJAM offered very few on-demand videos and no online livestream (as AJE did) because carriers required exclusivity. Retransmission agreements commonly proscribe the proportion of broadcaster programming that can go online. The channel's executives told staff they were contractually limited to posting no more than two clips per day, at most three minutes each, and they must be removed after a week.[45] Another ex-AJAM employee noted that managers said that distribution agreements include "restrictions on Internet," and that "our work can only go on air through television."[46] This brought about absurdities in programming, as a former AJAM staff member mentioned, such as not being allowed to Internet stream the show called *The Stream*.[47] The AJAM version of the program targeting online communities was short-lived due to this gap. The show was a forum for hearing from nontraditional media voices, activists, people of color, freelance journalists, and scholars.

Such limits also applied to televisual content that was not broadcast, including web-only and other AJ channels' videos—which effectively removed AJE from the country's news market. An Al Jazeera executive said they over-complied in geo-blocking AJE videos in the United States to avoid giving the companies cause to void agreements.[48] Al Jazeera English's media and politics program *The Listening Post* said in an email to fans of the show, "[d]ue to Al Jazeera America's licensing agreements, our shows are not available online in the US." Also, AJAM's website could not host video produced by other non-AJ outlets. A former digital team member mentioned that they had to remove an embedded video showing newsworthy content from C-SPAN out of fear it would upset carriers.[49] The channel's managers accepted this because they were overtly "risk averse" and "TV-first" because of their extensive backgrounds in the TV news industry. They believed, after all, that TV was their core product as it had been where they worked throughout their careers.[50]

Finally, AJ felt the need to counter perceptions of anti-Americanism. For example, AJAM did not carry the AJE show *Empire*, which critiqued American power and foreign policy. The decision was connected with a US branding study. In his email, Marwan Bishara mentioned the channel polled Americans in order to assess perceptions of the channel as "anti-American." When he found out the network geo-blocked *Empire's* archives in the United States (as it did with other AJE shows), Bishara wrote in an email to staff that this geo-blocking decision was not "communicated with staff, who spent years working on this [program]."[51] Bishara quoted a line producer for the show who found it "humiliating" and difficult to explain. He asked how they would persuade American guests to appear "if they don't get exposure in the U.S."

Al Jazeera's substantial investment in AJAM also made AJE more susceptible to flak. One instance was when AJE removed from its website Columbia University professor Joseph Massad's op-ed arguing that Zionism and anti-Semitism shared much in common.[52] The piece elicited sharp condemnation from commentators, including *The Atlantic's* Jeffrey Goldberg, who called it "one of the most anti-Jewish screeds in recent memory."[53] Though it was republished after a backlash against the perceived censorship, former AJE director Tony Burman noted that "it is widely believed that this was an effort by Al Jazeera's senior management to placate its American critics" in the lead-up to AJAM's initiation.[54] This boosted the perception that AJAM would be editorially timid.

Hiring

New York City boasts more media companies and "media jobs than any other city."[55] It was a natural port of entry for a large news media start-up. With the need for a rapid launch, AJAM was even more dependent on the city's labor pool. Finding the optimal TV personnel and moving them to a new city would delay launch preparations. Heavily local hiring was one reason AJAM became like a traditional US TV news source. What proportion of producers and executives working out of AJAM's New York headquarters were already based in the city? One employee estimated about "90% of the hires."[56] The author's analysis of AJAM senior producers' and executives' LinkedIn accounts revealed around 26 (75%) of the 34 in New York City were already in the city when AJAM hired them (see Appendix A). The rest came from London, Washington, DC, Dubai, Doha, and Philadelphia.

The overrepresentation of New York–based personnel was most pronounced among executives. Al Jazeera America boasted that its executives came from leadership positions in mainstream US networks, CNN, ABC, NBC, and CBS, and had extensive experience in the TV news industry. Al Jazeera America's president Kate O'Brian was a vice president at ABC News. Senior Vice President David Doss was previously with CNN as a senior executive producer for *Anderson Cooper 360* in New York City. Senior Vice President Marcy McGinnis was an associate dean of a journalism school after three decades at CBS News. Senior Vice President Shannon High-Bassalik joined from CNN in New York City. The only high executive who was not from New York City was the CEO, Ehab Al Shihabi. He was formally in charge of the business side and liaised with Doha, where he was previously based.

Al Jazeera America courted recognizable on-camera talent, many of whom were already in New York City. Ali Velshi was the first major on-air hire. He left CNN to join the channel. Joie Chen, host of the flagship *America Tonight*, was a CNN anchor and a correspondent with CBS. Richelle Carey, an anchor, moved over from HLN. Antonio Mora, who anchored *Good Morning America*, hosted a current events talk show and then the international news hour. Ray Suarez left PBS *NewsHour* to host *Inside Story*, a news talk show. John Seigenthaler was an anchor with NBC and MSNBC before joining AJAM. David Shuster, who anchored live news shows, was previously with MSNBC, Fox News, CNN, and Current TV. Almost all of the correspondents had similar pedigrees and most were already working in New York City.

DOMESTICATION THROUGH HIRING

Hiring from the US news media industry was instrumental to AJAM's domestication. A former manager said that AJAM was "trying to be 110% American" and speak with an American "accent."[57] This was a sore point for an ex-producer at AJAM who complained that the network stocked up on the same executives "who made US news so bad."[58] Former AJE managing director Tony Burman wrote that AJAM recruited "people who have driven US cable networks, including CNN, to a level of utter mediocrity."[59] The former producer claimed that executives who were trained in US television news had a "big influence in the newsroom."[60] They lacked basic knowledge about international affairs and were "provincial, too US-centric."

When AJAM was hiring, the network was only willing to transfer AJE's American employees. However, an ex-editor at AJE said many American colleagues at AJE preferred not to move based on the vision and early big name hires. They were familiar "with the nature of the U.S. news industry and its inherent biases" so "they just didn't think AJAM was worth coming home for."[61] They suspected AJAM would have a "real disconnection" from AJ's mission.[62] The former editor attributed AJAM's Americanness to the "motivating factors of that [New York–based] talent pool."[63] Most, but not all, of the AJAM hires joined the network as a career opportunity in a weakened industry. Jobs in TV news were disappearing as news budgets decreased. A former AJAM producer thought that many of the quick hires were recently unemployed journalists or simply seeking a higher salary.[64] Many joined AJAM because they were promised the chance to do real journalism, but that was steeped in what the ex-editor described as a "traditional US news mentality"[65]—one New York City's TV news industry codified as conventional wisdom.

An AJAM producer acknowledged that an upstart competitor would relish poaching industry veterans, but she lamented that many industry hires kept "the same cultural understandings" and "don't realize they have them."[66] The producer pointed to the controversy over AJE's editorial guidance over the term "terrorists," which was leaked to the *National Review* in January 2015.[67] It reproduced entries from the style guide, which discouraged using terrorist because of the adage, "one person's terrorist is another's freedom fighter." Those with the TV news backgrounds "were outraged that we couldn't say terrorists." Some US-trained personnel used the word "evil" in discussions about groups or individuals, showing a lack of familiarity with the "history and context" that "people working at Al Jazeera know." The "apparent biases" of many at AJAM showed they "don't totally get Al Jazeera's core identity."[68] This was a telling, microcosmic version of the epistemic gap in US–Arab relations, the same one that showed in the Bush administration's labeling of AJ as "the terror network."

Several AJAM insiders felt the channel betrayed AJE's critical eye in order to assimilate. There were instances where AJAM appeared too deferential to American officials, the producer complained, citing a story about a victim of a US drone attack who asked the government for a public apology. The AJAM producer said their story "gave the CIA the benefit of the doubt," and showed little sympathy for the victim.[69] Furthermore, a senior editorial decision-maker did not even want to cover the story since Americans did not care. The producer said the way they were "talking is not Al Jazeera." Given this distance from the channel's fundamental mission, multiple AJAM employees said the channel's identity was unclear—was it aimed at a narrow range of news junkies, for a wider audience, or for those demanding to hear the "voice for the voiceless"? How American was it supposed to be? This uncertainty produced editorial predicaments. For example, the producer speculated, it would not know how to decide between leading with a report of a massive attack that leaves many casualties in Syria or a Texas shooting that kills three Americans.[70] Those trained in US news organizations appeared conditioned to think "American lives are more important." At AJE, there was more of a principle of "all lives as equal." The producer asked rhetorically whether this is what "it actually means to be an American channel."[71]

Furthermore, there was an Americanized newsroom dynamic giving on-camera talent greater editorial influence. A former producer observed that AJAM overly subscribed to the US TV news standard that placed the news anchor as "the God of the newsroom."[72] Giving the anchor editorial power reflected how AJAM was, in the former staffer's opinion, "an American channel."[73] At AJE, by contrast, the anchors were news presenters or "readers" in the British tradition. They deferred to the journalists who produced the copy, and did not pretend to be subject-matter experts. Shows on AJE were less structured around the host than at AJAM, which reflected an American TV news norm about the familiar news anchor as a central editorial force and not just a deliverer of news. This was projected through the appearance of the names of AJAM's talent in the show's titles.

Part of the problem was AJAM's paradoxical objectives to both be an American channel and consistent with AJ's style of journalism. An interviewer asked Ali Velshi how that was possible if AJAM "hired a lot of old hands from CNN, ABC, etc." Rather than answer directly, Velshi responded that they "*had to hire up to 900 people*"—suggesting that staffing up quickly was the primary imperative.[74] How could they truly vet for fit 900 personnel in such a short amount of time? Later, the swift start-up was blamed for many of the channel's growing pains. Its second CEO, Al Anstey, said that AJAM's "aggressive timeline to launch . . . created certain challenges and certain disquiets."[75] The need for a tight timeline was due to the concern that they would lose the TV distribution contracts. Al Jazeera America did not enjoy the years of gestation period that AJE or AJ+ had. Staffing and programming urgently took precedence over the care of developing an organizational identity. This had the overall effect of making AJAM even more Americanized in the mold of a New York City news network.

Ratings

In early 2014, AJAM anchor John Seigenthaler appeared on *The Colbert Report* to discuss the new channel.[76] The veteran newsman ignored Stephen Colbert's playful banter about him being radicalized and explained that AJAM was a straight, hard news outlet with little room for opinion and celebrity obsession. "We have no angle," Seigenthaler told him. "It's just the news." Colbert's riposte was particularly telling of the channel's quandary: "[t]his is why your ratings are like 10,000 people a night." One way in which the language of commercial media became grafted onto AJAM was through the metric of audience ratings, which was to NYC's TV news industry what political implications were to Washington, DC's.

Al Jazeera America's concern about audience share was an outcome of the carriage deals. An executive producer for AJE and then AJAM, Bob Wheelock, observed that "[f]or the first time, because of the relationship with cable distributors, we need to meet some expectation for ratings."[77] Previously, AJ enjoyed "a luxury of not caring about ratings or revenue." But the need to renew cable and satellite television agreements meant meeting an audience threshold, Wheelock admitted. In other words, to be a television programmer on cable and satellite in the United States beckoned a fixation on audience ratings.

Within more than a year of launch, AJAM's numbers were less than Current TV's were before the handover. In the spring of 2015, more than 20 months after AJAM began airing, it could only claim an average prime-time viewership of between 20,000 and 30,000 viewers, according to Nielsen.[78] Current TV, by contrast, was getting 42,000 prime-time viewers on average in 2012, according to Horizon Media Inc.[79] These numbers paled next to CNN's 896,000 nightly viewers and the 2.48 million tuned in to Fox News. Externally, AJAM stressed that its numbers marked a gradual improvement of about 35% the first year.[80] It also estimated that approximately 20 million unique viewers tuned in. But that did not portend well. Extrapolating from the ratings, only a small percentage watched regularly, suggesting most of those exposed to its signal did not return. The ratings were so poor that when AJAM briefly surpassed MSNBC in viewers for two hours on one day in 2015, it was presented as proof of MSNBC's weakness, not AJAM's success.[81]

After publication of these abysmal numbers, some at AJAM suggested ratings were of secondary import. The anchorman Seigenthaler qualified that the "focus of this organization is producing quality news, not achieving a certain rating." He clarified that they wanted an audience and acknowledged that the "numbers are still small." He added, "we're on track for growth."[82] This was a contradictory reply. He downplayed the pertinence of ratings while stressing AJAM's potential improvement by the same measure.

On other occasions, AJAM executives requested patience when it came to audience performance. In Al Shihabi's August 6, 2014 email celebrating its first-year anniversary, he acknowledged, "there has been a lot of talk about ratings." While he qualified it by championing the journalism and its reception of industry awards, the CEO contextualized their disappointing numbers: "Let's put things in perspective. Other cable news networks have been on television for decades—we're a year old. We're still growing our brand awareness as well as our distribution." Al Jazeera America executives cited the slow starts of CNN and Fox News as a cause for optimism and forbearance.

Despite the weight given to its performance among viewers, AJAM was not willing to do whatever it took for a higher audience share. As the second CEO Al Anstey claimed, "[w]e could chase ratings" by doing "all sorts of stuff in the next week that could give us spikes in viewership." For example, he said, they could over-report on Donald Trump's presidential campaign, which drove ratings bumps at other networks.[83] While its commitment to a journalistic mission was a check, the ability to conjure an audience was necessary to justify the endeavor to the sponsor and please the distributors.

Advanced Producer Services

A port of entry domesticates foreign firms through its provision of advanced producer services, or locally situated complexes of firms and specialists that assist in industrial activity. New York offers the most media-industry support services in the United States.[84] It is a prerequisite to New York City's value as a port of entry. Many of AJAM's contracted services were based in New York. They helped acclimate AJAM to the national market.

Two New York companies were instrumental to shaping how AJAM appeared to Americans. The branding firm Siegel + Gale was one. In 2009, its associates held an event at the New York Public Library to celebrate four decades of its mantra, "simple is smart." A commissioner of Mayor Bloomberg's Office of Film, Theater, and Broadcasting delivered an official proclamation deeming Friday, October 16, 2009, "Siegel + Gale Day in the

City of New York." The renowned firm worked with AJAM to devise its brand design, identity, and strategy.

Al Jazeera America's website design was carried out by the New York company HUGEinc.com. Founded out of a Brooklyn apartment in 1999 by coworkers at another communications agency, HUGE is a digital company that provides marketing, design, and strategy services. Most of its 700 employees work in its headquarters in Brooklyn's DUMBO (Down Under the Manhattan Bridge Overpass). Once an industrial area where ferries boarded, it was developed into a mixed residential-commercial district to attract technology start-ups and now hosts nearly 500 technology companies.

Al Jazeera America contracted smaller local firms for visuals and footage. For the channel's launch promos, AJAM turned to Leroy & Clarkson, a group that advertises on its website that it "leads big brand turnarounds, launches classics, and strategically repositions iconic brands," including AMC, USA, TLC, PBS, and NBC.[85] Leroy & Clarkson helped develop AJAM's advertising motto "There's more to it" along with AJAM and other firms. The intent of the slogan was to signal that there is much more to news stories, as well as Al Jazeera, and that news consumers should expect better journalism. The channel's challenges, according to the New York–based firm, included figuring out how to "combat consumers' deep rooted misconceptions about a foreign-owned media organization" and how to establish a "position in an already saturated cable news marketplace." To address these, the firm wanted to show how American the new channel would be. It produced promos that featured "portraits of American news consumers," the sorts of audiences AJAM aspired to reach.[86] Their promos also showed ordinary American impacted by real news stories, suggesting the channel would be relevant to their lives, in contrast with the types of celebrity-centered stories the competition presented in excess.

Trollbäck + Company, a creative agency that designed graphics for Fox Sports and The Weather Channel, conceived buffer footage for AJAM to run at breaks. The firm wrote on its website that the "network wanted to connect warmly with both major US metros and the Heartland."[87] They developed a distinct visual that portrayed "ribbons of converging light" that flash "through glorious American landscapes," a visual metaphor for AJAM's movement into the country—an imagery of signals in motion that captured the movement through geographies suggested by the port of entry concept.

Media capitals attract and agglomerate symbiotic services that power and rely upon media industries. While firms may vary in their styles and methods, they are versed in the national market, offering to help acculturate a foreign company. While they work with multinational corporate entities, these sorts of outfits are distinctly locational, concentrated in places, and come to reflect basic characteristics of the relevant industry in its place.

Laws and Litigation

Foreign direct investment in a market subjects a firm to new laws, which also act to domesticate a foreign company. The principle of jurisdiction means that particular legal authorities overlap with certain territories. By setting up in a port of entry, a foreign company is operating within a different jurisdiction and must therefore abide by its rules and laws. In the United States, courts and government agencies have acted upon AJAM in three primary respects: commercial deals with distributors, civil litigation, and finally, labor unionization.

COMMERCIAL CLAIMS

Al Jazeera America faced more litigation in US courts than did all the other AJ services combined. At least six lawsuits over commercial disputes stemming from the carriage agreements followed the Current TV purchase. Some of them stemmed from the acquisition. Before signing the final deal, AJ and Current TV's owners set up an escrow account with $75 million of the sale price to indemnify against further costs in securing the agreements. Gore and Hyatt later took AJAM to court over the escrow account money. Al Jazeera America's claims against the account exceeded the total.[88] Separately, AJAM fought DirecTV and AT&T in court. The essential problem was that the contracts had "most favored nation" provisions that guaranteed that no carrier got preferential treatment. After the acquisition, the carriers conveniently found disparities and tried to use them as a pretense to get out of the contracts and to seek more favorable terms. Contract law and the power of courts domesticated AJ by expanding the leverage the carriers had over AJAM, magnifying their preferences for the channel's assimilation to US news values. The carriers used the legal process to extract payments and force AJAM's compliance with the legacy agreements. The network's desire to avoid bad publicity and to move forward motivated it to seek quick settlements.

CIVIL LITIGATION

Two workplace lawsuits highlighted the political and cultural discrepancies between AJ, as a network, and the norms of the New York news media milieu. Courts were made into forums where these differences played out. Whether or not the suits were legally viable, the cases relied on legal standards and norms at odds with what was permissible in the Doha newsroom, revealing a further way in which law domesticates media in motion.

High-Bassalik v. Al Jazeera America, et al.
Shannon High-Bassalik joined AJAM as a senior vice president of programming and documentaries in July 2013 after being with the short-lived CNN program

Starting Point with Soledad O'Brien. She sued AJAM in June 2015 for unlawful discrimination, hostile work environment, and retaliation. At the heart of her complaint was an allegation of systematic bias.

Al Jazeera America's "pro-Arabic [*sic*] prejudices" in substance and hiring practices were due to pressures from Doha, she alleged. Al Jazeera America had to "abandon all pretense of neutrality" by "putting the Arabic [*sic*] viewpoint front and center." There were "overtly anti-Israel" editorial pressures to which she objected. Around the 2014 Israeli invasion and bombardment of Gaza, she claimed, "the news and programming department was explicitly instructed to favor the Middle Eastern point of view and cast Israel as the villain, creating taglines such as 'Gaza under Fire.'" When others tried to offer "balanced news reports" on the Israeli attack, they were "accused by management of being 'very biased for Israel.'" Her lawsuit also stated that the company employees made "inflammatory statements" such as "Israelis are like Hitler" and "[a]nyone who supports Israel should die a fiery death." This, she argued, made for an "anti-Semitic" workplace. Her suit alleged that AJAM fired her for complaining about this in December 2014.

There was another controversial accusation, but one that got less press attention. The complaint stated that network management in Qatar relayed to AJAM "that many in the Arab world believed that the attacks that on American [*sic*] on September 11, 2001 were staged by the CIA to allow America to wage an unjust war on the Arabic [*sic*] world." High-Bassalik alleged that this was an "editorial viewpoint" the company was to take as "guidance."[†]

Furthermore, High-Bassalik claimed a discriminatory workplace environment where higher-ups showed preference to Arab and male employees, while treating others as "second class." High-Bassalik avowed that Arab employees were hired or promoted despite lacking qualifications. Furthermore, she argued that Al Shihabi undermined female employees by "giving them inconsistent instructions, as well as unreasonably short deadlines." Also, he supposedly excluded them from meetings. Male employees were treated more favorably and given light punishments for threatening and harassing coworkers. This allegedly led to the departure of other female executives.

Luke v. Al Jazeera America, et al.
Al Jazeera America hired Matthew Luke as the supervisor of media and archive management in May 2013. His suit was against AJAM and Osman Mahmud, manager of video production and editing.[89] Mahmud was promoted in February 2015 to senior vice president of broadcast operations and technology. Luke charged that he was fired for raising concerns about criticism of Israel and sexism.

[†] The suit did not cite any actual content to substantiate this accusation.

Luke painted Mahmud as unabashedly hostile to Israel and identified him as the utterer of the "fiery death" line referenced in High-Bassalik's suit. To evince this bias accusation, Luke claimed Mahmud sought to replace a Middle East correspondent's Israeli cameraman with a Palestinian one. Included as an exhibit in the suit was a Facebook post in which Mahmud criticized Israel in 2014. However, Luke argued there was a larger agenda at work. The suit also mentioned, "the CEO of AJAM felt the Middle East Correspondent's reporting was too biased toward Israel."

Luke's complaint also listed instances of Mahmud discriminating against and belittling women. On Mahmud's first day in his new role, he directed Luke to remove two female coworkers from an email chain that pertained to their project. He also told Luke to bypass a female lead editor in a correspondence. Mr. Mahmud fired an editor from *America Tonight*. When a female executive producer from the program confronted him, he became very upset and complained to Al Shihabi, the CEO.

Luke took the issue up with AJAM's human resources department and was fired 10 days later. They told him he "did not fit into the company culture." Luke alleged this was retaliation for protected workplace activity—complaining about discrimination. His complaint noted that AJAM never investigated Mahmud's conduct. Furthermore, a coworker who stood up for Luke was demoted. Why did the network go to great aims to protect Mahmud? Luke contended that Mahmud was only promoted because he "is well connected with the financiers and/or senior executives at the parent company of AJAM, specifically with Dr. Mostefa Souag, acting Director General." In a press interview, Mahmud confirmed that he had known Souag for nearly two decades; he denied that he had made the "fiery death" quote, that he wanted an Israeli cameraman fired, and that he mistreated women.[90]

UNIONIZATION

In September 2015, the nearly 50 members of AJAM's digital team joined the growing trend of new media unionization due to displeasure about pay differences, uncertain confidence in channel management, and a lack of clarity about the site's future.[91] At first, AJAM was unwilling to recognize the union. The workers voted in a National Labor Relations Board–administered poll to join the NewsGuild of New York, Local 31003.[92] The union's 2,600 members are mainly at New York news organizations, including Reuters, the *New York Times*, and Dow Jones. The union also belongs to the Newspaper Guild of the Communications Workers of America. Al Jazeera America's digital staff expected to later negotiate a collective bargaining agreement through the NewsGuild thanks to their unionization.

A port of entry presents a multinational and/or its subsidiaries with a new legal environment. High-Bassalik's and Luke's cases referred to New York City Administrative Code, for example. By contrast, Qatar offers no legal protections against discrimination. None of the alleged practices would have resulted in liability in Doha. There is no legal right to unionize there. New York City, with its industry unions, could therefore domesticate AJ in a way that gave more power to digital workers.

Legal processes do not occur in a vacuum. The larger cultural politics of post-9/11 America, including the question of support for Israel, patriotism, and the popular stereotypes of Middle Easterners, were projected on to AJAM through the plaintiffs' cases. As was likely intended, dozens of press reports picked up and repeated their charges. High-Bassalik's case was pushed into arbitration at the end of 2015 due to conditions in the employee contract and jurisdictional issues. Thus, AJAM and Al Shihabi never filed direct responses to her accusations. However, it was foreseeable that the charges would resonate with the prejudices of an American jury, which the litigants and their lawyers surely understood. Cultural politics seep into legal processes to be sure. To the extent that these lawsuits affected how AJAM developed, influencing its management and workplace culture, law became another way in which setting up in the United States, and New York City specifically, domesticated AJAM.

Emulation and Learning

Copying is an essential industrial milieu practice. Executives debated whether AJAM should more resemble Bloomberg News, specialized and pointed at an influential, elite audience, or seek a mass audience with straight news, as an updated version of CNN's glory days. Both visions relied on industrial emulation. Al Jazeera America programs further mimicked competitors. A senior executive producer, Kim Bondy, noted the flagship AJAM show *America Tonight* shared "some of the sensibilities of *CBS Sunday Morning*." It was planned to resemble "[NBC's] *Rock Center*, and we're stealing a couple pages out of [HBO's] *Real Sports with Bryant Gumbel*."[93] The goal was to seem familiar enough to be safe, while offering a product with extra news value. A former employee referred to this as an irony: "AJAM came in with a critique of US cable news stations yet replicated them."[94]

Fitting within the US news landscape also reflected in how certain stories were covered. Around the time of AJAM's launch in August 2013, the national news agenda was highly attuned to events in Syria. A chemical weapons strike in Syria tested President Obama's previous declaration that there was a "red line" forbidding such munitions. Many asked whether the American leader would take more action than training, arming, and supplying rebels. This was a significant event in the region AJ made its name covering. Naturally, those tuned into AJAM expected it to offer incisive coverage consistent with the company's comparative advantage. This was a clear opportunity for AJAM to stand out.

What they found on the channel, however, was not that different than other US channels. A Pew study of TV news media on the Syrian crisis that week showed that AJAM's coverage was more similar to its US competitors than the BBC.[95] The report said that as with "CNN, MSNBC and Fox News, Al Jazeera America devoted the biggest chunk of Syria coverage to the debate over whether the U.S. should become militarily involved in the conflict." It was a predictably US-centric frame. Furthermore, AJAM was more likely than CNN and MSNBC to feature the US president and administration as sources, as well as present and former US military officials or diplomats. Surprisingly, fewer of AJAM's datelines were from the Middle East (16%) than were CNN's (20%). It also featured Syrian sources at a lower rate, 7% to CNN's 12%. Finally, AJAM was more like CNN and Fox News in that around 10% of stories mentioned the Iraq War as a reason for caution in Syria, compared with more than 20% for MSNBC and BBC America. This was not the Al Jazeera its fans in the United States recalled.[†] These finds seemed to confirm suspicions that AJAM was overly domesticated.

Some viewers roundly objected to AJAM's perceived imitation of traditional US news channels. One wrote that AJAM offered a "downmarket" copy of the "parochial look and feel of the existing domestic cable outfits."[96] Others suggested that AJAM modeled itself on US TV news of yesteryear. USA Today's media columnist Rem Rieder called it a "throwback" to the sorts of "network newscasts of decades ago."[97] Its "plodding, responsible, in-depth and conventional approach to news," Jack Shafer opined, seemed more like PBS's NewsHour, a program whose audience was aging out.[§] The US public's reaction was more of a "shrug" than outrage or interest.[98] The notion that AJAM implemented an older style of journalism came out in a comment Al Shihabi made about how AJAM related to competitors: "A lot of news is moving toward entertainment. We are going completely the opposite way."[99] The "opposite way" is the past.

Appearing as a traditional news channel let AJAM stand out from the crowd, while not being too international or Middle Eastern. Nevertheless, AJAM produced

---

[†] Bebawi's study of Al Jazeera English (2016), however, found that many of its stories were similarly crafted to the BBC's and CNN International's. She determined this based on comparing selected stories, which could miss systematic agenda-setting disparities. Notably, though, she found AJE diverged in certain topics, especially Middle East reports.

[§] That was not the first time someone compared an AJ service with PBS. Ackerman (2006) speculated AJE would also be like the public broadcaster.

journalism on many under- or misreported issues pertaining to Native Americans and "people of color in cities such as Baltimore, Detroit, New Orleans and Chicago."[100] It offered original reporting not seen on other channels. Journalism industry groups recognized AJAM with various awards: Peabody, Emmy, Gracie, Eppy, and DuPont, among others. As valuable as its contribution to American journalism was, AJAM did not gain an audience worthy of the investment.

Al Jazeera America Struggled, Then Closed

Al Jazeera America's aspiration to attract a wide TV audience was ambitious from the start. The channel was not welcomed by a highly receptive public opinion. The author conducted a September 2013 telephone poll gauging public interest (see Appendix A). It revealed a limited appetite for AJAM. Of the 507 respondents, less than one in ten reported hearing positive reactions about AJAM, while almost one-third reported hearing "negative" takes; 13% heard neutral reactions.** The rest, about half, did not hear anything at all about AJAM. In terms of interest in watching, one in three reported they would like to see the channel in the future. However, those most interested primarily obtained their news via social media, newspapers, and news websites. Respondents who depended on cable television first were among the least intent on watching AJAM. The channel's fundamental flaw was that it did not seek distribution via the platforms where its natural audience went for news.

Getting wide penetration via cable and satellite—AJ's goal for so long—was a Pyrrhic victory then. Al Jazeera America was immediately relegated to relative marginality in the US public sphere, cited less frequently by other news outlets and unable to attract the same level of attention AJE did for its reports. So much of AJAM's broadcast content was kept offline, away from the news junkie audience that could have been its core. News consumers who were AJ's most immediate target audience turned more to video-on-demand distributors, news aggregators, social media platforms like Facebook and Twitter, and other new delivery means that undercut traditional TV carriers.[101] A former AJAM producer rued that AJ "invested in a dinosaur."[102] Many at the network thought from the beginning that "AJAM was a mistake," according to a channel employee.[103]

The public was mostly unfamiliar with AJAM, according to a 2014 Pew poll, which asked questions about media use and trust.†† As Chart 5.1 indicates, given

---

** The margin of error was 4.2%.

†† These numbers were "drawn from the first wave of the Pew Research Center's American Trends Panel, conducted March 19–April 29, 2014 among 2,901 web respondents. The panel was recruited from a nationally representative survey" ("Where News Audiences Fit . . ." 2014).

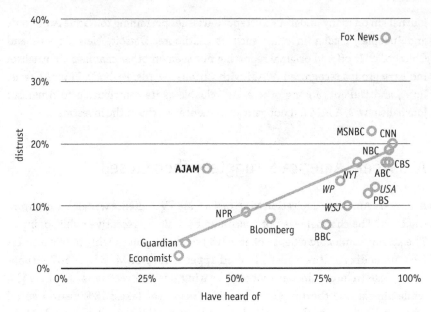

Chart 5.1 Americans and news sources: distrust given awareness. Source: Pew Research Center's American Trends Panel, conducted March 19–April 29, 2014 among 2,901 web respondents.

the relatively low level of awareness (42%) compared to competitors, AJAM was still subject to a high degree of distrust (16%), suggesting there was still popular prejudice against the brand.

This does not necessarily explain the low ratings. Americans, after all, showed considerably more distrust toward the higher-rated MSNBC and Fox News. Poor access to target audiences was a problem for AJAM, since it kept most Americans unaware of the channel and therefore unable to decide for themselves. Most basic cable subscribers could not discover AJAM by flipping through their channels. For all the resources of acclimation New York City offered, it could not overcome this distributional trap.

As the weight of its poor nightly performance mounted, there were reports of turmoil in the newsroom, including controversies, leaks, and high-profile departures. In early 2015, the head of communications and the director of human resources, as well as her deputy, left around the same time. All three were females. One of them, Marcy McGinnis, who started as head of newsgathering and was moved to senior vice president of outreach, wrote a resignation letter. She mentioned Al Shihabi's challenge that "anyone who felt they could not support the decisions or direction set forth by him and the Al Jazeera Media Network would be welcome to leave."[104] She told the *New York Times* there was a "culture of fear" within the network due to Al Shihabi's managerial style and that people who challenged him lost their jobs.[105] At a staff meeting, employees complained about women being fired, fears of retaliation for complaining, the poor marketing and promotion, and the lack of clarity over internal review standards.[106] McGinnis further complained that Al Shihabi, who was supposed to be an administrative executive, was interfering editorially. Due to these embarrassing episodes, poor ratings, and its excessive costs, the network removed Al Shihabi as CEO and replaced him with Al Anstey, AJE's managing director. Many in the network saw AJAM as Al Shihabi's project—he came up with a business case for an American channel years before the Current TV purchase and marshaled it into existence.

In the spring of 2015, there were signs that the channel was going to be dramatically revamped. Internal rumors and then public reports painted the network as facing looming cuts due to the steep fall in oil and natural gas prices—which account for half of Qatar's GDP.[107] It did not help that, as many AJ staffers believed, the new emir, Tamim bin Hamad Al Thani, was reluctant to back the entire network due to the diplomatic problems it caused the government.[108] He took power six months after the purchase of Current TV. Several employees mentioned it was his father, the previous emir, who kept the network afloat by demanding continued state support.

With budget cuts due, corporate leadership moved to trim the network. Al Jazeera management previously decreased AJAM's hours, filling the rest of the airtime with AJE programs. By late 2015, AJAM programming was reduced to about half of the broadcast time per day. As of January 2016, there was internal debate at the channel over its future. It appeared beyond repair and had a scant audience to show for the $2 billion it spent for its first two years.[109] The network studied how to integrate it with AJE entirely. An employee expected AJAM to integrate with AJE as a super-sized broadcasting center.[110] Some advocated scaling back TV and redirecting content production specifically for digital distribution. "So far," this source said, "they are taking steps to do the latter." Al Jazeera America, for example, had advertised for vice president of digital distribution just months before. The "writing is on the wall that TV will be nixed and livestream brought back again." Al Jazeera America's website was to become more multimedia even if it meant losing the cable and satellite deals.[111] Despite their expectations of drastic changes, everyone at AJAM was surprised by what came next.

On January 13, 2016, three years after AJ purchased Current TV, the network told employees in an all-hands meeting that AJAM was going off the air at the end of April 2016. The entire channel, the television and digital media departments, was to be shuttered. Al Anstey, who had been at the helm for six months, stated that the "business model" was unsustainable "in an increasingly digital world" and with "current global financial challenges."[112] A network insider said that Doha found it more sensible to cut AJAM than to pick apart pieces and revise it incrementally.[113] There was another reason for the closure. An employee intimated that the various contractual obligations with carriers and employees made both integration with AJE and down-scaling implausible; it had to dissolve in its entirety.[114] The day after the news came out, many of the staff members were consoled by generous severance packages giving them time to seek employment. Many tried to provide comfort by telling coworkers there would be bountiful media and communication job openings in New York.[115] Al Jazeera had to pay to break various contractual obligations, including office leases. Lawsuits with carriers were anticipated to require hefty settlements. Just as its birth was mired in contractual disputes with a highly litigious distribution industry, so was its demise.

Conclusion

By choosing New York City over San Francisco as the ideal media port of entry for Al Jazeera America, the network was prone to model the upstart channel on a legacy, American cable TV news outlet. Due to the need for a rapid launch, AJAM became even more conventional and "New York–centered," in the words of a former employee.[116] New York's TV news industry, with its attendant support services, is organized institutionally toward assisting in market performance through traditional TV distribution, appealing to a national audience: from the talent and staffing agencies, to design and production companies, advertising and law firms, and audience measurement firms. Through this media port of entry, the commercial impetus of TV carriage went from being an obstacle, as it was for AJE, to a source of coloration that fundamentally inflected AJAM.

This was foreseeable, or so the former owners of Current TV claimed. In Gore and Hyatt's later lawsuit, they admitted that when they weighed selling to AJ, they reasoned that domestication was a probable outcome. The suit stated that they knew the company's "large-scale entrance into the United States mass media marketplace would likely result in a significant improvement of its journalism."[117] Their usage of "improvement" was code for it becoming more favorable to the United States and more amenable to the structural inducements to Americanize. Consistent with the domesticating incentives and pressures of market entry, the suit said, "AJ's presence in the United States would likely result in more influence by the United States on AJ as opposed to more influence by AJ on American viewers."[118] This is the trap of media ports of entry. They lure with the promise of access but incur the cost of compromise. Anchor Ali Velshi expressed how the logic of domestication manifests through market entry. Al Jazeera America did what it had "to do to survive" on TV channel lineups. While he made clear that no one at AJAM wanted to betray Al Jazeera's reputation for quality international reporting, "at the same time, we do need to have cable carriage." To maintain or expand on its carriage by the TV news industry's chief means of distribution, AJAM necessarily appealed to Americans' preferences.[119] Cable and satellite delivery were taken for granted as the industrial standards.

As much as it was an extension of AJ's mission, AJAM also operated in an immediate milieu defined by an industry with engrained conventional wisdom about US TV news and its audiences. Naturally, there was tension between the localized pull of American news tastes and the institutional context with AJ's pronounced identity. Al Jazeera America's president Kate O'Brian made clear the perception that being American was simply safer; she insisted to reporters that on the channel, "the formats, the talent, the producers" were American: "this is an American channel."[120]

Eventually, due to internal protests that AJAM over-assimilated, CEO Ehab Al Shihabi came to insist that the company was "not Al Jazeera America but 'Al Jazeera in America.'" It had to report with more edge, assume a more provocative editorial perspective on the Middle East, and staff needed to be brave and critical, he urged. High-Bassalik's complaint against AJAM charged that Al Shihabi was pushing for the channel to promote Arab and Muslim perspectives in the United States due to what Al Shihabi said was a need to please "Doha." This pressure became unavoidable because low ratings and poor publicity justified the network's intervention. Still, the channel did not manage to attract Al Jazeera English's alienated viewership, which preferred international news coverage. This revealed the mismatch between Doha's vision and the port of entry's prototype of an American television service.

Ultimately, AJAM could not successfully utilize this television city to break into the national market. Al Jazeera America's failure to be future-facing or develop a pioneering news style and voice were functions of how the planners designed the channel as a reincarnated, legacy television station, contractually obligated to be at the margins of the standard, but increasingly outmoded, cable TV distribution system. In both regards, AJAM reflected its place of production.

6

AJ+

Al Jazeera's Digital Start-up in San Francisco

> The real key is we're not in Doha and not in New York City
> under Al Jazeera America.
> —An AJ+ manager.

> We're on the frontier, but we're not pioneers.
> —An AJ+ producer.

Introduction: The Story of AJ+ in San Francisco Told Through Office Space

AJ+'s headquarters are located at 118 King Street, in the SOMA (South of Market) section of San Francisco. The nondescript building is a converted coffee warehouse located across the street from the baseball stadium that the city's Major League Baseball team, the Giants, call home. From King Street's sidewalk, the broad windows display AJ+ branding, giving it an on-street presence. South of Market, or SOMA, is an industrial district for new media and software application developers. This part of the city was referred to as "Multimedia Gulch" for its high concentration of start-ups.[1] The heart of this new media district was the South Park neighborhood, which AJ+'s building borders.

This former warehouse was one of many in the area located near the historic docks. San Francisco had an active shipping port, but that changed due to the rise of high-capacity container ships—one of the main engines of the globalization of trade in goods.[2] With their ability to carry far greater loads, the mammoth ships required more space for larger docks, better rail access, and larger warehousing. As a result, the city of Oakland, located across the bay, overtook San Francisco as the primary port in the 1960s. The city's leftover warehouses offered cheap real estate. In the typical pattern of postindustrial urban development, after the warehouses were abandoned, the areas became blighted, underused or occupied by the homeless and downtrodden. Then artists in search of low rent started moving in. Soon after, developers turned the buildings into lofts and mixed-use real estate projects, before the tech entrepreneurs finally took over.[3] The area no longer offered affordable housing, which is lacking in what has become one of the most expensive markets in the country. Nevertheless, the building AJ+ works out of is a material testament to San Francisco's shift from an actual port function to the metaphoric port of entry concept at the center of this book. It is through that former warehouse that AJ+ was emplaced in a particular new media industrial milieu.

Inside the former Current TV headquarters, one finds what can only be described as the stereotypical new media workspace. The unfinished walls revealed exposed bricks, which supported various large posters, signage, and patterned backdrops giving visual identity to the outlet's space of inner working. It is reminiscent of Pratt's description of new media workplaces' "stock aesthetic" as "'industrial chic,' or 'raw space'" in the mid-1990s, nearly two decades before AJ+. The "common layout" he witnessed in SOMA new media firms— "an open plan office scattered with grouped open desks upon which individuals' computers were placed"—could very well describe AJ+.[4]

Its internal aesthetics mixed activism and fun, gravitas and levity—a reflection of its organizational culture. A visitor inside could not help but notice the large, colorful posterized images of rebellious personas and international figures, such as Nelson Mandela, Aung San Suu Kyi, and the Guy Fawkes mask, overlain with activist words, like "SEIZE," "TRUTH," or "EMPOWER." They also bore AJ+'s logo: the branded stylistics of progressive politics. One large black and white backdrop on the main floor resembled a graphic diagram of a computer circuit, with the evocative words emboldened in large print, as Figure 6.1 portrays. There were alternative seating arrangements and chairs, such as bean bags, high chairs, suspended chairs, and brightly colored sofas. In the kitchen well-stocked with snacks, there were M&M candy and trail mix dispensers. The second floor had a foosball table that AJ+ employees mastered. AJ+ branded hoodie sweatshirts hung from the backs of chairs.*

Background

The basic concept behind AJ+ was not new, a technologist with the network noted.[5] The foundational plans dated to 2010. They began as a blueprint for a

---

* Pratt linked the tendency of Bay Area tech companies to design workplaces as campuses or as "cool" or "funky" places with fun elements to lure recent graduates and skilled tech workers away from freelance careers that gave them the liberty to freely jump from project to project (2002, 38–41).

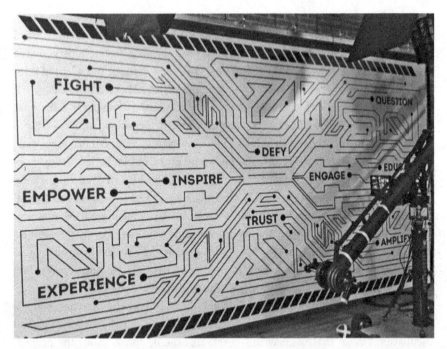

Figure 6.1 The large backdrop on the ground floor at AJ+'s studios resembles a computer circuit board. By highlighting the keywords of its identity, it projects AJ+'s combination of technology and brand of journalism. Photo: author.

digital channel targeting Spanish-language audiences, with a particular focus on Latin America. The plan's progenitors were a group of technology-centered staff members working to push new media projects, helping develop, deploy, and administer mobile apps and network social media accounts. With the Arab uprisings, the team shifted to assisting the network's coverage, finding ways to harness communication technologies, solicit user-generated content, and build wider distribution means. The plan for a digital-only Spanish enterprise was shelved. It would have involved multiple firsts for the network, not just in being a foray into a language market the network was yet to tap, but as an online video channel. This previous plan and its underlying thinking beyond a broadcast TV mindset was at the behest of then–director-general Wadah Khanfar. He guided the network through its rise to prominence and subsequent expansion before resigning in 2011. With Khanfar gone and the network consumed with covering the many regional conflagrations, there was less time and no mandate for ambitious new online projects.

The team finally had the chance to present the plans with the network's purchase of Current TV in early 2013. This move gave the technologists working in new media an opportunity to nudge the network to "be more aggressive on the digital front," according to an AJ+ staff member who helped with planning and implementation. After the Current TV purchase, the network gathered many of its experienced employees to plot the launch of AJAM and to brainstorm ideas. The director-general at the time, Sheikh Ahmed bin Jassim Al Thani, entertained proposals for post–Current TV acquisition projects. The technologists dusted off the prior plans for a digital-only Spanish YouTube channel and adapted it for the American market. They submitted it would complement AJAM.

Al Jazeera America's cable-first strategy meant sacrificing AJE's Internet presence in the United States. Al Jazeera America presumed AJE's audience would watch the new channel on television. However, more and more Americans were only getting their news online. The Innovation and Incubation Group from the Doha headquarters realized this and pushed the idea of launching something novel in the digital space. AJ+'s mandate to originate fresh content separate from AJAM resulted from cable TV agreements limiting AJAM adapting "broadcasting TV content on the web," according to a member of the Group.[6] With AJE out of the US market, AJ+ could approach the American online video news market without competing against other AJ subsidiaries, thereby avoiding overlap, contradiction, and sparking bureaucratic rivalry.

Al Jazeera first announced AJ+ in the fall of 2013 at the international TV trade show MIPCOM in Cannes. Moeed Ahmed, head of the Innovation and Incubation Group that oversaw AJ+'s establishment, spoke about the project, suggesting it filled the online gap AJAM created as a result of cable TV exclusivity.[7] The audience lost in the AJAM transition included online-first news consumers. Ahmad referred to reaching "a generation of people who wants to go beyond the box." This segmented the target audience as those who did not get their news from TV. This generation, Ahmad was quoted as saying in an October, 2013 press release, are active consumers.

> They instinctively turn online to consume news. They share, like, Tweet, comment, interact and forward. To reach them requires a fresh approach. We're working hard to bring this to the world. It will be engaging and at times entertaining—but always with purpose.[8]

This reflected market research the Incubation and Innovation Group analyzed. Trends in news consumption pointed to the growth of digital sources. Even though TV was still a dominant medium for news as of 2013, it was trending downward, especially among younger generations.

THE BRAND

The name "AJ+" began as a working moniker, a placeholder, during the early developmental phases. In the press release cited above, the naming sounded tentative: "[t]he channel is currently referred to internally as AJ+." As a trademark, AJ+ is suggestive of being supplementary. The "+" is additive, as if to build upon and complement a core. Broadcast TV in this case is the network's centerpiece medium, though it has branched out into publishing web reporting, books, and magazines, and producing documentaries. The name also emulated Google+, the tech giant's social networking platform that attached to its massive email service. The name alone indicated that AJ+ was a tech-oriented project.

Calling it AJ+ was also a middle ground in the perpetual debate over branding that racked each new service's establishment. Internally, there were conflicting views over the Al Jazeera brand in the United States and whether the subsidiaries should adapt the name. People at the network rightfully saw the brand as a powerful one globally, and they were also aware of the political liabilities in the United States. Some insisted it was necessary to hold on to the brand to improve it, which certainly happened after the Arab uprisings to a great degree. Others feared that hiding the name appeared disingenuous and invite conspiracy theories. AJ+ was suggestive, or indirect, with its status as an Al Jazeera property; it was more identifiable than the network's sports channel, Bein Sports, which shed the name Al Jazeera Sport and picked up wider distribution in the United States. Branding consultants proposed many alternatives to AJ+, including "Brew."[9]

THE LAUNCH

AJ+'s "hard launch" took place September 2014—three months after it started publishing videos online during its "soft" phase. Beginning with its "beta" launch, borrowing a software development term, the operation produced and uploaded publicly accessible clips to test out work processes and formats. Unlike television, which requires as perfect and impressive a public rollout as possible after the piloting stages, an online news site can launch relatively quietly, in an imperfect state, and make adjustments along the way. There had been the typical prelaunch fits and starts: nixed formats, ideas bandied about without implementation, and it was all amidst rumors that the network might axe the entire project. Even the name was undecided. AJ+ was only its working title. Before going live, the network's commitment to launch was questioned by some at the San Francisco office. This uncertainty was quite consistent with the frequently evoked notion among its staff and managers that AJ+ was a "start-up," despite being a property of an established media conglomerate.

Its September 15, 2014, rollout event had all the ritualistic makings of a technology industry event, with large screens, prominent branding, minimalist décor, and presenters dressed in all black (Figure 6.2). The San Francisco Cre8 Agency provided "brand ambassadors," or "ambiance models," as it had for other mobile app launch parties.[10] The agency described them as "six extremely intelligent and attractive male and female spokes models" who "served as greeters [and] posed for photos with guests." They were tasked to embody and perform tech

Figure 6.2 AJ+'s rollout in San Francisco had the markings of a typical tech company product launch. September 15, 2014. Photo: Cre8 Agency.

sophistication, which they displayed by teaching attendees how to use the app and encouraging them to download it on the spot. At one point during the launch party, these six "brand ambassadors took the stage and held phones displaying the app" as Dr. Bishr spoke about AJ+. It had all the trappings of a San Francisco tech "corporate event." Despite it being future-facing, the network's Director-General Dr. Mostefa Souag was reminded of the past: "AJ reshaped media in 1996 when it launched, Sept 15th marks the new phase of change with AJ+."

AJ+ represented a shift in thinking about strategy and direction. In a company press release after launching in September 2014, the head of the Corporate Development and Strategy department, Yaser Bishr, outlined the rationale for AJ+, noting that it will be oriented toward keeping up with changing "news consumption habits."[11] This required "innovation" of "a new digital destination for journalism." Recognizing the increasing multimedia competition for "attention," consistent with this "era of rapid change in the news industry," AJ+ sought to "captivate, and empower global conversations" by going to where young audiences in particular consume their news—mobile phones and social media. AJ+ took the opposite course of AJAM's "field of dreams" TV channel.[†] AJ+ further aimed primarily at a particular demographic group, millennials. As an audience research analyst with AJ+ noted, they appeal to those who are "globally-minded and educated."[12]

At the same time Bishr and Ahmad were careful to frame this as consistent with "Al Jazeera's mission." Ahmad noted that AJ+ would "give voice to the voiceless" while communicating with "the widest possible audience"—two principles espoused by AJE since it launched. AJ+'s top-level managers

---

[†] Al Jazeera English had previously used social media actively for reporting and content distribution, it is important to note (Ellis 2011).

identified very specifically what sort of audience it sought and, implicitly, how it differed from the other AJ subsidiaries in moving ahead of the technological curve in news consumption. Even with these essential ingredients, articulated by planners in Doha, working out of San Francisco shaped how AJ+ carried this vision out.

As of late December 2014, there were around 80 employees, 66 of whom worked in the San Francisco headquarters. Some of the remaining staff were in Doha, but there were also several global "engagers," social media producers/reporters stationed in different parts of the world, including Washington, DC and the United Kingdom. Around half the employees worked on the editorial side, whereas around 17 were on the engagement team and eight managed the platforms, the technological backbone.

Formats and Distribution

AJ+ launched as a free iOS and Android application for mobile phones and tablets. The app conveyed content through a "cards and stacks" system of display that became ubiquitous among mobile media applications. Each card displayed a type of content. Stacks are collections of cards organized by a single title (often with a hashtag) that signifies a topic or unifying theme. For example, "#RefugeesWelcome" represented stories about the positive reception of Syrian refugees in Europe; "#2016Elex" collected cards pertaining to the US elections. The app's starting point is essentially the most recently updated stacks, meaning those with the newest cards, appear at the top. The user could peruse the different stacks by scrolling down. Clicking on a stack allows the user to swipe through different cards. This was intended to make "the delivery and consumption of news fast, dynamic and simple," according to a September 15, 2014 company press release.

The cards offered several types of formats. Most commonly, a card contains an embedded video. The longest are 10-minute mini-documentaries, called "stories." Then, there are three-to-five-minute videos with presenters; these offer "context" to current news, provide background for understanding issues and events, or function more like opinionated video essays. Some of their event coverage reports are this length as well. Most videos are roughly one minute long "real time" bits. Usually based on images and text alone, rather than narration, they may be animated, info-heavy explainers, short updates on unfolding events, photo galleries, or quirky news kernels likely to be shared by users.

Besides videos, cards include conversation questions inviting debate and exchange in the comments section. For example, under the #PoliceBrutality stack, which they refer to as a "story" in the app, an opinion card asked, "What's been your experience with police?" The story titles, designated by hashtags—consistent with the Twitter convention of using keywords to organize similarly themed Tweets—are often tongue-in-cheek. A stack on North Korea was organized as #DontMessWithKim, a reference to the eccentric dictator, Kim Jong-un. The same stack includes a quiz—another card format—about the North Korean leader. It presented a bizarre tale and quizzed the user whether it was a "myth" or "fact." Some cards featured images only, with very succinct captions that offer explanations and some factual background in order to make sense of the photo. Cards also display social media content by others, including witnesses or the people a given story was about.

Not all stacks were issue oriented; some were overall themes. The stack #PicOfTheDay identified particularly powerful or evocative images and used them to present a news story. The May 29, 2015, image, for instance, showed a crowd of both tourists and migrants fleeing war in the Middle East standing under a police station's overhang as it rained on the Greek island of Kos. The card noted that over 200 migrants arrived there daily in the previous months. Other stacks are oriented toward commentary, advocacy, or critical thematic journalism. For example, #RepresentationMatters looked at Hollywood and other film and TV industries' portrayal of minorities and especially women. Another example is the #Islamophobia stack. Although these stacks of cards on the app were termed "Stories," they were not tied together coherently within an overarching narrative, as the word "story" suggested. They were more akin to categories or keywords that brought together bits of content, short reports, and the other card formats. The cards in a story primarily related to each other thematically. The app organized content in nonlinear fashion, a far cry from the sequential presentation of stories in TV production.

Aware of differences between social media platform affordances and uses, AJ+ developed different formats for various platforms. Such "optimization" meant, for example, producing even shorter clips for Twitter, because its users were less likely to watch longer videos. Twitter was designed for sifting through a high quantity of succinct comments, informational kernels, and links, rather than intensive attention to one content piece. AJ+ data analysts also noted that YouTube visitors tended to watch videos for longer than did Facebook users, suggesting the former was a better platform for the lengthier mini-docs. Unlike the broadcast siblings, AJ+ was not "platform agnostic," as one AJ+ employee called it. Al Jazeera English, by contrast, posted unaltered broadcast clips on its website and YouTube page, without regard for the medium. AJ+'s greater sensitivity to the particularities of each medium and those who used them was a step toward narrowcasting, the micro-targeting and customization of content for individual audience members based on their past behaviors. Social media platforms made this easy, whereas it was impossible through the broadcasting model of linear television. The mode of distribution in effect structured how AJ+ created and circulated its content.

Distance from Doha

In mid-2015, the acting director-general of Al Jazeera, Mostefa Souag, told one of the heads at AJ+'s San Francisco office that he was very encouraged by the "energy" of the operation. It reminded the veteran newsman of the excitement over the Arabic channel in its early, heady days. Souag was involved in its establishment and served as the director of news. He also told the AJ+ manager to "keep doing what you're doing." According to the manager, Souag added "don't worry about Doha." AJ+ was starting to attract more internal attention and some criticized its unorthodox content, but his remark insinuated that AJ+ had freedom from the network's center. While such autonomy could be formalized through structural provisions, like clear lines of decision-making authority, one source of protection from interference or oversight is the many miles and time zones separating Doha and San Francisco.

While AJ+'s production was headquartered in San Francisco, it was managed at the executive level by the Doha-based Innovation and Incubation Group. The director was previously the head of Al Jazeera's New Media team, which worked on digital means of distribution and enhancing audience engagement for the network's many properties. The Innovation and Incubation Group could be described as the research and development component of the network; it tested, developed, and adapted new technologies. This unit was housed within Yaser Bishr's Corporate Development and Strategy department.[‡] He carved out the space for projects outside the domain of the traditional news departments. It took some time to work out this administrative jurisdiction. AJ+ was originally meant to fall under the authority of Al Jazeera America. Housing it away from news departments allowed a team of other new media-oriented technologists to evolve AJ+ as an R&D project. Dr. Bishr's background suggested an understanding of organized innovation processes in a corporate context. He appreciated the need to shelter the project. Other, established departments would seek control, assimilating it within their practices and conceptions of news production. To develop, it had to be shielded from bureaucratic politics, namely the contestation over the

---

[‡] Yaser Bishr's background ranged from an academic post in Germany to entrepreneurship and corporate America. Before joining AJ, he was the chief strategist and business development director at Lockheed Martin, which is based in Washington, DC. There, he led "the transformation of its intelligence and cyber business from government focused to commercial." His academic interests included geospatial engineering, as well as "interoperability and knowledge management," and he founded start-up companies specialized in "location based services," according to his bio ("Dr. Yaser Bishr" 2016).

allocation of resources and influence within an organizational setting—which one former AJAM producer likened to a "game of thrones."[13] Dr. Bishr secured corporate support for AJ+ as a project within the purview of his office.

While it was carved out as a distinct project in the Corporate Development and Strategy department, affording it some internal autonomy, San Francisco's distance from Doha allowed it to minimize the sorts of scrutiny that working in the same vicinity as senior network personnel tends to entail. Physical proximity would have made AJ+'s editorial independence more difficult to maintain. For network senior executives or editorial superiors to monitor AJ+ required more effort and initiative. For the most part, AJ+ staff did not interact with colleagues in other channels as they might have if they worked from Doha. This strengthened the firewall on its own. The reason distance mattered is that it is longitudinal, giving way to a wide time zone difference. Doha and San Francisco's working times did not overlap due to the 11-hour time gap: the long turnover in correspondence gave AJ+ more breathing room. It made strong editorial oversight less likely. The executives in Doha and editors in San Francisco were in their prime working hours during different daily schedules. The dominant news agendas of the workday were staggered between the two, meaning they could not coordinate perfectly at all levels.

By the same token, the freedom granted by physical distance can produce tension. A manager at AJ+ felt that its editorial independence put it at more risk of upsetting Doha. An AJ+ employee noted this was a frequent problem for any sort of "rebellious outpost" that is "not in the mothership."[14] There was a natural tension, he acknowledged, from not being "on the same campus." He cited the natural "sibling rivalry" emanating from bureaucratic competition. Yet, distance limited the means by which central controls and internal politics could rein in the rebels. AJ+'s relatively small budget helped it avoid the sights of bureaucratic snipers. The above-cited AJ+ employee did not feel there was tremendous contestation, a sentiment shared by an executive producer with experience working for both AJE and AJAM. The latter called the budget for AJ+ tiny compared to the broadcasting channels' expenses. This meant that initially, the stakes were lower.[15]

Several employees with experience in Doha noted the benefit of the distance. As one producer who previously worked in Doha noted, there was much more editorial freedom, as well as autonomy in developing its unique "language," style of "presentation," and "leeway to take stances."[16] He noted it was "freer" and "more casual" than if under AJE's or AJAM's control. They would want the news to be hard and traditional, he surmised. AJ+ enjoyed the advantage of being "out of sight, out of mind" from the perspective of editorial executives at the other services in Doha. Even with the intentionally "insulated" position in AJ's corporate bureaucracy, just being in Doha would have meant attracting interest from channel executives seeking to establish control of the project. In his assessment, some saw its "success as a threat" and wanted it under their authority to protect their influence. Another AJ+ employee felt AJ+ was "better off" not being based in Doha given that it wanted to be something fresh and novel.

This distance took a material form in its disjointed information infrastructure. Partially as a result of AJ's very quick development of AJ+, it relied upon different internal work technologies and incompatible systems vis-à-vis the other services. To address this, the network launched an initiative, the Al Jazeera Workplace Transformation (AJWT) program to move all the services to a central Content Management System (CMS) with shared servers so that the different subsidiaries could easily draw upon shared resources. As of 2016, the technological infrastructures of each derivative service were disconnected. Separate servers meant that accessing network-produced footage was very difficult. AJ+ used third-party-agency footage and images often—even for events the Arabic or English channels covered—because their platforms were easier to search and use, and therefore more accessible. Being off the network's Intranet entrenched AJ+'s administrative distance from Doha.

Freedom to Experiment

A benefit of distance and relative autonomy is the freedom to experiment with types of content that are not normally associated with Al Jazeera. One member of the Context team noted many of the differences between AJ+ and the straight news reporting of AJAM and AJE. Calling AJ+'s output "totally different" than the sister channels', AJ+ professes its own news perspective, engages in commentary, and openly tries "to get people to care" about the news and events.[17] While "there is a need for the dry news reports of AJE," AJ+ appealed to a "different intellectual register"—an activist-oriented one. AJ+ steers a course between entertaining without pandering to its audience, while respecting its intelligence, the context team member claimed. The attractive disposition was due to them "not talking down" but "talking as a friend." This sort of quasi-social voice and advocacy disposition was distinct among AJ properties.

In terms of visual style, AJ+'s content was highly produced in contrast with its sister channels, which are marked by a sort of sober minimalism consistent with the BBC or PBS. The Context team member noted that AJ+ was, by contrast, "fast and moving," with "quick cuts."[18] Many of the video pieces were "over-produced" in this journalist's view: there were "too many close-ups," and cutaway shots to punctuate certain words or sentences. Over-production is "less authentic." This was a flaw because of the importance of perceived "authenticity" in "cultivating an audience" in online media.

One of the most significant departures from the traditional AJ news product was in the use of entertainment. As Moeed Ahmed said about AJ+ at the hard launch announcement, it would be "engaging and at times entertaining—but always with purpose." AJ+ termed one of its series, "investigative humorism." AJ+ staffers referred often to news satirists like Jon Stewart, the former host of *The Daily Show* on Comedy Central, and John Oliver, who became well-known for his HBO news and commentary program, *Last Week, Tonight*. An AJ+ manager noted the power of humor to "move the needle on an issue."[19] He said that the idea of investigative humorism started as "an experiment." The popularity of the videos in the series encouraged them to produce more toward this "different type of story-telling." Another AJ+ staff member noted this felt risky: "humor for Al Jazeera is like the Bermuda Triangle."[20] Its relative distance from Doha gave it the latitude to try original formats and an edgy persona.

Journalists with other AJ services derided AJ+ as being less serious than traditional news output. One AJAM employee based in New York City derided it as "letting the kids play." AJ+ staff reported hearing from other network employees that they were concerned it steered into lighter subjects or "fluff" and over reported on social and lifestyle issues at the expense of hard news. An ex-AJAM reporter said it was indicative of the general direction of news, for "short attention spans," and did not "think it's a good thing for the world."[21] Another former AJAM employee based in Washington, DC said that her colleagues "don't talk about AJ+."[22] She only knew its work because the videos often showed up on her Facebook timeline. AJ+ enjoyed a freedom from such pressures and judgments to emerge on its own terms. This was not just spatial, a consequence of locationality, but temporal as well. Its experimentation was foundational to its development of formats and style; as AJ+'s former Engagement Lead Jigar Mehta insinuated, it had an initial "stage" when they enjoyed the "ability to be experimental and try stuff just to see if it works."[23] The industrial and placial characteristics of the local milieu pervaded AJ+'s maturation from its beta form and on.

San Francisco as a Port of Entry

Freed from strong oversight, AJ+ enjoyed a freedom in formation that allowed it to draw upon industrial influences. It acclimated itself within, and thereby reflected, its local milieu of production, San Francisco. As the chief location of AJ+'s productive activities and a port of entry to the national market, San Francisco was influential in both direct and environmental ways: hosting the labor pool from which it drew upon; outlining performance metrics; inspiring spatial organization inside the workplace; locating its collaborators and partners; and positioning it within the Pacific Standard Time (PST) zone. Its proximity to the tech industry was most visible in an early internal debate about whether AJ+ was more a start-up tech company or a media company.

A TECH OR A MEDIA COMPANY?

Many employees and managers referred to AJ+ as a "start-up within the Al Jazeera network."[24] AJ+'s self-conception reflected its status as an experimental, conditional pilot project that treaded new ground within AJ, but it also shows how the company adopted the lexicon of the local milieu. AJ+ was unsure as to whether it would get the network's full backing before it launched. Even into their second year, managers were not confident that the network's funding would increase beyond the first-year amount, despite their plans for global growth and the development of a Spanish-language version and separate Arabic operation. This gave it the tenuousness of a start-up.

There was a debate over whether AJ+ was a tech company or a journalistic enterprise. Predictably, those working as journalists saw it as a news media operation principally. Staff working on the distributional platforms and audience engagement were more likely to consider it a hybrid at the nexus of tech and media. One producer insisted AJ+ is principally about "journalism."[25] A member of the Context team also saw their work as reporting first and foremost, but recognized AJ+ "started as a project of [Al Jazeera's] techies." At the same time, this interviewee questioned whether AJ+ should identify as a "start-up," which sounds "fledgling, like a passion project," when "we're part of a multi-national."[26]

One technologist admitted AJ+'s ability to innovate new technologies beyond its mobile phone application was limited. AJ+ relies on technologies developed by others; its sole tech innovation was the mobile app. Creating and improving technologies is too resource-intensive and requires more programming capacity than AJ+ employs. However, working at the meeting point of tech and media means optimizing use of others' platforms[27]—what an AJ+ executive producer referred to as "platform intelligence."[28] It strives to be ahead of the curve in planning for impending changes within the primary third-party applications. For example, it was one of the first news media outlets to use Twitter images to present news knowledge quizzes.

One locational advantage in this realm, a manager noted, is that their contact with the tech companies whose platforms they use can lead to advanced notice about functional changes. Staying abreast of platform changes is a direct benefit of being based in San Francisco. The same manager noted that just running into friends and acquaintances who work locally helps him stay up-to-date and learn more about various trends. This is the sort of informal avenue of learning through social interaction Neff discussed.[29] However, the location also made the claim to be a tech company more ecologically situated than it would have if launched in Doha. Furthermore, it would have been under the wings of larger news departments, and unable to incrementally build its own editorial voice.

EDITORIAL LEADERSHIP

One consequence of its identity crisis and deep social media integration was that AJ+ was slow to design clear editorial lines of control. Employees exercised more influence on the output. AJ+'s startup identity also involved a relatively flat hierarchical structure, especially when compared with traditional newsrooms built on long-developed norms. A member of the Context team declared, "each person who's been here has shaped the content and the voices of AJ+ tremendously." It was to an extent "you're not going to see at any media organization."[30] A short-term executive producer with decades of broadcast TV experience observed this, as well. He attributed this to AJ+ being younger and influenced by its status as a tech organization. While a more–democratically-structured newsroom sounds ideal, it led to various problems in editorial coherence. The culminating confusion demanded editorial structures. Who would determine what was newsworthy? Which kinds of stories to tell and how? The answers showed how AJ+ came to reflect both the network and the place in which it is based.

When AJ+ launched, editorial direction and authority were still under-developed. Just a few months before the soft launch in mid-2014, one AJ+ employee noted this was an issue that needed to be worked out. He observed that AJ+'s designers and earliest employees were more focused on technology, show formats and branding than in really establishing the substantive direction of its journalism and content creation. One of AJ+'s planners, Riyaad Minty, noted around the time of AJ+'s hard launch that "[o]ur engagement team is as big as our editorial team."[31]

This was rectified when more experienced editorial managers were brought in to guide the news agenda. The composition of the editorial leadership showed how the enterprise blended Al Jazeera's traditional journalism, new media sensibilities, and external influences. Roughly half of the executive producers (EPs) transferred from AJE or AJAM. The rest of the executive producers were new to the network, but had digital news and traditional journalist backgrounds with San Francisco–based news and tech entities. Ultimately, the mix in personnel, hiring both within and outside of the company, was essential to the hybridity of AJ+ as both an extension of the Al Jazeera mission and as a novel enterprise that pushed the network's boundaries. An executive producer claimed that founding AJ+ with "human capital" outside of the organization was essential because "new, fresh talent" helped them "tackle new problems" and showed them ways of "doing it differently."[32] He gave the network credit for locating "as far from HQ as one can get." While the top executives are based in Doha, the day-to-day editorial leadership resided in the San Francisco office as of 2016.

HIRING AND THE STAFF

Agglomerated media industries tend to attract pools of specialist labor.[33] Such places are magnets for "creative migration."[34] Being based in San Francisco, AJ+ had access to a distinct labor pool, one working at the nexus of two converging fields. Due to budgetary limitations, the richness of the local labor pool, managers' preexisting connections, and the need to staff quickly, most of the creative workforce came from the immediate area. AJ+ hired away from a handful of local new and traditional media enterprises, nonprofit groups, technology companies, and integrated Current TV staff after the acquisition. Local freelance journalists, producers, and documentary filmmakers also joined AJ+. It developed a recruitment pipeline from University of California–Berkeley's school of journalism. Some interviewees remarked that recent Berkeley journalism graduates were overrepresented. Several of the animators and other design talent came out of Ex'pression College, an Emeryville, CA-based digital arts and design institute. Not all the hires were local. Some staff moved across the network, from other channels, and many others came from other media and non-media organizations from both the United States and beyond.

Despite the advantages of staffing a hybrid tech-media enterprise in the Bay Area, there was a challenge in that "everyone else is hiring," a manager proclaimed.[35] AJ+ cannot compete with well-funded start-up salaries and benefits, as one technologist observed. Several job candidates had turned down offers from AJ+ because it could not match competing offers. On balance, despite the robust competition for employees, the manager thought the larger milieu is in general favorable to AJ+ as a new project given the "Bay Area culture of getting things done."[36] In Doha, by contrast, this manager saw much less urgency on productive work practices. Later, the peril of AJ+'s success showed as competing companies, like the ABC-Univision joint venture Fusion Media Network, poached AJ+ talent for their own digital enterprises.

CALIFORNIAN IDEOLOGY

The reliance on local hires was one of the main impetuses by which AJ+'s reporting came to reflect northern California as a place renowned for its progressive socio-politics. It is difficult to detect Qatari foreign policy or the country's dominant socially conservative outlook in AJ+'s output. Neither could one consider AJ+'s content particularly mainstream American. Instead, its outlook is closer to "Californian ideology," reflecting the characteristically "San Francisco values" that articulate through progressive positions on social and political matters. San Francisco has long been associated with socially libertarian views toward sexuality, drugs, alternative lifestyles, and other counterculture staples. It also championed social and political movements. One AJ+ employee observed that AJ+

had a particular "enthusiasm for protests."[37] In this sense AJ+ is much more an expression of San Francisco than Qatar, where the predominant religious affiliation of its citizens is a conservative strain of Islam.

"Californian ideology," according to Barbook and Cameron, is a "new faith" resulting from "a bizarre fusion of the cultural bohemianism of San Francisco with the hi-tech industries of Silicon Valley," bringing together "the free-wheeling spirit of the hippies and the entrepreneurial zeal of the yuppies."[38] Central to this "amalgamation of opposites" is a central belief in "the emancipatory potential of the new information technologies." While these two strains can conflict, they come together at the core of AJ+'s identity and content as a technology-oriented media company. Fred Turner wrote about the role of early tech journalists in adapting and protecting antiestablishment counterculture in the evolution of a notion of cyberculture as both hip and liberatory.[39] AJ+'s output includes the sorts of issues that Barbook and Cameron say were "pioneered by West Coast radicals," including "feminism, drug culture, gay liberation, (and) ethnic identity." These are very common themes in AJ+'s content, indicating that AJ+ often mirrors its immediate milieu more so than its distant sponsor. The impulse to report on such topics was reflective of the place of production and the people who staffed AJ+.

SHARABILITY AND METRICS

How AJ+ gauges its success further reflects its positioning as a media-tech company. In one of my interviews with an AJ+ manager, he differentiated the active, sharing news consumer that AJ+ sought to cultivate from the passive audience of television. AJ+ was not designed to simply be watched, but to pursue active engagement, including sharing and online conversation, as its primary metrics of success. These metrics were artifacts of tech platforms, social media namely.

The AJ+ manager said they aimed for 20 million engagements as a goal for 2015. An engagement is a social media share, in which the end user reposts or otherwise passes on the content within her online networks. The manager noted that roughly 12% of the viewers partake in this sort of activity, which is three to four times greater than most news companies. AJ+ is more sharable because it designs its content to maximize its currency on social media. The videos are shorter, punchier, visual, and more casual and conversational in tone. The videos often end with "invites" to viewers to "converse." The context videos explicitly direct questions to the viewer at the end—mainly "what do you think?"—while a graphic text beckons the viewer to "share this story." Optimizing for sharability gives them greater distributional reach through viewers' social networks. As opposed to the linearity of TV distribution, AJ+ is designed to travel to friends of friends/followers of followers on social media—what tech and media circles refer to as a distributed content strategy.[40] Even as their Facebook page had many fewer "likes" than AJE's, AJ+'s videos were seen by more people on Facebook because AJ+ published videos directly to Facebook and more people shared their videos. AJ+ assimilated the logic of social media in its production, while AJE and AJAM produced video for broadcast, firstly. AJ+ was the third-most-popular Facebook video creator in December 2015, behind Buzzfeed's *Tasty* food program and *NowThis News*, according to Tubular Labs. AJ+ garnered 592 million views in one month, its greatest to date.[41]

As AJ+ evolved, its approach of "platform intelligence" involved closer adaptation to how different platforms attract different audiences—a move toward the sorts of narrowcasting that AJAM and AJE did not adopt. AJ+'s data science research revealed how much variation there is among different platform users. For instance, its YouTube audience skewed male, were more international (40%), and took a higher interest in war and conflict. Facebook users showed more gender equity. Interestingly, YouTube viewers watched the videos for longer. Another factor was that YouTube users sought out AJ+'s content, whereas Facebook news users come across it in their feed. Similarly, AJ+ modified its content for Twitter, where snippets were more effective than lengthy videos. By contrast, AJE and AJAM are "platform agnostic." The traditional broadcast mindset approached online video was simply repackaged broadcaster matter.

AJ+ was more data-oriented than either AJE or AJAM. It took "analytics more seriously," as an AJ+ manager noted. AJ+ had two small teams dedicated to better understanding audience behavior. There was a small team of two data scientists who track views, as well as platform and social media engagement (sharing, liking, re-Tweeting, and so on). They pulled the metrics of interest from all the platforms AJ+ used, as well as its native mobile-phone application. The team generated reports for the executive management in Doha and the rest of AJ+'s staff. In both the head of engagement and the data scientists' offices, monitors showed running tallies of views and engagements across Facebook, YouTube, Twitter, and the app. By contrast, AJAM's executives were concerned most directly with traditional media measures, namely the gold standard of television metrics, the Nielsen ratings, and industry awards, and to a lesser extent, website visits and page views. The measures of success reflected respective industrial standards.

The audience development team used the data to assess the performance of particular videos. They conducted postmortems to gauge variables of performance, focusing on anomalies, videos that performed above and below the means, a member of the audience team explained. An AJ+ manager identified his default formula for assessing videos as over- or underperforming. The baseline ratio for Facebook-posted videos was that 25% of those a video reached should view the video for more than three seconds. Of those who watched, one-tenth should engage, that is comment, like, or share the video. The analysts, audience, and executive teams paid special attention to videos that were exceptionally high or low. They published evaluations internally for all to see and comment on. Members conducting the postmortem analyses suggested this process was for learning and improvement, not for editorial direction. However, production personnel reported feeling pressure to create videos that performed well according to these engagement metrics. This reflected a discrete logic, an industrial rationale, that viewed the audience as active, quite different than the expectations of broadcasting at AJAM and AJE's TV services.

"WORKFLOW," SOFTWARE, AND SPACE

One of AJ+'s institutional challenges as a hybrid tech-media operation was how to structure the "workflow." They tried to "make a factory out of it," said one technologist. This refers to the formation and deployment of templates, style guidelines, editorial directives, work calendaring, meeting schedules, and so forth. Instead of running belts, the primary technological architecture consisted of hardware and software. AJ+ managers also emphasized the spatial organization of the workplace. In both of these, the influence of the regional milieu was recognizable.

Among the primary software applications used by AJ+'s teams were Slack and Quip, which were common in the tech sector before being adopted by news media organizations. Slack was a workplace instant-messaging platform that replaced email, the primary software tool in the network's work. Quip was a cloud-based document-creation and sharing portal. These structured the real-time coordination within and between the various teams. AJ+ was nimble in adopting new software. Normally workplace software adoption required staff training on software, but they rarely conducted trainings. A manager suggested that AJ+'s digital-native employees adapted easily to the new applications. At AJE's Doha office, on the other hand, the web team was subject to compulsory training for a new Content Management System. Neither AJAM or AJE used Slack or Quip as of mid-2015, preferring email and Microsoft Word instead.

The concern with spatial arrangement in workplaces to advance creative productivity has been a modern infatuation in business. Fordism and Taylorism, for example, sought to coordinate production process and spatial movement to maximize efficiency in manufacturing and office work. Such principles were applied in orthodox fashion in corporate workplace design.[42] Newer thinking on workplace organization in creative work emphasized fluidity, flexibility, and quality of interactive space, believing these generate the requisite creativity that the knowledge economy requires. While less arduous than its industrial predecessors, such approaches to work design and culture are also geared toward productivity and long ago took a hold among Bay Area tech companies. AJ+ mixed the spatial characteristics of a start-up and a traditional media outlet. It did not draw on an established set of news media desks, as with AJAM's broadcasting side, where the functions were more or less clustered together so that teams that worked together were seated in proximity. Traditional news functions were diffused at AJ+. This was pointed out during one scheduling meeting among the Context team. A producer with broadcasting experience observed that anyone can book guests and that AJ+ did not require a central desk as would a TV network.[43] The diffuse work processes and sharepoint software applications made more flexible seating possible, yet many teams still clustered together.

Jigar Mehta, head of engagement for AJ+, kept on his shared office's coffee table a book on this subject: *Make Space: How to Set the Stage for Creative Collaboration*, by Scott Doorley and Scott Witthoft of the Hasso Plattner Institute of Design at Stanford University (d.school). When I asked him about the book, Mehta mentioned he was a fellow at the institute several years before. Experimenting with collaborative space design was common in the tech industry. AJ+'s internal workplace drew on principles of "Human-Centered Design." In 2012, Mehta spoke on an "Intro to Design Thinking" panel at the 2012 Online News Association conference in San Francisco. The panel included Justin Ferrell, the Fellowships Director of the d.school, as well as media workers who trained there. An excerpt from the panel's description gives a fitting insight into the intent of fashioning AJ+'s workplace:

> "Human-Centered Design" isn't just about making good web pages, it's a way of conceptualizing stories, projects and even your workspace. Toss in concepts of "show don't tell," "rapid prototyping" and "radical collaboration" and you've got *Silicon Valley–style innovation* jumpstarting your editorial and production process.[44]

The phrase "Silicon Valley–style" captured the influence of the larger milieu. Mehta contrasted this with *The New York Times*, where he once worked as a video journalist during the newspaper's first forays into online televisual content. Their workspaces were largely stationary and built around traditional, rigid floor plans.

Competition, Collaborations, and Partnerships

AJ+ engaged in joint productions with various organizations. Several of them were based locally, although not all. AJ+ collaborated with the San Francisco–based Electronic Frontier Foundation, which describes itself as a "nonprofit organization defending civil liberties in the digital world," to put together a series on avoiding online surveillance. Managers sought to foster relationships with other sorts of organizations based locally, including the IDEO design group. In the fall of 2014, I accompanied an AJ+ manager who met with OpenIDEO, a project that crowdsourced competitive and collaborative ideas for addressing specific world problems. It called itself an "open innovation platform" for a "global community to solve big challenges for social good."

AJ+ entered into agreements with and patronized the services of tech and other companies present in San Francisco. It hired Ixonos, for instance, to design its mobile-phone application. Although a Finnish company, Ixonos's San Francisco Design Studio was less than a mile from AJ+'s headquarters. The studio's Senior Vice President Sami Paihonen explained that the Helsinki-based firm opened an office in the city because it strategically "positions [the company] for working with some of the world's leading creative content companies." He went on to explain:

> San Francisco has always been a hot-bed of interactive design and offers us great access to next-generation mobile customers and partners. We are pleased to be part of the mobile revolution in the Bay Area.

In the context of AJ+'s desires to lead the way in mobile-phone- and social-media-distributed news, a presence in San Francisco was of central importance.

In discussing AJ+'s future plans, a technologist mentioned moving toward syndicating AJ+ content for various other video platforms and creating and deploying apps for smart watches, video-game boxes, and Internet-connected television.[45] In January 2015, the Watchup news video app announced it was adding AJ+, and other millennial-seeking news sources, *Fusion, The Verge, Vox.* Watchup CEO Adriano Farano said its "newest partners hit the content sweet spot our youthful users crave with distinct, irreverent and important voices."[46] This app aggregated news media video from over 100 sources, including the major broadcasters, but offered users a personalized stream based on their preferences, the news video equivalent of Pandora for music. The Watchup studio was based in nearby Menlo Park, CA. Its website declared, "we love sunshine and the entrepreneurial spirit of Silicon Valley." That was not the only new distributional boost for AJ+. Apple TV, the over-the-top TV distribution platform, started offering a fully dedicated AJ+ app in early 2016.[47]

AJ+ is inundated with pitches from outside companies, many of which offer technological "solutions" intended to improve conversion rates (the ratio of impressions to watched videos), to measure and understand the audience, and to improve the work of news production in general. The vast majority of these were local to San Francisco. AJ+ held these meetings regularly because they provided a chance to better understand the changing tech landscape. Receiving pitches and considering them are what one manager considered part of the "ethos of the place."[48] In San Francisco, a wide variety of start-ups approached AJ+ with pitches to promote their products or services.

Being located nearby, AJ+ sought to develop relations with tech companies. Twitter's headquarters are close. AJ+ met with them frequently. AJ+ enjoyed a closer relationship with YouTube, which gave them notice of impending changes, helping them with "adjusting workflows." However, being in the area does not guarantee access. Facebook, already a major power in online video and mobile applications, only called AJ+ to sell it ads, a manager complained.[49] The largest social media company did garner institutional relations with established outlets, such as ABC News and *The New York Times*. When it rolled out its native news hosting feature, Instant Articles, AJ+ was not named as a content partner despite being an early adapter to video publishing on the platform.

Despite the rich concentration of collaborators and service providers nearby, some of AJ+'s primary competitors were not based in San Francisco. In naming their competition, AJ+ employees focused on the major players in digital news and video, such as *Now This!, Vice News, Vox, Mic*, and other new media outlets, including *Fusion* and *The Verge*. They also named the chief legacy incumbents who increasingly distributed their content online and through mobile apps with greater sophistication. Most of those outlets cited as competitors were headquartered in traditional news media capitals, New York City or Washington, DC.

REPORTING FROM SAN FRANCISCO

Its location in San Francisco structured AJ+'s reporting in two essential ways. First, it positioned AJ+ nationally and internationally within a lagged time zone, putting AJ+'s main production hours further down the daily news cycle. Being behind in the news cycle, located farther west than the main news capitals, was both a curse and a blessing. Second, due to its limited budget, a great deal of AJ+'s reporting outside of the office was in the Bay Area. Even as it focused on stories with larger resonance, it placed AJ+ within a particular place in the country for viewers. Its location became part of its projected identity.

Some of the producers lamented the location because of how late it was vis-à-vis the daily news agenda. Being in Pacific Standard Time puts AJ+ three hours behind the east coast, where the dominant news industries were located. Eastern Standard Time is the default time zone in national media. This means they were "off the news cycle," in one producer's words.[50] While being late in reporting news seems a formidable liability, others at AJ+ considered it liberating from the rush to break stories. AJ+ was not intended to compete in breaking news, as the technical aspects of spot reporting were thought beyond its capacity.

AJ+ still tried to be early in reporting on timely news. On occasion, AJ+ experimented with live reporting. It used Periscope, a live video streaming app, to broadcast interviews and reports concerning the protest group Black Lives Matter and the 2016 primary elections. While the Real-Time team aimed at timeliness, it reported in small, quick kernels, providing usually repackaged summaries of an unfolding story for the consumer with minimal time to follow news. Context pieces were focused on background and explanation, taking longer to produce. Being behind the primary, national news-media time zone somewhat relieved them of the need to be first in the news race, which meant it better concentrated on explanation, commentary, evergreen content, and non-breaking news. It lacked, however, an investigative reporting team.

Due to limits and uncertainty in the budget, much of AJ+'s original reporting was local to the Bay Area. San Francisco is at a great distance from the population centers where most big news events took place, making it harder and more expensive to deploy news teams. There were some big stories where AJ+ sent personnel to cover, including the Ferguson, MO, and Baltimore, MD, protests against police violence in 2015. The teams covered the protests using mobile phones. Two on-location producers worked with colleagues in San Francisco to livestream and create "breaking content that we published immediately to Twitter, Facebook and YouTube," according to an engagement producer who wrote about her work.[51] Also, AJ+ put out reports from cultural events, such as the Sundance Film Festival and the climate-change talks in Paris in 2015. Occasionally, it ran reports by freelancers located in other parts of the country as well as international locations. However, most of AJ+'s production was based on desk work; many of its videos were created or shot in the studio, using largely repackaged external footage. As of mid-2015, it did not have a substantial news gathering presence throughout the rest of the country, nor was it well integrated with the rest of the network, making it less likely to incorporate AJAM's or AJE's original footage.

Most of the shoots where its hosts went into the field, outside of its head-quarters, were local, which allowed AJ+ to project its emplacement in the Bay Area, giving it a contrasting identity to other news organizations. AJ+ hosts will often cover national or general issues, as they transpire locally. Some types of formats, such as *vox pop* pieces, where the reporter asks people on the street their views, require leaving the studio. In the Bay Area, this put AJ+ within a particular sociopolitical milieu in which leftist, outwardly progressive politics thrive. For example, in a December 2014 report on "White Privilege," an AJ+ host stood on a street in Oakland, CA, and asked people of various racial backgrounds about their views.[52] Most of these sorts of videos are identified as places around the Bay Area, and often the responses they showed typified left political leanings. In the White Privilege video, none of those asked denied or questioned it existed. People of color shared their stories of racism, while White interviewees admitted benefitting from racial hierarchy in society. Through this use of the Bay Area for stories and local scenery, AJ+ displayed itself as a Bay Area, California entity. This was a means of Americanization through an identifiably youthful, multicultural, and progressive locale.

As of mid-2016, AJ+ looked to enhance its international presence. It had small teams of producers and engagers in Washington, DC, and London, and had a slightly bigger team in Doha. This helped AJ+ offset its late positioning in the news cycle, while helping it broaden the scope of its coverage. It generated some dividends in terms of international news coverage. An AJ+ staffer noted that the Baltimore protests got more attention in the San Francisco headquarters than did the Nepal earthquake, which left nearly 9000 people dead in April 2015. While San Francisco focused on covering the protests, the Doha-based team reported on the Nepal earthquake. In sum, nevertheless, AJ+ was on the whole highly domestic in its news perspective.

IN THE LOCAL VERNACULAR

The dominant style of AJ+'s tone of address is the colloquial. Its performance of a youthful online persona is set within San Francisco as its primary site of production. This is not only reflected in a characteristically Californian politics, but in its vernacular, which is at times steeped in localisms. For example, AJ+'s August, 2016 report on the Department of Justice's investigation of the Baltimore City Police Department was organized around four main assessments of the findings, that the department engages in racist practices, and is ineffective, violent, and unaccountable.[53] To emphasize these points, the video presenter enumerated these points and added to each the slang term and intensifier, "hella," which was superimposed on the 90-second video, as Figure 6.3 shows. The term is a derivation of "hell of" and is uniquely associated with Northern California, from

Figure 6.3 Screenshot from "4 Ways Baltimore Has A Massive Police Problem," an AJ+ report posted on August 12, 2016.

where it originated.[54] Even through small symbols, San Francisco is imprinted on AJ+'s output.

Conclusion

One could question the impact of San Francisco as a port of entry by pointing out that its planners chose San Francisco as an ideal site. However, in this case, San Francisco came to house its headquarters incidentally, not by original design, as one who helped launch AJ+ described it.[55] Al Jazeera obtained the San Francisco location as a secondary outcome of the Current TV acquisition. Since AJAM headquartered in New York City and office space was limited, AJ+'s planners took over most of the San Francisco space by default. An AJ+ producer said this proved to be "kind of serendipitous." AJ+'s status as an independent project was furthered by having its productive functions at a distance from bureaucratic competition and network executives who sought to expand their authority by taking control of other projects. Distance from Doha was therefore essential to moving away from the network's dominant broadcasting logic—defined by the linear "TV mindset" as one manager put it[56]—to the flexibility needed to become a digital multimedia, multi-format enterprise. AJ+ was able to develop its own voice situated within the larger milieu of area's new media industry.

San Francisco engendered unique influences on AJ+. For example, had it been in New York City, it might have tapped into a more conventional and experienced labor pool. There would have been no hiring pipeline with Berkeley's journalism school. Would AJ+ have identified as a start-up, aspired to be a tech company, and reported in the Bay Area vernacular? It might not have had traits of the Californian ideology, as New York presents a different sociopolitical milieu. AJ+'s reporters were infused with the atmospherics of place. As a manager noted, "we live here, we consume news here, and are influenced by everything here."[57]

Importantly, most of AJ+'s competition is based in New York City, which Massing called a surprising "centralization" given the supposedly "democratizing potential" of online communication technologies: "*BuzzFeed, The Huffington Post, The Daily Beast, Gawker, Quartz, Business Insider, The Intercept, Talking Points Memo*, and *ProPublica* are all located a short walk from one another in lower Manhattan, forming a sort of journalistic counterpart to Silicon Valley and replicating the parochialism of the New York media elite."[58] Had AJ+ headquartered in New York, it may have felt more pressure to emulate that city's "media elite," to use Massing's phrase. *Vice News*, another competitor, was based in Brooklyn. From its perch in San Francisco, AJ+ could evade that nexus in forming its distinguishable identity.

That is not to say there are no sound reasons for locating in New York, however. It is, after all, the ideal time zone for news reporting on a national scale. The impetus to cover breaking news as a competitive pressure, to compete more directly with leading digital news outlets, would have been heightened. However, being in NYC may have been detrimental to AJ+'s earliest development because of the probability of falling into AJAM's orbit, becoming subject to the larger channel's direction and preferences. This is only a speculation of course since at its very genesis AJ+ began by chance, as an incidental outcome of the Current TV purchase and was barely on AJAM's radar. The big budget television channel had bigger problems to worry about. AJ+ was a modified implementation of a previously designed outfit, the Spanish-language digital platform. As a bureaucratically isolated R&D project, it was autonomous enough to acclimate to its place of operation with relative freedom. AJ+ could then develop its placeness and exhibit San Franciscan qualities, showing further how media ports of entry act upon even the more technologically inclined resident firms.

Although AJ+ was intended to be closer to a tech firm, it proved to be firstly a media operation engaged in "platform intelligence." It optimized its content for the affordances of other technological platforms and hardware. This was an artifact, also, of its distribution strategy, to be present on the applications the audience relied upon for news. It did not marry and tie itself exclusively within one industrial gatekeeper, as did AJAM. Locating in the Bay Area was advantageous to staying abreast of third-party platform developments and tapping into a creative, technologically innovative milieu. The second epigraph at the start of this chapter—about being on a frontier, but not being pioneers—gestured to an old trope about the West, one revitalized in the mid-1990s as a popular enthusiasm for Silicon Valley as a wild, reckless place where newfound riches could abound.[§] The producer's quote was a reference to AJ+'s position on the frontier that is the future of digital news, but the quotation's utterer acknowledged it was not able to really be a technological pioneer. It was a digital media company that produced content, first and foremost, within the preexisting platforms the audience relied upon.

[§] This sort of frontier discourse is evident in the title of Rheingold's *The Virtual Community: Homesteading on the Electronic Frontier* (1993). This is a recognizable extension of Frederick Jackson Turner's classic 19th-century argument that the American expansion, conquest, and settlement of frontiers were essential to American democracy (Turner 2010). In the Silicon Valley version, the outcome is liberatory technology.

Conclusion

Al Jazeera in US Ports of Entry

Media in Place

In 2012, senior Al Jazeera English (AJE) Correspondent Alan Fisher appeared on C-SPAN to discuss his employer.[1] The host asked him a straightforward question that should have produced a simple answer: "What does Al Jazeera mean?" Fisher took the question as one of translation, and replied that it "means the peninsula. It is essentially that island." He added that it "sums up exactly the geographic position." This question about the name was common enough to be included in the FAQ section of a network website. It was the third question listed, no less, after such basic inquires as "What is the Al Jazeera Media Network?" In the answer, it did not mention island, saying instead the name means "'peninsula.'"

This was not the first time the network insisted on the peninsular translation. In the years after the September 11, 2001, attacks, the flagship Arabic news channel operated out of Washington, DC, under the formal name, "Peninsula productions." This was inscribed on its offices in its early days. Its reporters seeking *vox pop* comments from people on the street identified their employer as "Peninsula News." It was camouflage to avoid the sort of hostile confrontations expected during the "war on terror" decade.

Selecting "peninsula" as the translation of its trademark was certainly evocative. It hinted at its patron. Qatar is a small peninsula that juts out from a more massive one, the Arabian peninsula. This was what Fisher alluded to when he said the name captured the "geographic position." Why, however, did Fisher mention "island" in his C-SPAN reply? The confusion may be in the fact that "Al Jazeera" directly translates into "the island." In Arabic, a peninsula is a modified island—*sheba al jazeera* (شبه الجزيرة), or semi-island. The network's brand is a shortened reference then, but it raises a question: to which peninsula did it refer, Qatar or the regional, Arabian one?

The Arabian peninsula is the largest in the world, and the central focus of the channel's ambitions. Qatar directly borders Saudi Arabia, the peninsula's geographically and politically dominant resident. Its position on the map is fitting as a metaphor for the geopolitical arrangement that Qatar long sought to escape: Saudi Arabia's regional hegemony. Al Jazeera, after all, grew out of the remnants of a failed Saudi media venture with the BBC.[2] Once the project was nixed, it left a pool of unemployed, well-trained TV news workers and reporters, the eventual core of the groundbreaking Arabic channel's human resources. As part of its novel, pioneering effort to bring debate and diverse views into Arab regional television, AJ aired dissidents who were effectively shut out of legacy media. This included rarely heard Saudi opposition activists.* Al Jazeera also had the temerity to report critically on its behemoth neighbor, costing them advertisers afraid to displease Saudi Arabia, a large, wealthy market.[3] The intention was for Qatar to assert itself in the region, which necessitated moving out of its larger neighbor's shadow. This regional ambition showed in the name. According to Miles, the chairman Sheikh Hamad bin Thamir Al Thani explained that the network's brand was a tribute to Qatar being "an important part of the greater Arabian peninsula."[4]

Recounting the brand name's exegesis further justifies the book's interest in media geography. Even though it was a pan-Arab network, it is impossible to detach the Al Jazeera Media Network's original raison d'être, foundational principles, and development from its basic locationality in Doha, Qatar, the Gulf region and the Middle East at large. Even at its genesis, then, Al Jazeera was deeply imbued with geographic properties. The news network that became famous for reporting critically on the nearby US-led wars on Afghanistan and Iraq under the Bush administration was undeniably a product of a Qatari gambit for regional and then global prominence, an intense, multi-actor geopolitical contest. Furthermore, it was only possible due to the geological resource-driven political economy that financed it (based on oil and natural gas).† This was all encoded in the name.

Still, the basis for AJ's origins and Qatar's motives in supporting the network are at best partially explanatory of what Al Jazeera built for the US market. Yes, Qatar pursued its goals of inflated prestige through an expanding Al

---

* Seib (2008) noted that this appeared to end when in 2007 AJ employees were given a directive to avoid criticizing Saudi without obtaining upper management approval, as *The New York Times* reported (Worth 2008).

† The state's reliance on oil and gas made it into yet another example of what political economists called a rentier state (Beblawi and Luciani 1987). This refers to states whose income, or rents, came not from taxes, not from their economy and citizens, but from another source such as foreign aid or remittances, but most often, natural resources. Such an arrangement lent itself to authoritarian governance; no taxation, no representation, in essence. Such undemocratic systems preclude functionally free media, generally speaking.

Jazeera media empire that set its aspiration upon the United States. The Doha headquarters designed and steered the subsequent global expansion that produced the three outlets reviewed in this book. But, actualizing its US plans was accomplished by integrating industrial wisdom from the places it located within, the three media capitals. What the ports of entry explanation contributes is a framework for thinking geographically and industrially about a media company's entree into a foreign country. Al Jazeera's mobility into the United States was negotiated through the three cities' production contexts and placial characters. In other words, being in the United States made AJ's outlets more than just simple extensions of the sum of Qatar-specific and institutional factors. Market entry through foreign direct investment fundamentally gave shape to what AJ's US-facing projects became because it authorized adjustment in and to these places.

Discussing the origin of the brand name in terms of the Gulf region was instructive because of how the infamous logo complicated the network's US expansion. In furtherance of the media port of entry framework, we can think of how the brand became translated through each subsequent media capital. In Washington, DC, politicos sanctified the brand once it was expedient with the Arab Spring in 2011. Al Jazeera America's brand was a limited attempt at an Americanization actualized through its adoption of the classic model of the sober, straightforward TV news broadcaster. In contrast, AJ+ innovated on the brand in such a way that somewhat obscured the original name and parent company while projecting itself as a next generation digital news start-up in the San Francisco tech mold.

Al Jazeera in US Ports of Entry

While media ports of entry are conduits to larger markets and therefore oriented around facilitating movement, they are self-contained industrial sites, cities, places. Thus, each of the city's industrial cores that AJ tapped into was also a "bubble." An AJ employee who worked at several of the company's services used that exact term to describe how the personnel experienced the places as disconnected islands.[5] As an example, he said that AJE was subject to Washington, DC's political rationale, which was dominated by Democratic–Republican partisanship. It cued the media-politics industry, framed much of the capital's political deliberation, and therefore carried more relevance and stake among the larger place of the Beltway than it did with any other city of production; this is especially so vis-à-vis San Francisco, a veritable capital of progressive politics. The city on the bay provided for a much different news-making context than did New York City and Doha, he observed. The bubble-like nature of each service entitled each its placeness in its respective port of entry. Such emplacement is the basis for the sustained clout of place in media globalization, showing how place matters for space of flows dynamics. As Aristotle's quotation in the introduction's epigraph suggests, we inquired into these bubbles because of Al Jazeera's motion into them, with an eye toward what these places did for their formation and eventual media production. As central as flows are to the emergence of these places, we must accept their relative detachment—making them more like an archipelago than nodes in a technologically fused network. This is to recognize the vibrancy of place against spatializing processes like media globalization and the power of networked technologies.

The Beltway bubble's influence was tangible in how Al Jazeera English's Washington broadcasting center strove for political relevance, which it thought requisite to currency in the larger national market. After all, AJ's Arabic channel faced political stigmatization during the Bush years. The negative stance by political figures in the capital carried over to popular suspicion of its international sister, AJE. Political validation seemed the natural remedy. No place in the United States but Washington could provide such rehabilitation. While AJE's broadcasting center was established there to cover the country's politics and the Americas at large, it came to embrace the locational advantages. This logic, while embedded into the essential fabric of Washington, DC's media-politics industry, showed itself in AJE's marketing, outreach, embrace of politicos at events, and guest booking, among other indicators.

Washington, DC, as a media port of entry is much more likely to produce specialist, influential, rather than mass appeal, media. The Beltway's media-politics industry is simply not oriented toward widespread market reach given its structural prioritization of insider status, its insularity, and its overt politicization as a center in a governance-oriented knowledge economy where being a wonk is a badge of honor. This is expected of a political capital, because they tend to utilize media industries toward logics of governance, partisanship, and other expediencies concerning the strategic actors of political centers. Washington, DC, of course, is more than just the government. It hosts a concentrated ecology of constituent, supplementary, and publicly oriented organizations, or civil society groups, that are heterogeneous. Even with AJE's stated calling to speak back to the global north being authored in Doha, AJE would not be out of place in a western political capital that attracted NGOs and IGOs that shared a similarly globalist mission to varying degrees. Striving for relevance still meant putting a premium on access, influence, and perceptions of import, which many at AJE associated with elite approval. Thus, Washington, DC's value as a media port of entry was framed within the aims of political allowance as the step to market legitimation. This strategy was exposed as flawed for the network's goals after the seeming moment of legitimacy came with its celebrated Arab Spring coverage. Political approval did not produce the desired results of mass distribution and the chance to gain television market share.

The subsequent spin-offs, Al Jazeera America and AJ+, addressed two distinct strategic shortcomings of AJE in the United States. Al Jazeera America tailored to American exceptionalism, shedding the internationalist repertoire of its sister channel; the carriers were convinced American demand for such news could not sustain a channel, especially a controversial one. This mattered not for AJ+, which moved ahead of the news technology-distribution curve by abandoning the hopelessly backward goal of cable and satellite distribution, the tightly controlled means to audiences. These outfits were located in different media capitals, New York City and San Francisco, centers of the media and tech industries, respectively. This locational distance mirrored the departures in their missions and modi operandi from each other's, and AJE's.

The America channel's design was based on an older American model of TV journalism. Its reporting sought depth and spoke in the objective, view-from-nowhere vocality that was the hallmark of broadcast news—a rejection of the opinionated tenor of cable news. Its news presentation moved at the slower pace reminiscent of television's yesteryear. One could not find the sort of spectacle that became cable TV news' standard fare. Despite claiming to reenact the golden age of journalism as its higher calling, it had to value audience ratings because it relied on highly commercial television distributors. This was a fact exacerbated by its placement in New York City among incumbent news programmers and broadcasters, following the network's purchase of Current TV. Al Jazeera America was in part the enactment of a model drawn from the industry it hired from, emulated, and thought it could improve upon. This recipe would, its progenitors believed, be simultaneously familiar—especially with known TV personalities in front of the camera—and a remedial step away from the partisanship and/or sensationalism that is commonplace on US TV news. They presumed the many Americans who were alienated by the state of TV news would welcome the channel. This strategy failed for several reasons, but most directly, it was due to an overreliance on the traditional gatekeepers of television, companies that are not especially hospitable to start-up hard-news programmers. Al Jazeera America failed to identify a clear target demographic of television viewers and appeal to them through the modes of distribution in which they consume their video news. The carriers see themselves as responsive to demand, and their conventional wisdom is that hard news audiences are fading from TV and audiences with high interest in international news are marginal. Furthermore, the companies are driven by a commercial calculus, and they can impose it on programmers through the terms of carriage agreements, feedback, monitoring for contract compliance, and various other carrots and sticks. Al Jazeera America was to represent a deeper US market ingress than AJE, in part because traditional TV distribution required Al Jazeera's Americanization.

The distribution agreements set severe limitations on how much content AJAM could post online. The commercial model of the distribution industry depends on principles like exclusivity, because it requires artificial scarcity to secure subscribers. Distributors want to be the only providers of programming, naturally. This could have cohered with AJ's primary goal to be widely seen and heard by as many people as possible in the United States if distributors gambled on the channel and made it available on basic packages—which AJ presumed was the best avenue toward mass audiences. However, in most markets, the cable companies saw AJAM as inherently niche, so they only made it available as an add-on channel to which preexisting customers had to subscribe. Motivated viewers had to pay extra for it or a bundle of less popular and similar channels. This reduced dramatically the chances of non-viewers discovering the channel. There was a fundamental mismatch between AJAM's raison d'être—to reach American audiences beyond those who tuned into AJE—and the TV carriage industry's profit motive to maintain traditional carriage formats and practices. While distribution companies recognize the need to adjust to a more complex media environment, only the most powerful programmers have been able to enjoy traditional distribution while experimenting with expansive digital distribution. Regular cable and satellite carrier practices of bundling and exclusive deals are becoming outmoded under the conditions of enhanced competition and expanded technologies of media delivery. Al Jazeera America's business strategy was to put itself at the mercy of the fading basic-distribution model rather than find ways to expand its availability. This proved costly to maintain and was ultimately fatal, as it locked AJAM into marginal status. As a media port of entry, New York shaped AJAM in countless ways, but it could not prevent the channel's failure. In fact, being situated in the capital of American television, AJAM was only affirmed on its erroneous course of outmoded distribution through the Current TV agreement. The channel was captive to the prevailing political economy of the commercial TV distribution model.

It was advantageous that AJ installed AJ+ in San Francisco, a milieu of technological innovation. From there, AJ+ emulated and engineered novel forms of digital video-news presentation, which slowly became ubiquitous among other new media outlets distributing news content via social media. It joined other news companies ahead of the media-technology curve, while legacy media played catch-up. Of the three channels, AJ+ achieved the furthest reach and penetration, relying on mobile and tablet applications and social media distribution to reach the friends of friends of its users, thus growing its audience in highly distributed, networked patterns of sharing, linking, and liking—in the nomenclature of its social media–centered distribution. The channel registered billions of online video views. The network celebrated this number as an achievement and indicator of success in its January 2016 announcement following news of AJAM's closure—a stark contrast of their fates. Network headquarters noted that post-AJAM it would "broaden its multi-platform presence" in the United

States, praised AJ+'s performance, and even held it out as a model for AJ's digital future in the United States and elsewhere.[6] Working out of San Francisco, AJ+'s style, edge, content, and dynamically evolving "platform intelligence" appeared at home in the city's tech sector.

How much of this story is captured by the media port of entry framework presented in chapter 2? Table 7.1 depicts in summary form how each subsidiary demonstrated various elements of the theoretical approach.

Takeaways for International Communication and Media Studies

To echo Michael Curtin, thinking about media's movement in the world through the built-up urban centers of industry bridges historic paradigms of international communication.[7] It puts media imperialism's legacy concern with power's desire to colonize the "communication space" into conversation with globalization theory's model of decentralized pluralism.[8] Localizing in foreign media capitals enabled Al Jazeera's attempt at contra-flow, allowing it a chance to report back to the most powerful media market. This refocusing on ports of entry dynamics encourages scholars of media contra-flow to consider how places themselves moderate media traveling against historical grains by being the ideal locations of foreign direct investment strategies, offering services for repackaging, versioning, and other means in which media are tailored for foreign, and especially difficult, markets.[9] As transnational spaces, media ports of entry tend to be hospitable to foreign firms, usually more so than the national or regional markets they serve. Contra-flow media—those that go from south to north—are more likely reliant on native interlocutory industries and firms given the complexity and maturation of the richer media markets in the target countries. Iwabuchi observed that local partners and services are "much more imperative for non-Western media industries targeting global (i.e., including Western) markets" than they are for established western companies expanding to weaker markets.[10] This is due to their elevated liabilities of foreignness. Media capitals are vital because they are industrially oriented toward mitigating the burdens of being different; they offer corporate services of assimilation.

Second, regarding *glocalization*, we can trace the prospects of institutional hybridization from two directions. On one hand, as with AJE, especially, the Washington, DC, center sought to localize the global, or domesticate the foreign, more accurately. In spreading multinational firms where central offices retain control, it is more likely the case that the globally conceived projects are localized. Thus, the Washington, DC, center was still in Doha's orbit, which made the city more a site of localization rather than local origination. On the other hand,

Table 7.1 **Summary of Media Port of Entry Effects**

	AJE in DC	AJAM in NYC	AJ+ in SF
Degree of Autonomy from Doha	Limited	Somewhat, changed over time	Most independent, as R&D project
Clustered services	• freelancers • studio designers • public relations • interns	• branding firm • website design • promos & bumpers design • advertising	• app design • event planning (release party) • other apps as distributors • Apple TV
Hiring and staffing	• greater mix of hires, including international	• majority of producers • almost all executives • most of on-air talent	• Berkeley journalism school pipeline
Learning	• astroturf campaign to reach cable • strategic guest booking	• models • program designs	• emulation • social interactions with industry
Collaborations & partnerships	• local NGOs • politicos • Newseum	n/a	• distribution platforms • nonprofit orgs, e.g. Electronic Frontier Foundation
Competition	• other international broadcasters, many based in DC	• cable TV news, most based in NYC	• new media in SF, but also NYC
Socio-political acculturation	• sought establishment validation • Beltway pressures	• sought to appear apolitical and safe	• Californian ideology
Legal-regulatory regimes	• sought post-9/11 clearance from Congress; found no issue	• New York human rights law • contract law (multi-state) • local unionization	n/a

Al Jazeera America and AJ+ were closer to the opposite directionality whereby localized formations—foreign media subsidiaries established and formed largely in distant media capitals—became national or globalized through the ports of entry. With AJ+ and AJAM, the network originated the sorts of firms that typify the New York and San Francisco media industries, but adopted them for the larger market. These scenarios are raised to highlight the variable array of glocalization patterns emanating from the different roles that ports of entry play within variable organizational structures.

Third, this study proposes that media studies scholars should commit more energy to the robustness of what Castells called "the space of places." The story of Al Jazeera in the United States reveals flaws in the overwhelming preference for thinking through the "space of flows." First, the obstacles presented in chapter 1 show that momentous impediments remain in the way of news and information circulation in the world. The presumed dominance of network logics—that technological interconnectedness redefines social life, including media consumption—runs against customary, robust barriers, such as the power of statism, lasting cultural preferences, and changing market terrains due to the rise of national and local firms and other media producers. Furthermore, the institutional underpinnings of flows are still emplaced, from origination to distribution. These processes are locatable through multiple mechanisms: the local sites of industries, the materiality of productive edifices and the biographical lives of the people who make, transmit and consume the stuff of flows. The tendency of the most networked of news media, the many new digital outlets, to congregate in media capitals rather than disperse, suggests the staying power of place. If we approach the built-up cities where multinational media institutions locate merely as simple hubs in a network, we might miss how they are uniquely organized as staging grounds for the production, transmission, rerouting, and repackaging of manufactured media content. Or we may not appreciate the impact of the cities as larger places. Ports of entry are more than hubs, as they bear their own influences beyond the network effects. The touch of place on a multinational is locatable, ceteris paribus, in the gap between what the corporate entity initially intended or designed and what finally results as its in-market presence and productions.

Fourth, this book points to the value of thinking infrastructurally about news media and recognizing more clearly the power of distribution in this era of supposed informational ubiquity. As Morley urged, the field should resurrect its ancestral interest in transportation to assess how structural patterns in media movement relate to their distributional systems.[11] Armand Mattelart wrote that the history of communication is first and foremost about transportation, which beckons a revitalized interest in the infrastructures through which media move.[12] The technical terminology of Internet technologies is, after all, centered on the coordinated motion of packets, encoded data, between computer servers.

The Internet is an infrastructural delivery system. As such, countries and cities vary in the quality and speeds of their Internet connections. The pipes of information transit are inherently skewed.

Circumscribed distribution was certainly a salient reason for Al Jazeera's market struggles. This beckons attention to how the presentation of information and expression is tailored to fit the technological affordances of the material hardware used to access the content and the software that delivers them. The companies controlling distributional access weigh gatekeeping power; and they, whether cable companies or social media platforms, have their own preferences and market evaluations that can determine market performance.[†] The sharp distinction between AJ's derivative entities, their products, and their distributional reach highlights this lesson about the importance of distribution for media companies. The three AJ services' very differing dispositions to the evolving modes of distributional infrastructures, and therefore the space of flows, correlated with the ports of entry in which they were emplaced.

Al Jazeera English could not get on television and it was the paramount means of delivering televisual news to Americans. Thus, AJE reached relatively few. It attracted a lot of interest only at extraordinary news moments and with online news consumers. Although widely accessible over the Internet, it was not designed for what became out of necessity its chief means of distribution. It was produced as linear TV and largely broadcast online while packages made for TV were posted on YouTube.

Al Jazeera America also designed its output for conventional television, and gained access to more households. However, it was only partially distributed due to its absence from basic cable subscriber lineups. Contractual obligations meant it fell behind online, just as digital news video was becoming more common through new delivery platforms like over-the-top services. Therefore, it underserved the growing demand for online video. Styled as old-fashioned TV journalism and tied to a diminishing distribution industry, it reached very small audiences and could not compete with competition that was highly partisan and more prone to blending news and entertainment.

AJ+ catered its formats to digital audiences and their devices. It would be illegible on traditional television as a news producer with nonlinear output. Rather than merely trying to magnetically draw viewers to its own preselected

---

[†] While gatekeeping power is most apparent in cable and satellite TV companies, it is also true for tech companies like video-hosting sites and social media platforms. YouTube may be much more accessible and democratic for a host of new users, but it has its own ways of privileging certain producers. When Facebook offers a new function like Articles, it chooses which news organizations can utilize it first; or it can decide to eliminate a type of page, which in effect disconnects a page's sponsor from its audience. In 2016, it announced it would give priority to friends' and family's posts on timelines, which would push organizations', publishers', and other institutions' posts further down timelines (Jackson 2016).

distributional mechanisms, AJ+ went to the audience directly via the social media platforms they were already using. It deployed a multiplicity of modes of distribution based on being highly accessible on as many social networks and devices as possible in order to build extensive reach. Operating from the tech center where the companies at the forefront of new media are based, San Francisco, AJ+ grew into a quintessential digital news operation. While AJ+ was most prototypical of a venture designed to navigate the space of flows, with its emphasis on social media distribution and aspiration to appeal to an online community, it was also arguably the most embedded within and reflective of its respective port of entry. This may have been due to it enjoying the most bureaucratic independence as a research and development project.

Finally, the inventory of ports of entry effects provides a framework for subsequent research on media in motion through cities in the world. It starts with the clustered industrial cores to which media cities and media industries research has given much attention. Second, no analysis can ignore the anthropological aspects of media capitals as cities with their own medleys of identities and social-cultural, political lifeworlds. The power of the confluence of these two components upon resident media firms is conditioned upon internal bureaucratic independence because it allows these subsidiaries, branch offices, bureaus or spin-offs more latitude for assimilative stances vis-à-vis their host ports.

Zooming in on the actual organizational outlay through cities reveals the limits of macro-scale analysis. It is instinctual to follow the standards of international communication research and analyze Al Jazeera's globalization into the United States as a story of attempted international contra-flow against the traditional imperial center, or through a lens of the complicated geopolitics of US–Arab relations and/or Qatar's influence-peddling. Conventionally, we would presume a methodological nationalism that treats the United States as a unitary, homogenous media market.[13] There are deep flaws to only conceptualizing media organization extension as between countries, at the national scale, or beaming into a region, or as globally circulating through networked technologies. Such abstractions do not show so clearly in the lived sites of media-making: the places where the observable practices of transnationalism occur. Global, regional, and national media are not ethereal, do not operate purely in a cloud or network, but are grounded at particular loci—creative and informational milieus that revise what gets produced as global and by whom.

Emphasizing these media capitals as arenas of localized differentiation rooted in variable industrial cores and anthropological characters is a call to examine the power of cities on media movement in the world. The construct of ports of entry expresses the function of certain cities as strategically diverse pivot points for media on the move. Al Jazeera's subsidiary hybridization in these places produced the three derivative outlets as neither fully foreign, nor domestic; they intertwined peculiar institutional contexts and mandates with the industrial forms, models, cultures, and technologies clustered in the respective ports of entry. None of the resulting entities were institutionally pure, either as a product of Doha or as a perfectly assimilated reflection of the respective port's dominant logic.

That is not to repudiate all macro-level studies of media. For a full accounting of how media globalization takes shape, it will be instructive to catalog and weigh the ambit of scalar dimensions of influence, from the global, to the transnational, institutional, and local, and how they intersect. This call accords traction to gauging the broader macro and national structural impediments as they trend all the way down to the particular milieus of execution, design, production, and distribution. The primary contribution of the book's framework is that it refocuses and informs attention to the local faculty of place and its influence on situated media work and forms.

Ports of Entry in Other Contexts

Every globalizing company makes an initial choice of entry mode—simple export, joint venture, or direct investment—to determine the extent and quality of their in-market investment. These presuppose various degrees of dependency on locationality, with simple export hinging the least on geographic factors and direct investment, the most. Second, many target markets are served by multiple ports of entry offering variable benefits and costs. Krätke and Taylor documented the most interconnected media cities.[14] Their findings demonstrate that multiple, competing media capitals serve large national, linguistic, and regional markets. For example, a Spanish media company seeking a presence in Latin America may choose where to establish its derivative entities, offices, or branches between cities like Mexico City, Miami, Bogota, Buenos Aires, and so on. Therefore, firms must resolve between the optional locations to optimize their advantages. There are multiple directions research on ports of entry could take. To better present the utility of the media ports of entry framework for making sense of how companies are impacted by locational strategies, it is useful to consider examples of other cases ripe for study in this vein.

One could examine Al Jazeera's competitors in global news. For example, when CNN International planned its reach into the Asia Pacific, it chose Hong Kong as the city in which to base its regional operations. Certainly, it could have chosen Singapore or Tokyo, for example. Each provided marked disincentives, however. Singapore has an unfriendly regulatory environment with its strict media regulations. Tokyo may have been costlier and the English-language media scene there is less developed, meaning there is a smaller talent pool to draw on. CNN International South Asia based some of its staff in New Delhi, India, the political capital. What if it had chosen Bangalore instead; what different influences, pressures and resources would have shaped it as a subsidiary? Those are very differently oriented media capitals. Of course, CNNI's integration into and dependence upon these cities depends on how independent it is from the central headquarters in Atlanta. While CNN appeared interested in differentiating these in the early 2000s, it scaled back the efforts so that much of the programming is the same, while advertising and weather reporting differ. Inquiry into the locational aspects of such market expansions have to weigh several questions: To what extent are the subsidiary operations empowered with autonomy in editorial authority, staffing decisions, and in contracting domestic specialists and services? How great are the demands that they adjust to local norms and regulations? The answers could drive analysis of how setting up in Hong Kong and New Delhi mattered in ports of entry terms.

There are other global news competitors worth noting. Iginio Gagliardone's study on China's strategic media expansion into sub-Saharan Africa is illustrative.[15] In 2006, the Chinese news agency Xinhua moved its African regional editorial center from Paris to Nairobi, Kenya—an emerging tech and news hub in its own right. This preceded the international broadcaster Chinese Central Television's (CCTV) establishment in 2012 of a unique Africa channel based in Nairobi—it was designed to cover and reach English-speaking Africans throughout the continent. Chinese Central Television Africa promotes China's image in Africa by reporting on Africa with perspectives and a "positive" editorial agenda in contrast to the European and American broadcasting agencies (coverage of China proved to be positive as well, he noted). Through its staffing, it sought "an African face": of the 100 staff members, "around 70 were African (mostly Kenyans) and 40 Chinese."[16] Many of the employees were local, consistent with a port of entry effect. The center, however, also managed a string of bureaus in major cities, such as Johannesburg, Lagos, and Cairo, among others. One of the advantages of being in Nairobi was that the Kenyan media scene was "exceptionally vibrant" compared to its region. In industrial fashion, CCTV poached some of the "most familiar and talented anchors" in Nairobi to present its programs.[17] He reported that Kenyan reporters initially met the project with skepticism; they doubted that they would be free to report and that there was an African audience for a Chinese broadcaster. Part of CCTV's locational strategy was to facilitate a continental domestication, to be made palatable for a heterogeneous target market. As for bureaucratic independence, one of Gagliardone's interviewees insisted that "our Chinese colleagues learned to give us freedom, they adapted quickly."[18] Kenyan journalists acknowledged that their training in journalism, which they saw as "western," sometimes clashed with the editorial vantage point of the institution, showing how Nairobi became a site for the meeting of multiple journalistic contexts.[19] This case from a different international broadcaster in another region raised the possibility of media port of entry tactics and issues not apparent in this book's story of Al Jazeera.

There are emerging media sites worth attending to, and they can be approached comparatively. To reach Francophone Africa, French media companies have deployed through various emerging media cities.[20] The French media consortium Canal+ launched A+, a family entertainment channel. Though the African subsidiary is based in Canal+'s headquarters in the Parisian suburb Boulogne-Billancourt, its team is divided between France and Abidjan, Ivory Coast. The French Lagardère group opened television facilities in Dakar, Senegal. Most significantly, the pan-European broadcaster Euronews established the Africanews multiplatform media project in Brazzaville, the capital of the Republic of Congo, with regional offices dotting the continent.[21] The multilingual channel is designed to be editorially independent of the parent company. What are the relative benefits of each city: Abidjan, Dakar, and Brazzaville, and how do they imprint themselves upon these media projects? A related research question could be whether ports of entry effects are weaker in smaller or emerging media capitals. If these cities do not have robust media industries in place or if the markets they serve are less competitive, we might expect they have less inflective power, especially if the companies planting within them are well-resourced. Such questions demand further inquiry.

Another starting point is to study how government-planned media cities function as ports of entry. Several media companies seeking to grab a share of the news market in India have established joint ventures or subsidiaries in Noida, Uttar Pradesh. Noida is a planned development set up in the mid-1970s; its name stands for New Okhla Industrial Development Authority. Film City is a hub for major news channels and studios. Due to the short distance from Delhi, the capital, it has attracted various news channels. Cable News Network–Indian Broadcasting Network (CNN-IBN), for example, was a joint venture established in 2005 to reach a wider audience than CNNI, which attracted elite viewers. The American business news channel CNBC has a presence there as well. They are co-located with competing Indian news broadcasters like Zee News, NDTV, ABP News, TV Today group, PTC News, NewsX, and India TV, who headquartered or maintain significant operations in Noida. As a district intended to promote development proximate to Delhi, it offers benefits and costs compared with other news media capitals in India. Bloomberg TV India, for example, opened in Mumbai in a partnership with the Walt Disney–owned conglomerate, UTV Software Communications Ltd. While a national film-industry capital, Mumbai also hosts business news, sports, and entertainment channels with a national audience. Some research questions include: how do such planned industrial cities function as other ports of entry?

In these quick sketches, we can see an impetus for examining how media globalization transpires through media capitals that work upon the resulting hybridized operations of foreign-owned subsidiaries. This book's contribution of media ports of entry is built on a conception of how media emplacement in media capitals and the anthropological ecologies of cities influence resident, foreign-owned media. It offers an analytical framework for thinking through the locational outlays of multinational media, and why media capitals offer arrays of advantages and costs for market entrants. Often, the easiest context to overlook in the information age is the local, the immediate place in which media happen in their first instance. Location still matters.

Afterword

Points of Clarification

Every book is a victim of unintended interpretations. There are claims this book may seem to make, but does not. For the sake of clarity, it is worth enumerating potential points of confusion, especially the ones I could not fault an innocent reader for producing.

The most likely mistaken impression—a claim that this book *did not* advance—is that the cities in this story, Doha, Washington, DC, New York, and San Francisco, were singularly determinant of Al Jazeera's subsidiaries and their fates in the United States. The corporate headquarters in Doha was ground zero for origination and control, the source of many institutional pressures, and determined subsidiary distance in physical and bureaucratic terms, which involved variable degrees of autonomy. As for the US cities, this made them, inversely, more or less influential relative to the authority of headquarters in Doha. Rather than being deterministic, places *shape* traveling media organizations that set up in them. Media products are a sum of multiple factors, geographic and not, and so thinking through the influence of place requires weighing a multitude of other factors. It begets complex, multivariate analysis.

This book *does not* claim that AJ's fate in the United States was purely a matter of its agency, that is, its will and strategic decision-making. Zooming in on locational choices and their consequences may give the false impression that AJ was not subject to macro-level structural forces—but those were outlined in chapter 1 in order to paint the magnitude of the challenge before the network. Structural forces constrained and framed the array of decisions available to the subsidiaries given the relative impenetrability of the highly saturated, matured, competitive TV news market. In combination with the first point above, this is to say that AJ neither enjoyed pure agency to enact its intentions nor was it purely a subject of structure—these forces combine to give a nuanced picture familiar to critical media studies approaches.[1] Nevertheless, corporate decision-making was consequential. Al Jazeera, after all, had the power of design, the capacity to plan, and the resources to implement the results.

Finally, the preceding analysis might be seen as glorifying or neglecting the serious critiques one could and should levy against the network and its channels.

Al Jazeera must be as scrutinized as any other media company. Admittedly, readers could confuse some of the appropriation of the company's talking points as the author's wholesale acceptance of their veracity. For example, the book made frequent mention of Al Jazeera's mission to serve as a "voice for the voiceless," but without reflecting critically on this corporate mantra. The book's interest was more on AJ's self-presentation and discourses around its identity. Excluding critiques like one former AJAM reporter's point that "[n]obody is voiceless to begin with" should not be taken as wholesale endorsement or validation of this motto.[2] This book, as was stressed to interviewees, was not intended as an exposé or a media critique, but as a theoretical treatment on media geographies. This could have the unintended effect of glossing over the many legitimate criticisms.

One valid critique merits further mention. Like any news institution, Al Jazeera's employees were cautious in reporting on issues that were vaguely taboo or editorially sensitive areas; and one result included acts of self-censorship. Among its workforce and executives, there were diverse motivations, normative expectations, modes of working, interpersonal sensibilities, and political agendas. These resulted in prejudices, skews, and lapses in editorial judgment to be certain. Many present and former employees I interviewed accused their and other services of patterned bias (pro- or anti-American/Israeli/Muslim Brotherhood), of discriminatory hiring practices (most flagrantly in Doha), of ethno-religious favoritism and cliquishness, and of poor journalistic, managerial, and other practices betraying questionable professionalism.[*] I could not generalize from such anecdotes without making this the focus of more systematic research; it is unsurprising given its institutional complexity, the often informal business practices of the network, and the vying and bureaucratic infighting ubiquitous in any human institution. The most urgent, distinct critique has been the evidence of Al Jazeera's instrumentalization as a Qatari foreign-policy tool, which sacrificed what makes it valuable, its independence—discussed in chapter 1. This tension between editorial independence and pleasing the sponsor is well known to international broadcasters, and is deeply consequential since it implicates the programmers' credibility with its employees, audiences, and larger news media industry. Al Jazeera's former director-general Wadah Khanfar used to assert that violating the network's editorial independence would undermine its value, which, he claimed, was why the emir would not allow it. He left the position under unclear circumstances in 2011.

[*] As for reasoned critiques of Al Jazeera, there are a rich number of statements or press articles (Booth 2010; Koblin 2015; Bordelon 2015; Bond 2015a) and critical scholarly inquiries (Zayani and Sahraoui 2007; Figenschou 2013; Samuel-Azran 2013; Abdul-Nabi 2015; Bebawi 2016) that document them.

As of the summer of 2016, the future of Al Jazeera in the United States appeared to be digital. In late July, the acting managing director and director of programs, Giles Trendle, sent an email to AJE staff that it was hoping to relaunch Al Jazeera English digitally after clearing legal hurdles related to the network's contractual obligations to distributors following Al Jazeera America's closure. His email announced that the international English channel will again be made "available in the USA, across digital platforms" contingent on "the green light from our Legal team, who have been concluding deals with the cable carriers of AJAM."[3] By September, 2016, AJE unblocked its livestream, making it accessible by Americans again.

Methodology

This book's main method is the theoretically motivated comparative case study.[1] Al Jazeera English in Washington, DC; AJAM in New York; and AJ+ in San Francisco are presented as unique cases, and compared along the dimensions enumerated in the port of entry framework (chapter 2). The basis for comparison is strong given they are part of the same parent company, which had a consistent overriding mission, political economy, and, for the most part, leadership at the highest levels. While accounting for the differences, each case study tracks the subsidiaries from the points of design, to production, content, distribution, and finally audience reception.

The primary data for the case studies come from over 60 confidential interviews with AJ employees and executives since 2010. In order to secure their full participation and to ensure no harms accrue to them for speaking to me, I promised confidentiality, consistent with the ethical obligations a researcher owes voluntary participants. In this text, I sought to limit descriptions that accidentally may reveal their identities. Thus, interviewees were described generally by their position and where they worked. I also provided dates of the interviews in the citations for reference purposes. Most of the interviews were semi-structured, beginning with a list of questions.[2] However, responsive questioning was used to stimulate further insights. No interview lasted more than an hour in order to respect informants' time. Half of the interviews were recorded with a digital audio recorder or smartphone. For the rest, I relied on handwritten notes. I offered to share quotations with participants to ensure accuracy—"member checks"—but only a few wanted to check them. Only one interviewee insisted on a change due to the high chance they could be identified by a quotation. I removed it.

Chapter 4 references an online study, which the author conducted between February 23 and March 5, 2011, in collaboration with Katie Brown, who was then a colleague at the University of Michigan. The study's 179 participants were Americans recruited using Amazon's Mechanical Turk (MTurk), an online worker platform. Participants were paid $0.25 or $0.50. The mean participant age was 30.29, with a range of 17 to 67. About 66% of the participants were female. The average participant (59%) lived in a suburb, though 22% described their residential area as "urban" and 19% as "rural." Resembling national education-attainment data, the average participant has completed some college coursework. Half of the participants identified as Christian, 17% as agnostic, and 13% as atheist. The majority of participants (80%) were white. Other ethnicities represented include Asian Americans and Pacific Islanders (10%), African Americans (4%), Latino/as (4%), and Arab American (less than 1%). The mean political ideology on a 7-point scale was 3.55, firmly in the moderate, centrist range. The vast majority of participants (98%) do not watch AJE or CNNI regularly. However, CNN was the most popular source of TV news among respondents (18%), followed by Fox News (16%). While this sample is not representative, and the value of MTurk to researchers has been debated, it provided more representative samples than do the other study pools available to university researchers.[3] The study measured Arab American prejudice using Bushman and Bonacci's items on the Arab American Prejudice scale.[4] It is an 11-question inventory, but was reduced to six questions for purposes of this study.

Chapter 4 also presents Al Jazeera English's website traffic data for the American cities where the most hits came (Table 4.1). The original data came from Google Analytics, which the network installed for its own internal website-traffic observation. The population numbers were drawn from the United States' 2010 Census.[5]

In chapter 5, there was a presentation of the findings from a content analysis of AJAM employees' profiles on LinkedIn, the professional social media platform where many in the media industry post their resumes and network with others in the industry. The author searched for AJAM personnel who were producers, editors, executive producers, vice presidents, and presidents in June 2015, and built a database of 48 personnel, representing 5–10% of AJAM's total staff. The author marked down their current and previous titles, the three past employers and where they were located. It is possible this database excluded some executives but the list appeared exhaustive.

Also in chapter 5, there is a reference to a telephone survey (n = 507; margin of error was 4.2%.), conducted in September 2013 by the MPO Research Group. The questions asked were: (1) As you may know, Al Jazeera recently launched an American TV news channel. What kind of reactions have you heard about the channel? (2) Have you watched Al Jazeera America TV news? Other questions about political views and demographics were included as well. The results presented are after demographic weighting, which was, according to MPO Research Group, based on the latest US Census 2010 population statistics (which are the most up-to-date population numbers available), using population, age, ethnicity, and gender control totals. It was weighted using the raking survey method developed by Deville, Särndall and Sautory, also known as iterative proportional fitting modeling (IPF), which aimed to find weights applied to the sample data that will give the same proportions found in the actual population.[6] These ratios were computed and applied in the form of weights to each sample observation. The result was an extrapolated view at the national level based on the proportions of each control variable according to demographic census data.

Notes

Introduction

1. Douglas Quenqua, "Al Jazeera Steps Up Efforts to Establish Presence in US," *PR Week*, January 13, 2003, accessed August 5, 2016, http://www.prweek.com/article/168049/al-jazeera-steps-efforts-establish-presence-us.
2. Tal Samuel-Azran, *Al-Jazeera and US War Coverage* (New York: Peter Lang, 2010).
3. Mohamed El-Nawawy and Adel Iskandar, *Al Jazeera: How the Free Arab News Network Scooped the World and Changed the Middle East* (Cambridge, MA: Westview, 2002).
4. Hugh Miles, *Al Jazeera: How Arab TV News Challenges America* (New York: Grove Press, 2005), 94–95.
5. Interview, October, 20, 2010.
6. Stephen Brook, "Al-Jazeera Is World's Fifth Top Brand," *The Guardian* [UK], February 1, 2005, accessed August 6, 2016, http://www.theguardian.com/media/2005/feb/01/marketingandpr.broadcasting.
7. Brian Steinberg, "Al Jazeera America's New Chief Hopes to Change Network's Image," *Variety*, November 2, 2015, accessed August 5, 2016, http://variety.com/2015/tv/news/al-jazeera-america-al-anstey-1201631317/.
8. Robert McChesney, *Rich Media, Poor Democracy: Communication Politics in Dubious Times* (Urbana: University of Illinois Press, 1999), 106.
9. Roland Robertson, "Glocalization: Time-Space and Homogeneity-Heterogeneity," in *Global Modernities*, ed. Mike Featherstone, et al. (London: Sage, 1995), 25.
10. Khalil Rinnawi, *Instant Nationalism: McArabism, Al-Jazeera, and Transnational Media in the Arab World* (Lanham, MD: University Press of America, 2006).
11. Robertson, "Globalization," 28.
12. Victor Roudometof, "The Glocal and Global Studies," *Globalizations* 12, no. 5 (2015): 775.
13. Jeremy Tunstall, *The Media were American: U.S. Mass Media in Decline* (New York: Oxford University Press, 2008).
14. Isabel Jijon, "The Moral Glocalization of Sport: Local Meanings of Football in Chota Valley, Ecuador," *International Review for the Sociology of Sport* (2015), accessed August 7, 2016, doi: 10.1177/1012690215572854.
15. Ingrid Volkmer, "Deconstructing the 'Methodological Paradox': Comparative Research Between National Centrality and Networked Spaces," in *The Handbook of Global Media Research*, ed. Ingrid Volkmer (Malden, MA: Wiley-Blackwell, 2012), 117.
16. "The Flow of News" (Zurich: The International Press Institute, 1953); Terhi Rantanen, "The New Sense of Place in 19th-Century News," *Media, Culture & Society* 25, no. 4 (2003): 436.
17. Haoming Denis Wu, "Investigating the Determinants of International News Flow: A Meta-Analysis," *International Communication Gazette* 60 (1998): 493.

18. Daya Thussu, "Mapping Media Flow and Contra-Flow," in *Media on the Move: Global Flow and Contra-Flow*, ed. Daya K. Thussu (London: Routledge, 2007b).

19. Annabelle Sreberny, "The Global and the Local in International Communications," in *Media and Cultural Studies: Keyworks 2006*, rev. ed., ed. Meenakshi G. Durham and Douglas M. Kellner (Malden, MA: Blackwell, 2006).

20. Nitin Govil, "Thinking Nationally: Domicile, Distinction, and Dysfunction in Global Media Exchange," in *Media Industries: History, Theory, and Method*, ed. Jennifer Holt and Alisa Perren (Walden, MA: Wiley-Blackwell, 2009); Terry Flew and Silvio Waisbord, "The Ongoing Significance of National Media Systems in the Context of Media Globalization," *Media, Culture & Society* 37, no. 4 (2015).

21. Joseph S. Nye Jr., "Soft Power," *Foreign Policy* 80 (1990); Olivier Da Lage, "The Politics of Al Jazeera or the Diplomacy of Doha," in *The Al Jazeera Phenomenon: Critical Perspectives on New Arab Media*, ed. Mohamed Zayani (London: Pluto Press, 2005).

22. Volkmer, "Deconstructing the 'Methodological Paradox,'" 120.

23. Ulrich Beck, "The Terrorist Threat. World Risk Society Revisited," *Theory, Culture & Society* 19, no. 4 (2002b): 51–52.

24. Brian Joe Berry, "Cities as Systems Within Systems of Cities," *Papers of the Regional Science Association* 13 (1964); Larry S. Bourne and James W. Simmons, *Systems of Cities* (New York: Oxford University Press, 1978).

25. Larry S. Bourne, *Urban Systems: Strategies for Regulation* (Oxford: Clarendon Press, 1975).

26. David Harvey, *Social Justice and the City* (London: Edward Arnold, 1973); Manuel Castells, *The Urban Question: A Marxist Approach*, trans. Alan Sheridan (Cambridge, MA: MIT Press, 1979); Henri Lefebvre, *The Production of Space*, trans. Donald Nicholson-Smith. (Blackwell: Oxford, 1991), 26.

27. Castells, *The Urban Question*. Originally published as: Manuel Castells. *La question urbaine* (Paris: Maspero, 1972).

28. Harvey, *Social Justice and the City*.

29. David Harvey, *The Condition of Postmodernity*, vol. 4. (Oxford: Blackwell, 1989).

30. Jane Jacobs, *Cities and the Wealth of Nations* (New York: Vintage, 1984).

31. John Friedmann and Harold G. Wolff, "World City Formation: An Agenda for Research and Action," *International Journal of Urban and Regional Research* 6, no. 3 (1982); Fernand Braudel, *The Perspective of the World* (London: Collins, 1984); Peter J. Taylor et al., *World City Network: A Global Urban Analysis* (London: Routledge, 2004).

32. Saskia Sassen, "Global City: Introducing a Concept," *Brown Journal of World Affairs* 11, no. 2 (2005): 27; Saskia Sassen, *The Global City: New York, London, Tokyo* (Princeton, NJ: Princeton University Press, 2001).

33. Stefan Krätke and Peter J. Taylor, "A World Geography of Global Media Cities," *European Planning Studies* 12, no. 4 (2004): 459–477.

34. Janet Abu-Lughod, *Before European Hegemony: The World System, AD 1250–1350* (New York: Oxford University Press, 1989).

35. Taylor, *World City Network*, 9.

36. Manuel Castells, *The Rise of the Network Society*, 2nd ed. (New York: Blackwell, 2010).

37. Ibid., 453.

38. Ibid., 458.

39. Ibid., 443.

40. Ibid., xxxii.

41. Ibid., 417.

42. Interview, January 2, 2016.

43. Aswin Punathambekar, *From Bombay to Bollywood: The Making of a Global Media Industry* (New York: New York University Press, 2013); Jennifer Holt and Alissa Perren, eds., *Media Industries: History, Theory, and Method*, (Malden, MA: John Wiley & Sons, 2011); Timothy Havens and Amanda Lotz, *Understanding Media Industries* (New York: Oxford University Press, 2012).

44. Alfred Marshall, *Principles of Economics*, 8th ed. (London: Macmillan, 1920); Paul Krugman, *Geography and Trade* (Cambridge, MA: MIT Press, 1991); Paul Krugman, "What's New

About the New Economic Geography," *Oxford Review of Economic Policy* 14, no. 2 (1998); Michael E. Porter, "Location, Competition, and Economic Development: Local Clusters in a Global Economy," *Economic Development Quarterly* 14, no. 1 (2000).

45. Anthony Giddens, *Central Problems in Social Theory: Action, Structure, and Contradiction in Social Analysis* (Los Angeles: University of California Press, 1979); Anthony Giddens, *The Constitution of Society: Outline of the Theory of Structuration* (Berkeley: University of California Press, 1984).

46. Timothy Havens, Amanda Lotz, and Serra Tinic, "Critical Media Industry Studies: A Research Approach," *Communication, Culture & Critique* 2, no.2 (2009): 234–253.

47. Taylor, *World City Network.*

48. Stefan Krätke, *Medienstadt. Urbane Cluster and Globale Zentren der Kulturproduktion,* (Opladen: Leske & Budrich, 2002).

49. Taylor, *World City Network,* 95.

50. Ibid.

51. Krätke and Taylor, "A World Geography," 466.

52. Michael Curtin, *Playing to the World's Biggest Audience: The Globalization of Chinese Film and Television* (Berkeley: University of California Press, 2007).

53. Ibid., 19.

54. Edward S. Casey, *The Fate of Place: A Philosophical History* (Berkeley: University of California Press, 1997).

55. Ibid.

56. David Morley, "Communications and Transport: The Mobility of Information, People and Commodities," *Media, Culture & Society* 33, no. 5 (2011): 744.

57. Charles Landry, *The Creative City: A Toolkit for Urban Innovators* (London: Earthscan, 2000).

58. Herbert Schiller, *Communication and Cultural Domination* (New York: International Arts and Sciences Press, 1976); Herbert Schiller, "Not Yet the Post-Imperialist Era," *Critical Studies in Mass Communication* 8 (1991): 13–28; Herbert. I. Schiller, *Mass Communications and American Empire,* 2nd ed. (Boulder: Westview Press, 1992); Edward S. Herman and Robert W. McChesney. *The Global Media: The New Missionaries of Corporate Capitalism* (London: Cassell, 1997); Edward Herman and Noam Chomsky, *Manufacturing Consent: The Political Economy of the Mass Media* (New York: Pantheon, 2002); Daya K. Thussu, "Mapping Media Flow and Contra-Flow," in *Media on the Move: Global Flow and Contra-Flow,* ed. Daya K. Thussu (London: Routledge, 2007b).

59. Philip Seib, "Hegemonic No More: Western Media, the Rise of Al-Jazeera, and the Influence of Diverse Voices," *International Studies Review* 7, no. 4 (2005); Tal Samuel-Azran, *Al-Jazeera and US War Coverage* (New York: Peter Lang, 2010); Oliver Boyd-Barrett and Shuang Xie, "Al-Jazeera, Phoenix Satellite Television and the Return of the State: Case Studies in Market Liberalization, Public Sphere and Media Imperialism," *International Journal of Communication* 2 (2008); Abeer. I. Al-Najjar, "How Arab is Al-Jazeera English? Comparative Study of Al-Jazeera Arabic and Al-Jazeera English News Channels," *Global Media Journal* 8 (2009).

60. Kai Hafez, "Guest Editor's Introduction: Mediated Political Communication in the Middle East," *Political Communication* 19, no. 2 (2002): 121.

61. Thussu, "Mapping Media Flow," 24.

62. Naomi Sakr, "Challenger or Lackey? The Politics of News on Al-Jazeera," in *Media on the Move: Global Flow and Contra-Flow,* ed. Daya K. Thussu (London: Routledge, 2007), 116.

63. Saba Bebawi, *Media Power and Global Television News: The Role of Al Jazeera English* (London: IB Tauris, 2016).

64. Tine U. Figenschou, "A Voice for the Voiceless? A Quantitative Content Analysis of Al-Jazeera English's Flagship News," *Global Media and Communication* 6, no. 1 (2010). Tine U. Figenschou, "Content: The Messages of AJE's News," in *Al Jazeera English: Global News in a Changing World,* ed. Philip Seib (New York: Palgrave Macmillan, 2012), 52.

65. Shawn Powers and Mohamed El-Nawawy, "Al-Jazeera English and Global News Networks: Clash of Civilizations or Cross-Cultural Dialogue?" *Media, War & Conflict* 2, no. 3 (2009).

66. Philip Seib, *The Al-Jazeera Effect* (Washington, DC: Potomac Books, 2008).

67. Mohammed El-Nawawy and Shawn Powers, *Mediating Conflict: Al-Jazeera English and the Possibility of a Conciliatory Media* (Los Angeles: Figueroa Press, 2008).

68. El-Nawawy and Iskandar, *Al Jazeera: How the Free Arab News Network Scooped the World*.

69. Marc Lynch, *Voices of the New Arab Public: Iraq, Al-Jazeera, and Middle East Politics Today* (New York: Columbia University Press, 2006).

70. Seib, "Hegemonic No More"; Boyd-Barrett and Xie, "Al-Jazeera, Phoenix Satellite Television"; Zainab Abdul Nabi, "Based on the Peace Journalism Model: Analysis of Al-Jazeera's Coverage of Bahrain's Uprising and Syria's Chemical Attack," *Global Media and Communication* 11 (2015).

71. Tine U. Figenschou, *Al Jazeera and the Global Media Landscape: The South is Talking Back* (New York: Routledge, 2013); Philip Seib, ed., *Al Jazeera English: Global News in a Changing World* (New York: Palgrave Macmillan, 2012); Bebawi, *Media Power and Global Television News*.

Chapter 1

1. David Marash, "TV News Creates Ignorant Americans," *Milwaukee Journal-Sentinel*, April 13, 2008, accessed August 5, 2016, http://www.jsonline.com/news/opinion/29558064.html.

2. Joe Pompeo, "Al Jazeera America: A Unicorn Is Born," *New York Magazine*, July 11, 2013, accessed August 5, 2016, http://nymag.com/daily/intelligencer/2013/07/al-jazeera-america-a-unicorn-is-born.html.

3. Assem Nasr, "Al-Jazeera and the Arab Uprisings: The Language of Images and a Medium's Stancetaking," *Communication, Culture & Critique* 7, no. 4 (2014): 410; Shawn Powers, "The Origins of Al Jazeera English," in *Al Jazeera English: Global News in a Changing World*, ed. Philip Seib (New York: Palgrave Macmillan, 2012), 21.

4. Amy Goodman, "Media Blackout in Egypt and the U.S.: Al Jazeera Forced Off the Air by Mubarak, Telecommunications Companies Block Its Expansion in the United States," New York, NY: *Democracy Now*, February 1, 2011, accessed August 5, 2016, http://www.democracynow.org/2011/2/1/media_blackout_in_egypt_and_the.

5. Dennis Carlton and Jeffrey M. Perloff, *Modern Industrial Organization* (New York: Harper Collins College Publishers, 1994).

6. Jeremy Dahl, "I Want My AJE," *Guernica*, May 15, 2008, accessed August 5, 2016, http://www.guernicamag.com/features/588/limited_access_1/.

7. Srilata Zaheer,"Overcoming the Liability of Foreignness," *Academy of Management Journal* 38, no. 2 (1995): 343.

8. Tunstall, *The Media Were American*.

9. Kaarle Nordenstreng, "Three Theses on the Imbalance Debate," in *Politics of News: Third World Perspective*, ed. Jaswant S. Yadava (New Delhi: Concept Publishing Company, 1984).

10. Ibid., 10–11.

11. Alejandro Portes, "On the Sociology of National Development: Theories and Issues," *American Journal of Sociology* 82, no. 1 (1976).

12. Schiller, *Communication and Cultural Domination*.

13. Immanuel Wallerstein, *The Modern World System: Capitalist Agriculture and the Origins of the European World Economy in the Sixteenth Century* (New York: Academic Press, 1974).

14. Marc Raboy, "Media Pluralism and the Promotion of Cultural Diversity," A Background Paper for UNESCO, December 10, 2007, accessed August 6, 2016, http://media.mcgill.ca/files/unesco_diversity.pdf.

15. Arjun Appadurai. *Modernity at Large: Cultural Dimensions of Globalization* (Minneapolis, MN: University of Minnesota Press, 1996); Arjun Appadurai, "Disjuncture and Difference in the Global Cultural Economy," *Public Culture* 2 (1990).

16. Joseph Straubhaar, *World Television: From Global to Local* (Los Angeles: Sage, 2007), 8.

17. Jeremy Tunstall, "Part IV: International-Regional-National: The National Media System as the Lead Player," *Global Media and Communication* 3, no. 3 (2007); Kai Hafez, *The Myth of Media Globalization*, trans. Alex Skinner (Cambridge: Polity Press, 2007).

18. Meredith L. Clausen, "Localizing the Global: 'Domestication' Processes in International News Production," *Media, Culture & Society* 26, no. 1 (2004). Kristina Riegert, "Pondering the Future for Foreign News on National Television," *International Journal of Communication* 5 (2004).
19. Tunstall, *The Media Were American*, 2008.
20. Haoming Denis Wu, "Investigating the Determinants"; Haoming Denis Wu, "Systematic Determinants of International News Coverage: A Comparison of 38 Countries," *Journal of Communication* 50, no. 2 (2000); Guy Golan, "Inter-Media Agenda Setting and Global News Coverage: Assessing the Influence of the *New York Times* on Three Network Television Evening News Programs," *Journalism Studies* 7 (2006); Timothy M. Jones, Peter Van Aelst, and Rens Vliegenthart, "Foreign Nation Visibility in US News Coverage: A Longitudinal Analysis (1950–2006)," *Communication Research* 40, no. 3 (2011).
21. Herman and McChesney, *Global Media*.
22. Tunstall, "Part IV," 322.
23. Daya K. Thussu, "Introduction," in *Media on the Move: Global Flow and Contra-Flow*, ed. Daya K. Thussu (London: Routledge, 2007a); Hartmut Wessler and Manuel Adolphsen, "Contra-Flow from the Arab World? How Arab Television Coverage of the 2003 Iraq War Was Used and Framed on Western International News Channels," *Media, Culture, Society* 30, no. 4 (2008).
24. Sakr, *Challenger or Lackey?*, 116.
25. Rashid Khalidi, *Resurrecting Empire: Western Footprints and America's Perilous Path in the Middle East* (Boston, MA: Beacon Press, 2004).
26. Sahar Khamis, "The Role of New Arab Satellite Channels in Fostering Intercultural Dialogue: Can Al Jazeera English Bridge the Gap?," in *New Media and the New Middle East*, ed. Philip Seib, (London: Palgrave Macmillan, 2007); Majid Tehranian, "Peace Journalism in West Asia," *Global Media Journal: Mediterranean Edition* 1 no.1 (2005); El-Nawawy and Powers, *Mediating Conflict*; Mohammed El-Nawawy and Shawn Powers, "A Conciliatory Medium in a Conflict-Driven Environment?," *Global Media and Communication* 6, no.1 (2010).
27. David E. Sanger, "Under Pressure, Dubai Company Drops Port Deal," *New York Times*, March 10, 2006, accessed August 5, 2016, http://www.nytimes.com/2006/03/10/politics/10ports.html?pagewanted=all&_r=0.
28. Louis Goodstein, "Across Nation, Mosque Projects Meet Opposition," *New York Times*, August 7, 2010, accessed August 5, 2016, http://www.nytimes.com/2010/08/08/us/08mosque.html.
29. Edward Said, *Orientalism* (New York: Vintage, 1979).
30. Ibid., 231.
31. Samuel P. Huntington, *The Clash of Civilizations and the Remaking of World Order* (New York: Simon & Schuster, 1996).
32. Brian Whitaker, "Al-Jazeera Causes Outcry with Broadcast of Battle Casualties," *The Guardian* [UK], March 25, 2003, accessed August 6, 2016, http://www.guardian.co.uk/media/2003/mar/24/broadcasting.Iraqandthemedia.
33. Robert W. Jackman and Ross A. Miller, "A Renaissance of Political Culture?" *American Journal of Political Science* 40, no. 3 (1996), 635.
34. Daniel Hallin and Paolo Mancini, *Comparing Media Systems: Three Models of Media and Politics* (New York: Cambridge University Press, 2004).
35. Scott Allan, *News Culture*, 2nd ed. (Buckingham: Open University Press, 2004).
36. Michael Schudson, "The News Media as Political Institutions," *Annual Review of Political Science* 5, no. 1 (2002).
37. Mark Deuze, "National News Cultures: A Comparison of Dutch, German, British, Australian, and US Journalists," *Journalism & Mass Communication Quarterly* 79, no. 1 (2002).
38. Ulrich Beck, "The Cosmopolitan Society and its Enemies," *Theory, Culture & Society* 19, no. 1–2 (2002a); Ulrich Beck, *The Cosmopolitan Vision* (Cambridge: Polity Press, 2006).
39. Pippa Norris and Ronald Inglehart, *Cosmopolitan Communications: Cultural Diversity in a Globalized World* (Cambridge: Cambridge University Press, 2009).
40. Appadurai, "Disjuncture and Difference."

41. James T. Hamilton, "The (Many) Markets for International News: How News from Abroad Sells at Home," *Journalism Studies* 11, no. 5 (2010): 653–654; Samuel J. Best, Brian Chmielewski and Brian Krueger, "Selective Exposure to Online Foreign News during the Conflict with Iraq," *International Journal of Press/Politics* 10, no. 4 (2005).

42. Tunstall, "Part IV," 322; Hess, *International News and Foreign Correspondents* (Washington, DC: The Brookings Institution, 1996), 9.

43. James Curran et al., "Media System, Public Knowledge and Democracy: A Comparative Study," *European Journal of Communication* 24, no. 1 (2009). Shanto Iyengar et al., "Cross-National Versus Individual-Level Differences in Political Information: a Media Systems Perspective," *Journal of Elections, Public Opinion and Parties* 20, no. 3 (2010).

44. Pew Research Center, "Where News Audiences Fit on the Political Spectrum," October 21, 2014, accessed August 6, 2016, http://www.journalism.org/interactives/media-polarization/table/overall/.

45. Robert D. Jacobson, *New Nativism: Proposition 187 and the Debate over Immigration* (Minneapolis: University of Minnesota Press, 2008), xxi.

46. John L. Esposito and Ibrahim Kalin, eds. *Islamophobia: The Challenge of Pluralism in the 21st Century* (New York: Oxford University Press, 2011).

47. Andrew Shryock, "Introduction: Islam as an Object of Fear and Affection," in *Islamophobia/Islamophilia: Beyond the Politics of Enemy and Friend*, ed. Andrew Shryock (Bloomington: Indiana University Press, 2010), 9.

48. Jon B. Alterman, "The Challenge for Al Jazeera International," *Transnational Broadcasting Studies* 14 (2005).

49. Deborah Circelli, "Daytona State College Faces Complaint over Public TV Programming," *Daytona Beach News-Journal*, February 10, 2011, accessed August 5, 2016, http://www.usasurvival.org/home/ck02.10.11–2.html.

50. Cliff Kincaid, "How Al-Jazeera Kills Americans," *Accuracy in Media*, Feburary 28, 2011, accessed August 5, 2016, http://bigjournalism.com/aim/2011/02/28/how-al-jazeera-kills-americans/.

51. David Marash, "Why Can't You Watch Al Jazeera English?," *Television Quarterly* 37, no. 3/4 (2007): 46–47.

52. Ibid., 47.

53. Marisa Guthrie, "Al Jazeera Unit Renews U.S. TV Push," *Broadcasting & Cable*, October 1, 2007, accessed August 5, 2016, https://www.highbeam.com/doc/1G1-169306612.html.

54. Dahl, "I Want My AJE."

55. Vincent Mosco, *The Political Economy of Communication* (London: Sage, 1996), 25.

56. Boyd-Barrett and Xie, "Al-Jazeera, Phoenix Satellite," 211.

57. Mehran Kamrava, *Qatar: Small State, Big Politics* (Ithaca, NY: Cornell University Press, 2013).

58. Mohamed Zayani, "Introduction" in *The Al Jazeera Phenomenon: Critical Perspectives on New Arab Media*, ed. Mohamed Zayani (London: Pluto Press, 2005), 13.

59. Robert Worth, "Al Jazeera No Longer Nips at Saudis," *New York Times*, January 4, 2008, accessed August 6, 2016, http://www.nytimes.com/2008/01/04/world/middleeast/04jazeera.html?pagewanted=all.

60. Shibley Telhami, *The World Through Arab Eyes* (New York: Basic Books, 2013), 47.

61. Da Lage, "The Politics of Al Jazeera."

62. Ibid., 49.

63. William L. Youmans, "Al Jazeera English After the Arab Spring: The Changing Politics of Distribution in the United States," in *Al Jazeera English: Global News in a Changing World*, ed. Philip Seib (New York: Palgrave Macmillan, 2012).

64. Colin Sparks, "China's Media in Comparative Perspective," *International Journal of Communication* 4 (2010): 553.

65. Miles, *Al Jazeera*; Lynch, *Voices*; Mohammed El-Nawawy and Adel Iskandar, *Al-Jazeera: The Story of the Network that is Rattling Governments and Redefining Modern Journalism* (Cambridge, MA: Westview, 2003).

66. Tom Finn, "Qatar's Support for the Entire Al Jazeera Operation Is in Question, Diplomats Say," *Reuters*, January 27, 2016, accessed August 6, 2016, http://www.jpost.com/Middle-East/Al-Jazeera-America-closure-marks-a-quieter-Qatar-442972.

67. Robert Booth, "WikiLeaks Cables Claim al-Jazeera Changed Coverage to Suit Qatari Foreign Policy," *The Guardian* [UK], December 5, 2010, accessed August 5, 2016, http://www.the-guardian.com/world/2010/dec/05/wikileaks-cables-al-jazeera-qatari-foreign-policy.

68. "Scenesetter for Senator Kerry's Visit to Qatar," *Wikileaks*, February 8, 2010, accessed August 5, 2016, https://wikileaks.org/plusd/cables/10DOHA52_a.html.

69. Tony Burman, "Al Jazeera America Has the Odor of Disaster," *Toronto Star*, June 1, 2013, accessed August 5, 2016, http://www.thestar.com/news/world/2013/06/01/al_jazeera_america_has_the_odour_of_disaster_burman.html.

70. Pete Pattison, "Revealed: Qatar's World Cup 'Slaves'," *The Guardian* [UK], September 25, 2013, accessed August 5, 2016, http://www.theguardian.com/world/2013/sep/25/revealed-qatars-world-cup-slaves.

71. Dan Sabbagh, "Al-Jazeera's Political Independence Questioned Amid Qatar Intervention," *The Guardian* [UK], September 30, 2012, accessed August 5, 2016, http://www.theguard-ian.com/media/2012/sep/30/al-jazeera-independence-questioned-qatar.

72. Glenn Greenwald, "Al Jazeera Deletes its Own Controversial Op-Ed, then Refuses to Comment," *The Guardian* [UK], May 21, 2013, accessed August 5, 2016, http://www.the-guardian.com/commentisfree/2013/may/21/al-jazeera-joseph-massad-retraction.

73. Richard Currier, "Al Jazeera Blocks Anti-Saudi Arabia Article," *The Intercept*, December 18, 2015, accessed August 6, 2016, https://theintercept.com/2015/12/18/al-jazeera-blocks-anti-saudi-arabia-article/.

74. Amy Goodman, "'Shouting in the Dark': Film Chronicles Bahrain's Pro-Democracy Uprising Against U.S.-Backed Rule," *Democracy Now*, April 6, 2012, accessed August 5, 2016, http://www.democracynow.org/2012/4/6/shouting_in_the_dark_film_chronicles.

75. Mohamed Fahmy, "How Qatar Used and Abused Its Al Jazeera Journalists," *New York Times*, June 2, 2015, accessed August 5, 2016, http://www.nytimes.com/2015/06/03/opinion/mohamed-fahy-how-qatar-used-and-abused-its-al-jazeera-journalists.html?r=0.

76. "Egypt Releases Al Jazeera Journalists Fahmy and Mohamed," *BBC News*, September 23, 2015, accessed August 6, 2016, http://www.bbc.com/news/world-middle-east-34337595.

77. Fahmy, "How Qatar Used and Abused".

78. "Qatari Poet Final Verdict Expected in February," *Al Jazeera English*, January 27, 2013, accessed August 6, 2016, https://www.youtube.com/watch?v=ME15QDcGw94; "Qatari Poet's Life Sentence Cut to 15 years," *Al Jazeera English*, February 24, 2013, accessed August 6, 2016, https://www.youtube.com/watch?v=_Zr1dkd5mks; "Qatar Court Upholds Poet's Jail Sentence," *Al Jazeera English*, October 21, 2013, accessed August 6, 2016, http://www.aljazeera.com/news/middleeast/2013/10/qatar-court-upholds-sentence-against-poet-20131021123723850815.html.

79. Andrew Hampp, "Al-Jazeera English Looks to Build Audience Before Ads," *Advertising Age*, June 13, 2011, accessed August 5, 2016, http://adage.com/article/global-news/al-jazeera-english-build-audience/228094/.

80. Interview, October 19, 2010.

81. Interview, October 7, 2010.

82. Lorraine Ali and Marisa Guthrie, "Why American Cable Systems Won't Carry the Al Jazeera Network," *The Hollywood Reporter*, March 17, 2011.

83. Bob Wheelock (guest) and Libby Casey (host), "Al Jazeera's U.S.-Based News Channel [Television episode]," in *Washington Journal*. Washington, DC: C-SPAN, 2013, accessed August 6, 2016, http://www.c-span.org/video/?310901–4/al-jazeeras-usbased-news-channel.

84. Marvin Ammori, "TV Competition Nowhere: How the Cable Industry Is Colluding to Kill Online TV," *Free Press Report*, January, 2010, 38.

85. Sylvia Chan-Olmsted, "Market Competition for Cable Television: Reexamining its Horizontal Mergers and Industry Concentration," *Journal of Media Economics* 9, no. 2 (1996).

86. Eli M. Noam, *Media Ownership and Concentration in America* (Oxford: Oxford University Press, 2009).
87. Dan Brown, "Historical Perspectives on Communication Technology," in *Communication Technology Update and Fundamentals*, ed. August E. Grant and Jennifer H. Meadows (Burlington, MA: Focal Press, 2010), 27–28.
88. Edwin C. Baker, *Media, Markets, and Democracy* (New York: Cambridge University Press, 2002).
89. Curran et al., "Media System, Public Knowledge"; Shanto Iyengar et al., "'Dark Areas of Ignorance' Revisited: Comparing International Affairs Knowledge in Switzerland and the United States," *Communication Research* 36, no. 3 (2009).
90. Keach Hagey, "Al Jazeera US Cable Deal Signals New Era," *The National* [UAE], July 15, 2009, accessed August 5, 2016, http://www.thenational.ae/business/al-jazeera-us-cable-deal-signals-new-era.
91. William L. Youmans, "The Media Economics and Cultural Politics of Al Jazeera English in the United States" (PhD diss., University of Michigan, 2012b), 98.
92. William L. Youmans, "The Debate Over Al Jazeera, English in Burlington, VT," *Arab Media & Society* 13, May 21, 2011, accessed August 6, 2016, http://www.arabmediasociety.com/articles/downloads/20110601113558_Youmans_Burlington_VT.pdf.
93. Brown, "Historical Perspectives," 27–28.
94. Hagey, "Al Jazeera US Cable Deal."
95. Ali and Guthrie, "Why American Cable Systems."
96. Youmans, "Debate Over Al Jazeera."
97. Michael Calderone, "Time Warner Cable Will Consider Carrying Al Jazeera's U.S. Network," *Huffington Post*, January 3, 2013, accessed August 5, 2016, http://www.huffingtonpost.com/2013/01/03/time-warner-cable-al-jazeera-american2404879.html.
98. Wheelock, "Al Jazeera's U.S.-Based News Channel."
99. Interview, October 7, 2010.
100. David M. Levine, "The Fox News Revolution," *Adweek*, October 3, 2011, accessed August 5, 2016, http://www.adweek.com/news/television/fox-news-revolution-135385.
101. Christopher Helman, "Will Americans Tune to Al Jazeera?," *Forbes Magazine*, June 24, 2009, accessed August 5, 2016, http://www.forbes.com/forbes/2009/0713/comcast-al-qaeda-will-americans-tune-to-al-jazeera.html.
102. Interview, March 21, 2011.
103. Rowena Mason, "Al Jazeera English Focused on its American Dream," *The Telegraph* [UK], March 23, 2009, accessed August 5, 2016, http://www.telegraph.co.uk/finance/newsbysector/mediatechnologyandtelecoms/5039921/Al-Jazeera-English-focused-on-its-American-dream.html.
104. Ali and Guthrie, "Why American Cable Systems."
105. Quinn Klinefelter, "Al Jazeera TV Gets Toe-hold in Toledo," *Voice of America*, March 31, 2007, accessed August 5, 2016, http://www.voanews.com/english/news/a-13-2007-03-29-voa53.html.
106. "Al-Jazeera Draws Harsh Comments Online," *Sandusky Register*, March 15, 2007, accessed August 5, 2016, http://www.sanduskyregister.com/2007/mar/16/al-jazeera-draws-harsh-comments-online?similar.
107. "AIM Protests Ohio Cable Co.'s Decision to Air Al-Jazeera English Channel," *Accuracy in Media*, March 30, 2007, accessed August 5, 2016, http://www.aim.org/press-release/aim-protests-ohio-cable-cos-decision-to-air-al-jazeera-english-channel/.
108. Trevor Dawson, *Building Blocks: Buckeye CableSystem's Communications Revolution, From Printer's Ink to Cable to Fiber* (Lanham, MD: Hamilton Books, 2015), 183.
109. "Buckeye Cable System Adds Al Jazeera English," *Toledo Blade*, March 10, 2007, accessed August 5, 2016, http://www.toledoblade.com/TV-Radio/2007/03/10/Buckeye-CableSystem-adds-Al-Jazeera-English.html.
110. Dahl, "I Want My AJE."
111. Baker, *Media, Markets, and Democracy*.

112. Todd Spangler, "Cord-Cutting Alert: Pay-TV Business Declines for First Time During Q1," *Variety*, May 11, 2015, accessed August 5, 2016, http://variety.com/2015/biz/news/cord-cutting-alert-pay-tv-business-declines-for-first-time-in-q1-1201492308/.

113. Janko Roettgers, "Close to Half of All U.S. Households Subscribe to Netflix, Amazon Prime or Hulu Plus," *GigaOm*, June 6, 2014, accessed August 5, 2016, https://gigaom.com/2014/06/06/close-to-half-of-all-u-s-households-subscribe-to-netflix-amazon-prime-or-hulu-plus/.

114. Ali and Guthrie, "Why American Cable Systems."

115. Amanda Lotz, *The Television Will Be Revolutionized* (New York: New York University Press, 2007).

116. Nicholas Garnham, "Concepts of Culture: Public Policy and the Cultural Industries," *Cultural Studies* 1, no. 1 (1987): 31.

117. Hannah Allam, "New Al-Jazeera International Channel Sparks Conflict," *Knight Ridder*, March 2, 2006, accessed August 5, 2016, http://www.commondreams.org/headlines06/0302-08.htm.

Chapter 2

1. Michael Curtin, "Conditions of Capital: Global Media in Local Contexts," in *Internationalizing International Communication*, ed. Chin-Chuan Lee (Ann Arbor: University of Michigan Press, 2015), 112.

2. William Howarth, "Reading the Wetlands," in *Textures of Place: Exploring Humanist Geographies*, ed. Paul C. Adams et al. (Minneapolis: University of Minnesota Press, 2001), 58.

3. Theodore H. Moran, "Foreign Direct Investment," in *The Wiley-Blackwell Encyclopedia of Globalization*, ed. George Ritzer (Oxford: Wiley-Blackwell, 2012).

4. Tunstall, *The Media Were American*.

5. Porter, "Location, Competition, and Economic Development," 15.

6. Krugman, "What's New About."

7. Frank McDonald et al., "Is There Evidence to Support Porter-Type Cluster Policies?," *Regional Studies* 41, no.1 (2007): 39–49.

8. Krugman, "What's New About."

9. Andrew Ure, *The Philosophy of Manufactures; or, An Exposition of the Scientific, Moral, and Commercial Economy of the Factory System of Great Britain* (London: C. Knight, 1835); Porter, "Location, Competition, and Economic Development."

10. Curtin, *Playing to the World's*, 12–13.

11. Fred Cairncross, *The Death of Distance: How the Communications Revolution Is Changing Our Lives* (Cambridge, MA: Harvard Business Press, 1997).

12. Morley, "Communications and Transport," 745.

13. Richard Florida, *Who's Your City?: How the Creative Economy Is Making Where to Live the Most Important Decision of Your Life* (Toronto: Vintage Canada, 2010); Richard Florida, *Cities and the Creative Class* (New York: Routledge, 2005); Gina Neff, "The Changing Place of Cultural Production: The Location of Social Networks in a Digital Media Industry," *Annals of the American Academy of Political and Social Science* 597, no.1 (2005).

14. Peter Dicken, *Global Shift: Mapping the Changing Contours of the World Economy*, 5th ed. (Thousand Oaks, CA: Sage Publications), 18.

15. Michael Curtin, "Media Capital: Towards the Study of Spatial Flows," *International Journal of Cultural Studies* 6, no. 2 (2003); Michael Curtin, "Comparing Media Capitals: Hong Kong and Mumbai," *Global Media and Communication* 6, no. 3 (2010); Punathambekar, *From Bombay to Bollywood*; Michael Keane, "Once Were Peripheral: Creating Media Capacity in East Asia," *Media, Culture and Society* 28, no. 6 (2006).

16. Curtin, "Comparing Media Capitals," 265.

17. Charlie Karlsson and Robert G. Picard, "Media Clusters: What Makes them Unique?" In *Media Clusters: Spatial Agglomeration and Content Capabilities*, ed. Charlie Karlsson and Robert G. Picard (Northampton, MA: Edward Elgar Publishing, 2011), 4–5.

18. Curtin, "Conditions of Capital," 115.
19. Karlsson and Picard, *Media Clusters,* 3.
20. Curtin, "Conditions of Capital," 113–117.
21. Herbert I. Schiller, *Mass Communication and American Empire* (Boston: Beacon, 1969); Schiller, "Not Yet the Post-Imperialist Era."
22. Dwayne Winseck, "The State of Media Ownership and Media Markets: Competition or Concentration and Why Should We Care?," *Sociology Compass* 2, no. 1 (2008): 34–47.
23. Harvey, *Condition of Postmodernity.*
24. Curtin, "Conditions of Capital," 115.
25. Karlsson and Picard, *Media Clusters,* 8.
26. Ibid.
27. Richard Florida et al., "Music Scenes to Music Clusters: The Economic Geography of Music in the US, 1970–2000," *Environment and Planning* 42, no. 4 (2010): 785.
28. Allen J. Scott, *The Cultural Economy of Cities: Essays on the Geography of Image-Producing Industries* (London: Sage, 2000).
29. Karlsson and Picard, *Media Clusters,* 7.
30. Curtin, *Playing to the World's,* 14–15.
31. Florida, *Cities and the Creative Class.*
32. Harald Bathelt and Armin Gräf, "Internal and External Dynamics of the Munich Film and TV Industry Cluster, and Limitations to Future Growth," *Environment and Planning* 40, no.8 (2008).
33. Neff, "Changing Place," 136.
34. Ibid., 135.
35. Curtin, "Conditions of Capital," 116.
36. Scott, *The Cultural Economy of Cities*; Florida et al., "Music Scenes to Music Clusters"; Krätke and Taylor, "A World Geography."
37. Krätke and Taylor, "A World Geography"; Karlsson and Picard, *Media Clusters.*
38. Florida et al., "Music Scenes to Music Clusters," 800.
39. Daniel Mato, "Miami in the Transnationalization of the Telenovela Industry: On Territoriality and Globalization," *Journal of Latin American Cultural Studies* 11, no. 2 (2002); John Sinclair, "The Hollywood of Latin America: Miami as Regional Center in Television Trade," *Television & New Media* 4, no. 3 (2003).
40. Punathambekar, *From Bombay to Bollywood.*
41. Curtin, *Playing to the World's.*
42. Bathelt and Gräf, "Internal and External Dynamics."
43. Curtin, "Conditions of Capital," 117; emphasis in original.
44. Ibid., 115–116.
45. Michael Storper, "Globalization, Localization and Trade," in *The Oxford Handbook of Economic Geography*, ed. Gordon L. Clark et al. (Oxford: Oxford University Press, 2000), 148.
46. Castells, *Rise of the Network Society.*
47. Curtin, "Conditions of Capital," 111.
48. Ibid., 118.
49. Wayne K. Talley, *Port Economics* (New York: Routledge, 2009), 2.
50. Curtin, "Conditions of Capital," 112; emphasis in original.
51. Punathambekar, *From Bombay to Bollywood*, 11; Krätke & Taylor, "A World Geography," 461.
52. Curtin, *Playing to the World's,* 285.
53. Bathelt and Gräf, "Internal and External Dynamics," 1961–1962.
54. Marshall, *Principles of Economics,* 271.
55. Sassen, *Global City.*
56. Porter, "Location, Competition, and Economic Development," 21–22.
57. Curtin, *Playing to the World's,* 14–15.
58. Jean K. Chalaby, *Transnational Television in Europe: Reconfiguring Global Communications Networks* (London: IB Tauris, 2009), 225.
59. Marshall, *Principles of Economics,* 271.

60. Porter, "Location, Competition, and Economic Development," 22.

61. Michael Storper and Anthony Venables, "Buzz: Face-to-Face Contact and the Urban Economy," *Journal of Economic Geography* 4, no. 4 (2004).

62. Porter, "Location, Competition, and Economic Development," 16–17; Neff, "Changing Place."

63. Scott, *The Cultural Economy of Cities*, 33.

64. William Whyte, *City: Rediscovering the Center* (New York: Doubleday, 1988), 341; emphasis in original.

65. Porter, "Location, Competition, and Economic Development," 23.

66. Curtin, *Playing to the World's*, 285, 289.

67. Walter Lippmann, *Public Opinion* (London: Transaction Publishers, 1991); John Zaller, *The Nature and Origins of Mass Opinion* (Cambridge: Cambridge University Press, 1992); Timothy E. Cook, *Governing with the News: The News Media as a Political Institution* (Chicago: University of Chicago Press, 1998); W. Lance Bennett, "Toward a Theory of Press-State Relations in the United States," *Journal of Communication* 40, no. 2 (1990).

68. Anna L. Tsing, *Friction: An Ethnography of Global Connection* (Princeton, NJ: Princeton University Press, 2011); Emily S. Rosenberg, *Transnational Currents in a Shrinking World* (Cambridge, MA: Harvard University Press, 2014); Fien Adriaens and Daniel Biltereyst, "Glocalized Telenovelas and National Identities: A 'Textual Cum Production' Analysis of the Telenovelle Sara, the Flemish Adaptation of *Yo Soy Betty, La Fea*," *Television & New Media* 13, no. 6 (2012); Andy C. Pratt, "Microclustering of the Media Industries in London," in *Media Clusters: Spatial Agglomeration and Content Capabilities*, ed. Charlie Karlsson and Robert G. Picard, 120–135 (Northampton, MA: Edward Elgar Publishing, 2011).

69. Curtin, "Conditions of Capital," 113.

70. Zygmunt Bauman, *Liquid Modernity* (Malden, MA: Polity, 2000).

71. Doreen Massey, *Space, Place and Gender* (Minneapolis; University of Minnesota Press, 1994), 154.

72. Ibid.

73. Curtin, "Conditions of Capital," 116.

74. Doreen Massey, *World City* (Malden, MA: Polity, 2007), 21.

75. William J. Mitchell, *City of Bits: Space, Place and the Infobahn* (Cambridge, MA: MIT Press, 1995), 170.

76. Penny Harvey and Harvey Knox, "Ethnographies of Place," in *Understanding Social Research: Thinking Creatively about Method*, ed. Jennifer Mason and Angela Dale (London: Sage, 2013).

77. Paul C. Adams et al., "Place in Context: Rethinking Humanist Geographies," in *Textures of Place: Exploring Humanist Geographies*, eds. Paul C. Adams et al. (Minneapolis: University of Minnesota Press, 2001), xviii.

78. Bauman, *Liquid Modernity*, 102–104.

79. Harold M. Proshansky et al., "The Influence of the Physical Environment on Behavior: Some Basic Assumptions," in *Environmental Psychology: Man and His Physical Setting*, ed. Harold M. Proshansky et al. (New York: Holt, Rinehart & Winston, 1969), 32.

80. Harold M. Proshansky et al., "Place-Identity: Physical World Socialization of the Self," *Journal of Environmental Psychology* 3, no. 1 (1983).

81. Raymond Williams, *The Long Revolution* (Orchard Park, NY: Broadview Press, 2001), 63.

82. Ibid.

83. John A. Agnew, *Place and Politics: The Geographical Mediation of State and Society* (New York: Routledge, 2015).

84. Massey, *Space, Place and Gender*; Doreen Massey, "Politics and Space/Time," *New Left Review* 196 (1992): 65–84.

85. Massey, *World city*, 10.

86. Ibid., 23.

87. Ibid., 208–209.

88. Yi-Fu Tuan, *Topophilia: A Study of Environmental Perceptions, Attitudes, and Values* (Englewood Cliffs, NJ: Prentice-Hall, Inc., 1974), 93.

89. Yi-Fu Tuan, "Geography, Phenomenology, and the Study of Human Nature," *The Canadian Geographer* 15, no. 3 (1971): 181.

90. Christoph Henning, "Distanciation and Disembedding," in *The Blackwell Encyclopedia of Sociology*, vol. 3, ed. George Ritzer (Malden, MA: Blackwell Publishing, 2007), 1188.

91. Michael Schudson, "The Objectivity Norm in American Journalism," *Journalism* 2, no. 2 (2001); Mark Deuze, "What Is Journalism? Professional Identity and Ideology of Journalists Reconsidered," *Journalism* 6, no. 4 (2005); Barbie Zelizer, "Journalists as Interpretive Communities," *Critical Studies in Media Communication* 10, no. 3 (1993).

92. Casey, *Fate of Place*, 246.

93. Shaun Moores, *Media, Place and Mobility* (New York: Palgrave Macmillan, 2012), 10.

94. Mark Fishman, *Manufacturing the News* (Austin: University of Texas Press, 1980).

95. George Downey, "Making Media Work: Time, Space, Identity, and Labor in the Analysis of Information and Communication Infrastructures," in *Media Technologies: Essays on Communication, Materiality, and Society*, ed. Tarleton Gillespie et al. (Cambridge, MA: MIT Press, 2014), 148.

96. Andy C. Pratt, "Hot Jobs in Cool Places. The Material Cultures of New Media Product Spaces: The Case of South of the Market, San Francisco," *Information, Communication & Society* 5, no. 1 (2011).

97. Aurora Wallace, *Media Capital: Architecture and Communications in New York City* (Urbana: University of Illinois Press, 2012).

98. Susan R. Brooker-Gross, "Spatial Aspects of Newsworthiness," *Geografiska Annaler. Series B, Human Geography* 65, no. 1(1983): 8.

99. Harvey L. Molotch and Deirdre Boden, "The Compulsion of Proximity," in *Now Here: Space, Time and Modernity*, ed. Roger Friedland and Deirdre Boden (Berkeley: University of California Press, 1994), 267.

100. Pamela J. Shoemaker and Stephen Reese, *Mediating the Message: Theories of Influences on Mass Media Content*, 2nd ed. (New York: Longman, 1996), 118, 181.

101. Jingrong Tong, "The Importance of Place: An Analysis of Changes in Investigative Journalism in Two Chinese Provincial Newspapers," *Journalism Practice* 7, no. 1 (2013): 7.

102. Fishman, *Manufacturing the News*; Daniel Kreiss and Mike Ananny, "Responsibilities of the State: Rethinking the Case and Possibilities for Public Support of Journalism," *First Monday* 18, no. 4 (2013).

103. Alan Brown et al., *Digitizing Government: Understanding and Implementing New Digital Business Models* (London: Palgrave Macmillan, 2014).

104. Brooker-Gross, "Spatial Aspects of Newsworthiness," 2.

105. Wheelock, "Al Jazeera's U.S.-Based News Channel."

106. Ibid.

107. Herbert Zettl, *Television Production Handbook* (Stamford, CT: Cengage Learning, 2011), 196.

108. Fishman, *Manufacturing the News*, 48.

109. Nicholas Negroponte, *Being Digital* (New York: Vintage, 1996), 240.

110. Boden and Molotch, *The Compulsion of Proximity*.

111. Zvia Reich, "The Impact of Technology on News Reporting: A Longitudinal Perspective," *Journalism & Mass Communication Quarterly* 90, no. 3 (2013).

112. Boden and Molotch, *The Compulsion of Proximity*, 277.

113. Reich, "The Impact of Technology."

114. Fishman, *Manufacturing the News*, 144.

115. Casey, *Fate of Place*, 246.

116. Alessandro Duranti, "Husserl, Intersubjectivity and Anthropology," *Anthropological Theory* 10, no. 1–2 (2010).

117. Casey, *Fate of Place*, 241.

118. Ibid.

119. Stephen E. Bennett et al., "Citizens' Knowledge of Foreign Affairs," *Harvard International Journal of Press/Politics* 1, no. 2 (1996): 5.

120. Erik Ericson and Roger J. Hamilton, "Happy Landings: A Defense of Parachute Journalism," in *From Pigeons to News Portals: Foreign Reporting and the Challenge of New Technology*, ed. David D. Perlmutter and John Maxwell Hamilton (Baton Rouge: Louisiana State University Press, 2007), 143.

121. Mark Pedelty, *War Stories: The Culture of Foreign Correspondents* (London: Routledge, 1995), 110–112.

122. Shawn Powers, "The Geopolitics of News: The Case of the Al Jazeera Network," (PhD diss., University of Southern California, 2009), 161.

123. Lawrence Pintak, "Interview with Nigel Parsons, Managing Director of Al Jazeera International," *Transnational Broadcasting Studies* 15 (2005).

124. Timothy Mitchell, *Rule of Experts: Egypt, Techno-Politics, Modernity* (Berkeley: University of California Press, 2002), 15.

125. Silvio Waisbord, *Reinventing Professionalism: Journalism and News in Global Perspective* (Cambridge: Polity Press, 2013), 227.

126. Ibid.

127. Ibid., 230.

128. Shakuntala Rao, "Glocalization of Indian Journalism," *Journalism Studies* 10, no. 4 (2009).

129. Caitriona Noonan, "The BBC and Decentralisation: The Pilgrimage to Manchester," *International Journal of Cultural Policy* 18, no. 4 (2012).

130. Curtin, *Playing to the World's*, 12.

131. Ibid., 4.

132. Georgios Terzis, "The EU Correspondent," *Journalism* 9, no. 4 (2008).

133. John Price, "A Tale of Two Cultures: A Comparison of EU News Reporting by Brussels-Based and National-Based Journalists," in *Public Communication in the European Union: History, Perspectives and Challenges*, ed. Chiara Valentini and Giorgia Nesti (Newcastle, UK: Cambridge Scholars Publishing, 2010), 227.

134. Zaheer, "Overcoming the Liability," 343.

Chapter 3

1. Hagey, "Al Jazeera US Cable Deal Signals New Era."

2. Wheelock, "Al Jazeera's U.S.-Based News Channel."

3. Dan Zak, "K Street: The Route of All Evil, or Just the Main Drag?," *Washington Post*, February 5, 2012, accessed August 6, 2016, http://www.washingtonpost.com/lifestyle/style/k-street-the-route-of-all-evil-or-just-the-main-drag/2012/01/26/gIQAAnKdsQ_story.html.

4. Miles, *Al Jazeera*, 121.

5. Neil Irwin, "Landlord Snubs Al-Jazeera," *Washington Post*, June 9, 2003, accessed August 5, 2016, http://www.washingtonpost.com/archive/business/2003/06/09/landlord-snubs-al-jazeera/7d2f9286-5bdf-404a-b30a-69dc6f6260db/.

6. Ibid.

7. Ellen Gamerman, "Al-Jazeera Grows Boldly, Keeps Head Down in D.C.," *Baltimore Sun*, January 14, 2005, accessed August 5, 2016, http://articles.baltimoresun.com/2005-01-14/news/0501140086_1_arab-network-al-jazeera-international-arab-world.

8. Christopher Dickey, "The Al Jazeera Revolution," *Newsweek*, May 23, 2013, accessed August 5, 2016, http://www.newsweek.com/2013/05/22/al-jazeera-revolution-237390.html.

9. Gamerman, "Al-Jazeera Grows Boldly."

10. Ibid.

11. Pintak, "Interview with Nigel Parsons."

12. Interview, June 19, 2015.

13. James B. Cunningham, "Dave Marash: Why I Quit," *Columbia Journalism Review*, April 4, 2008, accessed August 5, 2016, http://www.cjr.org/the_water_cooler/dave_marash_why_i_quit.php?page=all.

11. "The Colbert Report. Ayman Mohyeldin interview," *Comedy Central*, March 22, 2011, accessed August 5, 2016, http://www.colbertnation.com/the-colbert-report-videos/ 378442/march-22-2011/ayman-mohyeldin.

12. Interview, June 22, 2015.

13. Keach Hagey, "Amjad Atallah to Al Jazeera English," *Politico*, May 1, 2011, accessed August 5, 2016, http://www.politico.com/blogs/onmedia/0511/Amjad_Atallah_to_Al_Jazeera_ English.html.

14. "Al Jazeera and Kidnapping Tapes," *Wikileaks*, February 13, 2006, accessed August 5, 2016, https://wikileaks.org/plusd/cables/06DOHA219_a.html.

15. Herman and Chomsky, *Manufacturing Consent*, 26.

16. "Al Jazeera and Kidnapping Tapes."

17. John Stephens, "Sierra Madre Residents Gather to Celebrate and Discuss the Death of Osama Bin Laden," *Sierra Madre Patch*, May 2, 2011, accessed August 6, 2016, http://patch.com/california/sierramadre/sierra-madre-residents-react-to-death-of-osama-bin-laden.

18. Sharon Otterman, "Students Take Time to Reflect on Bin Laden." *New York Times*, City Room Blog, May 3, 2011, accessed August 6, 2016, http://cityroom.blogs.nytimes.com/ 2011/05/03/students-take-time-to-reflect-on-bin-laden/.

19. Robert MacMillan, "Al Jazeera Fights 'Myths' in North American Push," *Reuters*, February 17, 2009, accessed August 5, 2016, http://www.reuters.com/article/ aljazeera-idUSN1738968120090218.

20. Bob Fernandez, "Al-Jazeera Seeks TV Distribution Deal with Comcast," *Philadelphia Inquirer*, February 25, 2011, accessed April 28, 2016, http://articles.philly.com/2011-02-25/business/28629801_1_mouthpiece-for-osama-bin-al-jazeera-officials-al-jazeera-english.

21. David B. Wilkerson, "Al Jazeera English Makes Case to Comcast," *MarketWatch*, March 1, 2011, accessed March 8, 2016, http://www.marketwatch.com/story/ al-jazeera-english-makes-its-case-to-comcast-2011-03-01.

22. Scott Malone, "Talking Heads Block Al-Jazeera TV in U.S.-Zucker," Reuters, February 7, 2011, accessed August 6, 2016, http://blogs.reuters.com/mediafile/2011/02/07/talking-heads-block-al-jazeera-tv-in-u-s-zucker/.

23. Carla Parks, "BBC World News Channel in 30m American Homes," *Ariel* (BBC internal news website), April 14, 2014, accessed August 5, 2016, http://www.bbc.co.uk/ariel/ 27487105.

24. Interview, October 20, 2010.

25. Interview, June 19, 2015.

26. Hagey, "Al Jazeera US Cable Deal."

27. Zach Coleman, "CNN Fends Off its Competitors in Foreign Markets," *Atlanta Business Chronicle*, August 8, 1997, accessed August 5, 2016, http://www.bizjournals.com/atlanta/ stories/1997/08/11/story7.html.

28. David Folkenflik, "Al-Jazeera English Struggles for U.S. Audience," *NPR*, February 24, 2009, accessed August 5, 2016, http://www.npr.org/templates/story/story.php?-storyId=101071599.

29. Lauren Feeney, "What's Al Jazeera's Problem?," *PBS*, April 29, 2009, accessed August 5, 2016, http://www.pbs.org/wnet/need-to-know/the-daily-need/whats-al-jazeeras-problem /3924/.

30. Lorne Manly, "Translation: Is the Whole World Watching?" *New York Times*, March 26, 2006, accessed August 8, 2016, http://www.nytimes.com/2006/03/26/arts/television/ translation-is-the-whole-world-watching.html?_r=0.

31. Dahl, "I Want My AJE."

32. Interview, October 7, 2010.

33. Clemons, "Al Jazeera English."

34. Interview, July 17, 2013.

35. Interview, June 19, 2015.

36. Interview, June 19, 2015.

37. Curtin, "Comparing Media Capitals," 266.

Chapter 5

1. Glenn Hunter, "The Selling of Al Jazeera America," *Front Burner*, October 8, 2014, accessed August 5, 2016, http://www.dmagazine.com/frontburner/2014/10/the-selling-of-al-jazeera-america/.

2. Joe Pompeo, "The Last Time Al Jazeera Had a Big American Strategy, It Was Rejected," *Politico*, July 15, 2013b, accessed August 5, 2016, http://www.capitalnewyork.com/article/media/2013/07/8531884/last-time-al-jazeera-had-big-american-strategy-it-was-rejected.

3. Liam La Guerre, "Al Jazeera Pays Boston Properties $45M for Midtown Lease Termination," *Commercial Observer*, February 4, 2016, accessed August 5, 2016, https://commercialobserver.com/2016/02/al-jazeera-pays-boston-property-45m-for-midtown-lease-termination/.

4. Interview, January 7, 2016.

5. Keach Hagey and Eliot Brown, "Al Jazeera in Site Hunt: Broadcaster Looks at Former New York Times, Other Offices for U.S. Operations," *Wall Street Journal*, March 11, 2013, accessed August 5, 2016, http://www.wsj.com/articles/SB10001424127887324128504578348711622224832.

6. Ibid.

7. Claire Atkinson, "Al Jazeera America Angers Staffers with Shift in Direction," *New York Post*, April 21, 2015, accessed August 5, 2016, http://nypost.com/2015/04/21/al-jazeera-america-angers-staffers-with-shift-in-direction/.

8. Terenzio v. Current TV, LLC, 2015 Cal. App. Unpub. LEXIS 8032 (2015).

9. Albert A. Gore, et al., v. Al Jazeera America Holdings I, Inc., 2015 Del. Ch. LEXIS 215 (2015).

10. Jeanine Poggi, "Al Jazeera America One Year Later: Is Gaza the Turning Point?," *Advertising Age*, August 8, 2014, accessed August 5, 2016, http://adage.com/article/media/al-jazeera-america-year-gaza-a-turning-point/294495/.

11. High-Bassalik v. Al Jazeera America, et al. 2015 U.S. Dist. LEXIS 150589 (2015).

12. Shannon Bond, "Al Jazeera America Shaken by Defections," *Financial Times*, May 4, 2015a, accessed August 5, 2016, http://www.ft.com/intl/cms/s/0/4b782a8e-f2a5-11e4-b914-00144feab7de.html#axzz3wkk79FtO.

13. "Mayor Bloomberg Announces Eight Initiatives to Strengthen the Media Industry in New York City," *NYC Economic Development Corporation* [press release], July 7, 2009, accessed August 5, 2016, http://www.nycedc.com/press-release/mayor-bloomberg-announces-eight-initiatives-strengthen-media-industry-new-york-city.

14. Janet Abu-Lughod, *New York, Chicago, Los Angeles: America's Global Cities* (Minneapolis: University of Minnesota Press, 1999), 20.

15. Morris Greenberg, *Branding New York: How a City in Crisis Was Sold to the World* (New York: Routledge, 2008), 50.

16. Braudel, *Perspective of the World*.

17. Greenberg, *Branding New York*, 51.

18. Ibid.

19. "Mayor Bloomberg Announces," 2009.

20. "Media. NYC. 2020. Final Report," *NYC Economic Development Corporation* (2009), 12, accessed August 6, 2016, http://www.nycedc.com/sites/default/files/filemanager/Industries/Media_EmergTech/MediaNYC2020_Report.pdf.

21. Ibid.

22. Jan Morris, *The Great Port: A Passage Through New York.* (New York: Oxford University Press, 1969).

23. Greenberg, *Branding New York*, 50.

24. Dylan Byers, "CNN Moves to Centralize in New York," *Politico*, May 22, 2014.

25. Michael Wolff, "Who Will Buy Al Gore's Current TV?," *USA Today*, November 12, 2012, accessed August 6, 2016, http://www.usatoday.com/story/money/business/2012/11/04/michael-wolff-currenttv/1677303/.

26. Hunter, "The Selling of Al Jazeera America."

27. "Al-Jazeera America Will Have to Work Hard to Win Viewers," *On the Media*, NPR, August 16, 2013, accessed August 6. 2016, http://www.onthemedia.org/story/312966-inside-al-jazeera-america/transcript/.

28. Wheelock, "Al Jazeera's U.S.-Based News Channel."

29. Poggi, "Al Jazeera America One Year Later."

30. Ibid.

31. Ibid.

32. Interview, January 15, 2016.

33. Interview, May 14, 2015.

34. Atkinson, "Al Jazeera America Angers."

35. "Al Jazeera America: Audience," *Allied Media Corporation*, accessed August 5, 2016, http://www.allied-media.com/aljazeera/america/aljazeera_america_audience.htm.

36. Ben Winsor, "Al Jazeera America Has an Ambitious Plan For Its Future in the US," *Business Insider*, September 18, 2014, accessed August 6, 2016, http://www.businessinsider.com/al-jazeera-americas-plan-towards-profit-2014–9.

37. Steven Perlberg, "Al Jazeera America Has Its First Major Shake-Up," *Wall Street Journal* [blog], April 14, 2014, accessed August 5, 2016, http://blogs.wsj.com/cmo/2014/04/14/al-jazeera-america-layoffs/.

38. Albert A. Gore, et al., v. Al Jazeera America Holdings I, Inc.

39. Atkinson, "Al Jazeera America Angers."

40. Liana Baker and Peter Lauria, "Al Jazeera Inherits Current TV's Distribution Woes," *Reuters*, January 4. 2013, accessed August 5, 2016, http://www.reuters.com/article/us-currentv-aljazeera-idUSBRE90301I20130104.

41. Interview, January 15, 2016.

42. DirecTV, LLC v. Al Jazeera America, LLC. 2015 Del. Ch. LEXIS 215 (2015).

43. High-Bassalik v. Al Jazeera America, et al.

44. Ibid., 8.

45. Interview, January 15, 2016.

46. Interview, January 16, 2016.

47. Interview, January 13, 2016.

48. Interview, March 11, 2014.

49. Interview, January 16, 2016.

50. Interview, January 16, 2015.

51. Interview, August 20, 2013.

52. Greenwald, "Al Jazeera Deletes its Own."

53. Joe Winkler, "Al-Jazeera Publishes, Pulls, then Reposts Joseph Massad Piece," *Jewish Telegraph Agency*, May 22, 2013, accessed August 6, 2016, http://www.jta.org/2013/05/22/arts-entertainment/al-jazeera-publishes-pulls-then-reposts-joseph-massad-piece.

54. Burman, "Al Jazeera America Has."

55. "Media. NYC. 2020 Final Report," 13.

56. Interview, June 19, 2015.

57. Interview, June 19, 2015.

58. Interview, May 14, 2015.

59. Burman, "Al Jazeera America Has."

60. Interview, May 14, 2015.

61. Interview, March, 10, 2014.

62. Interview, March 10, 2014.

63. Interview, March 10, 2014.

64. Interview, May 14, 2015.

65. Interview, March 10, 2014.

66. Interview, June 22, 2015.

67. Brendan Bordelon, "Internal Emails Show Al Jazeera English Banning Use of Terms Terrorist, Militant, Islamist," *National Review*, January 27, 2015, accessed August 5, 2016, http://www.nationalreview.com/corner/397320/internal-emails-show-al-jazeera-english-banning-use-terms-terrorist-militant-islamist.

68. Interview, June 22, 2015.
69. Interview, June 22, 2015.
70. Interview, June 22, 2015.
71. Interview, June 22, 2015.
72. Interview, May 14, 2015.
73. Interview, May 14, 2015.
74. John K. Engelhart, "Ali Velshi on Launching Al Jazeera America and the Future of TV," *MacLean's*, August 12, 2013, accessed August 5, 2016, http://www2.macleans.ca/2013/08/12/on-launching-al-jazeera-america-engaging-an-american-audience-and-the-future-of-tv/; emphasis added.
75. Shannon Bond, "Al Anstey Looks to Rewrite Al Jazeera America Headlines," *Financial Times*, September 28, 2015b, accessed August 5, 2016, http://www.ft.com/intl/cms/s/0/7bef7300-6304-11e5-a28b-50226830d644.html#axzz3wKB9JM00.
76. Patrick K. Day, "Colbert Interrogates John Seigenthaler about Al Jazeera America," *Los Angeles Times*, January 8, 2014, accessed August 5, 2016, http://articles.latimes.com/2014/jan/08/entertainment/la-et-st- colbert- interrogates-john-seigenthaler-about-al-jazeera-america-20140108.
77. Wheelock, "Al Jazeera's U.S.-Based News Channel."
78. Steinberg, "Al Jazeera America's New Chief."
79. Alex Sherman and Christopher Palmeri, "Current TV Said to Fetch $500 Million from Al Jazeera," *Bloomberg*, January 4, 2013, accessed August 5, 2016, http://www.bloomberg.com/news/articles/2013-01-03/al-jazeera-news-network-acquires-current-tv-to-expand-in-u-s-.
80. Winsor, "Al Jazeera America Has."
81. Andrew Kirell, "Al Jazeera America Beat MSNBC for 2 Hours in the Key 25–54 Ratings Demo," *Mediate*, March 31, 2015, accessed August 5, 2016, http://www.mediaite.com/tv/al-jazeera-america-beat-msnbc-for-2-hours-in-the-key-25-54-ratings-demo/.
82. Hunter, "Selling of Al Jazeera America."
83. Steinberg, "Al Jazeera America's New Chief."
84. "Media. NYC. 2020. Final Report," 12.
85. Leroy and Clarkson, "Homepage," accessed August 7, 2016, http://www.leroyandclarkson.com/.
86. Leroy and Clarkson, "Would You Like to Know More? Al Jazeera America Launch Campaign," accessed August 8, 2016, http://www.leroyandclarkson.com/work/ajam-launch.
87. Trollbäck + Company, "Al Jazeera America: Light + Voice," accessed August 6, 2016, http://trollback.com/al-jazeera-america/.
88. Albert A. Gore, et al., v. Al Jazeera America Holdings I, Inc.
89. Luke v. Al Jazeera America, et al. Supreme Court of the State of New York. [complaint, April 28, 2015] Index No. 154219/2015, accessed August 5, 2016, http://pospislaw.com/wp-content/uploads/2015/04/Complaint-Luke-v-Al-Jazeera.pdf.
90. Erik Wemple, "Former Al Jazeera Employee Sues Network, Alleging Anti-Semitism, Anti-Americanism," *Washington Post*, April 28, 2015, accessed August 6, 2016, https://www.washingtonpost.com/blogs/erik-wemple/wp/2015/04/28/former-al-jazeera-employee-sues-network-alleging-anti-semitism-anti-americanism/.
91. Brendan James, "Al Jazeera America Will Not Recognize Union: NLRB Elections Underway," *International Business Times*, September 29, 2015, accessed August 6, 2016, http://www.ibtimes.com/al-jazeera-america-will-not-recognize-union-nlrb-elections-underway-2118695.
92. James Warren, "Al Jazeera America Digital Workers Vote to Go Union," *Poynter*, October 6, 2015, accessed August 6, 2016, http://www.poynter.org/2015/al-jazeera-america-digital-workers-vote-to-go-union/377175/.
93. James, "Al-Jazeera America Will."
94. Interview, January 15, 2016.
95. Mark Jurkowitz, Amy Mitchell and Katerina E. Matsa, "How Al Jazeera Tackled the Crisis Over Syria," *Pew Research Center*, September 26, 2013, accessed August 5, 2016, http://www.journalism.org/2013/09/16/how-al-jazeera-tackled-the-crisis-over-syria.

96. David Tereshchuk, "Al Jazeera: Management Style Echoes Country-of-Origin," *Huffington Post*, May 21, 2015, accessed August 5, 2016, http://www.huffingtonpost.com/david-tereshchuk/al-jazeera-management-sty_b_7377190.html.
97. Rem Rieder, "Can Al Jazeera America Flourish?" *USA Today*, January 27, 2014, accessed August 6, 2016, www.usatoday.com/story/money/columnist/rieder/2014/01/27/can-al-jazeera-america-flourish/4938253/.
98. Jack Shafer, "What's More Rare, a Unicorn or an Al Jazeera America Viewer?," *Reuters*, July 9, 2014, accessed August 5, 2016, http://blogs.reuters.com/jackshafer/2014/07/09/whats-more-rare-a-unicorn-or-an-al-jazeera-america-viewer/.
99. Rieder, "Can Al Jazeera America."
100. David Zurawik, "What Al Jazeera America's Death Means to TV News," *Baltimore Sun*, January 15, 2016, accessed August 6, 2016, http://www.baltimoresun.com/entertain-ment/tv/z-on-tv-blog/bs-ae-zontv-al-jazeera-20160115-story.html.
101. Poggi, "Al Jazeera America One Year Later."
102. Interview, May 14, 2015.
103. Interview, January 7, 2016.
104. Bond, "Al Jazeera America Shaken."
105. John Koblin, "Al Jazeera America, Its Newsroom in Turmoil, Is Now the News," *New York Times*, May 5, 2015, accessed August 5, 2016, http://www.nytimes.com/2015/05/06/business/media/al-jazeera-network-in-turmoil-is-now-the-news.html?_r=1.
106. Ibid.
107. Bond, "Al Anstey Looks to Rewrite."
108. Interview, January 7, 2016.
109. Atkinson, "Al Jazeera America Angers."
110. Interview, January 7, 2016.
111. Interview, January 7, 2016.
112. Joe Pompeo et al., "Al Jazeera America Shutting Down," *Politico*, January 13, 2016, accessed August 5, 2016, http://www.capitalnewyork.com/article/media/2016/01/8587929/al-jazeera-america-shutting-down.
113. Tom Kludt and Brian Stetler, "Al Jazeera America to Shut Down in April," *CNN Money*, January 13, 2016, accessed August 5, 2016, http://money.cnn.com/2016/01/13/media/al-jazeera-america/.
114. Interview, January 14, 2016.
115. Interview, January 14, 2016.
116. Interview, January 15, 2016.
117. Albert A. Gore, et al., v. Al Jazeera America Holdings I, Inc.
118. Ibid.
119. James, "Al-Jazeera America Will."
120. Ibid.

Chapter 6

1. Pratt, "Hot Jobs in Cool Places," 35.
2. "The Humble Hero," *The Economist*, May 18, 2013, accessed August 5, 2016, http://www.economist.com/news/finance-and-economics/21578041-containers-have-been-more-important-globalisation-freer-trade-humble?fsrc=nlw|hig|5-16-2013|5722602|34886579.
3. Pratt, "Hot Jobs in Cool Places," 39.
4. Ibid., 41.
5. Interview, May 15, 2015.
6. Interview, May 15, 2015.
7. Jessica Toonkel, "Al Jazeera to Launch English Language Digital Streaming Service in U.S.," *Reuters*, July 21, 2016, accessed August 5, 2016, http://ca.reuters.com/article/tech-nologyNews/idCAKCN1012PF.

8. "Al Jazeera to launch dedicated online channel," *Al Jazeera Media Network* [press release], October 9, 2013, accessed August 6, 2016, http://pr.aljazeera.com/post/63541421248/al-jazeera-to-launch-dedicated-online-channel.

9. Interview, May 15, 2015.

10. "Cre8 Agency Talent at Another Successful Mobile Launch Party," *Cre8 Agency* [press release], October 14, 2014, accessed August 6, 2016, http://cre8agency.com/cre8-agency-talent-at-another-successful-mobile-launch-party/.

11. Peter Kovessy and Shabina S. Khatri, "Al Jazeera Launches Digital Channel AJ+ in Bid to Woo Younger Viewers," *Doha News*, September 15, 2014, accessed August 6, 2016, http://dohanews.co/al-jazeera-launches-digital-channel-aj-bid-woo-younger-viewers/.

12. Interview, May 12, 2015.

13. Interview, May 14, 2015.

14. Interview, May 15, 2015.

15. Interview, May 14, 2015.

16. Interview, June 3, 2015.

17. Interview, May 14, 2015.

18. Interview, May 14, 2015.

19. Interview, May 14, 2015.

20. Interview, May 14, 2015.

21. Interview, February 10, 2016.

22. Interview, June 22, 2015.

23. Ricardo Bilton, "Al Jazeera's Distributed Content Unit Generated 2.2 Billion Facebook Video Views in 2015," *Digiday*, January 13, 2016, accessed August 5, 2016, http://digiday.com/publishers/al-jazeeras-distributed-content-unit-generated-2-2-bil-facebook-video-views-2015/.

24. Alastair Reid, "Beyond Websites: How AJ+ is Innovating in Digital Storytelling," *Journalism.co.uk*, April 17, 2014, accessed August 6, 2016, https://www.journalism.co.uk/news/beyond-websites-how-aj-is-innovating-in-digital-storytelling/s2/a564811/.

25. Interview, May 14, 2015.

26. Interview, May 14, 2015.

27. Interview, May 15, 2015.

28. Interview, May 13, 2015.

29. Neff, "Changing Place."

30. Interview, May 14, 2015.

31. Abigail Edge, "How Al Jazeera's AJ+ Aims to Engage Millennials," *UK Journalism*, September, 2014, accessed August 5, 2016, https://www.journalism.co.uk/news/how-al-jazeera-s-aj-aims-to-engage-millennials-/s2/a562464/.

32. Interview, May 13, 2015.

33. Scott, *The Cultural Economy of Cities*.

34. Michael Curtin, "Thinking Globally: From Media Imperialism to Media Capital," in *Media Industries: History, Theory, and Method*, ed. Jennifer Holt and Alisa Perren (Walden, MA: John Wiley & Sons, 2009); Florida, *Cities and the Creative Class*.

35. Interview, May 15, 2015.

36. Interview, May 15, 2015.

37. Interview, May 12, 2015.

38. Richard Barbrook and Andy Cameron, "The Californian Ideology," in *Crypto Anarchy, Cyberstates, and Pirate Utopias*, ed. Petr Ludlow (Cambridge, MA: MIT Press, 2001).

39. Fred Turner, *From Counterculture to Cyberculture: Stewart Brand, the Whole Earth Network, and the Rise of Digital Utopianism* (Chicago: University of Chicago Press, 2006).

40. Bilton, "Al Jazeera's Distributed Content."

41. "Tubular Labs Ranks the Top Video Brands and Influencers in December 2015," *Business Wire* [press release], January 19, 2016, accessed August 6, 2016, http://www.businesswire.com/news/home/20160119005795/en/Tubular-Labs-Ranks-Top-Video-Brands-Influencers.

42. Martha Crowley et al., "Neo-Taylorism at Work: Occupational Change in the Post-Fordist Era," *Social Problems* 57, no. 3 (2010): 421–447.

43. Interview, May 15, 2015.
44. "Intro to Design Thinking," presentation at the annual convention of the Online News Association, San Francisco, CA, September 20, 2012, accessed online August 7, 2016, https://ona2012.sched.org/event/18HiCGr/intro-to-design-thinking.
45. Interview, May 15, 2015.
46. Mark Joyella, "Watchup Adds Fusion, The Verge, Vox and AJ+," *TV Newser*, January 6, 2015, accessed August 5, 2016, http://www.adweek.com/tvnewser/watchup-adds-fusion-the-verge-vox-and-aj/251494.
47. Janko Roettgers, "Al Jazeera's AJ+ Gets Its Own Apple TV App," *Variety*, January 19, 2016, accessed August 5, 2016, http://variety.com/2016/digital/news/ajplus-apple-tv-app-1201682896/.
48. Interview, May 13, 2015.
49. Interview, May 13, 2015.
50. Interview, June 3, 2015.
51. Shadi Rahimi, "How AJ+ Reported from Baltimore Using Only Mobile Phones," *Poynter*, May 1, 2015, accessed August 6, 2016, http://www.poynter.org/news/mediawire/341117/how-aj-reported-from-baltimore-using-only-mobile-phones/.
52. "What Is White Privilege? Here's What People on the Street Have To Say," *AJ+*, December 12, 2014, accessed August 8, 2016, https://www.youtube.com/watch?v=aQK8H0z-irM.
53. "4 Ways Baltimore Has A Massive Police Problem," *AJ+*, accessed August 12, 2016, https://www.youtube.com/watch?v=wC5Cne0oe7o.
54. Mary Bucholtz et al., "Hella Nor Cal or Totally So Cal? The Perceptual Dialectology of California," *Journal of English Linguistics* 35, no. 4 (2007): 342.
55. Interview, May 15, 2015.
56. Interview, October 8, 2014.
57. Interview, May 13, 2015.
58. Michael Massing, "Digital Journalism: The Next Generation," *New York Review of Books*, June 25, 2015, accessed August 5, 2016, http://www.nybooks.com/articles/archives/2015/jun/25/digital-journalism-next-generation/.

Conclusion

1. Fisher and Casey, "Al Jazeera English Foreign."
2. El-Nawawy and Iskandar, *Al-Jazeera: The Story*, 30–31.
3. Miles, *Al-Jazeera*, 346.
4. Ibid., 10.
5. Interview, January 2, 2016.
6. "Al Jazeera to Expand Digital Services in US," *Al Jazeera Media Network* [press release], January 14, 2016, accessed August 5, 2016, http://www.aljazeera.com/news/2016/01/al-jazeera-160113151725873.html.
7. Curtin, *Playing to the World's*, 9.
8. Oliver Boyd-Barrett, "Media Imperialism Reformulated," in *Electronic Empires: Global Media and Local Resistance*, ed. Daya K. Thussu (New York: Hotter Arnold, 1998).
9. Thussu, "Mapping Media Flow"; Tunstall, *The Media Were American*.
10. Koichi Iwabuchi, "Contra-Flows or the Cultural Logic of Uneven Globalization? Japanese Media in the Global Agora," in *Media on the Move: Global Flow and Contra-Flow*, ed. Daya K. Thussu (London: Routledge, 2007).
11. David Morley, "For a Materialist, Non-media-centric Media Studies," *Television & New Media* 10, no. 1 (2009).
12. Armand Mattelart, *The Invention of Communication*, trans. Susan Emanuel (Minneapolis: University of Minnesota Press, 1996).
13. Taylor, *World City Network*.
14. Krätke and Taylor, "A World Geography."

15. Iginio Gagliardone, "China as a Persuader: CCTV Africa's First Steps in the African Mediasphere," *Ecquid Novi: African Journalism Studies* 34, no. 3 (2013).
16. Ibid., 29–30.
17. Ibid., 30.
18. Ibid., 33.
19. Ibid., 36.
20. Parker, "Francophone Africa Is the New Land of Opportunity for the French Media Industry," trans. Lova Rakotomalala, *Global Voices*, June 15, 2015, accessed August 5, 2016, https://globalvoices.org/2015/06/12/francophone-africa-is-the-new-land-of-opportunity-for-the-french-media-industry/.
21. "Africanews Launches Vision of Unbiased Information, Embracing Diversity," *Euronews*, January 7, 2016, accessed August 5, 2016, http://www.euronews.com/2016/01/07/africanews-launches-vision-of-unbiased-information-embracing-diversity/.

Afterword

1. Havens et al, "Critical Media Industry Studies."
2. Interview, February 8, 2016.
3. Toonkel, "Al Jazeera to Launch."

Appendix A

1. Alexander L. George and Andrew Bennett, *Case Studies and Theory Development in the Social Sciences* (Cambridge, MA: MIT Press, 2005).
2. Tom Wengraf, *Qualitative Research Interviewing: Biographic Narrative and Semi-Structured Methods* (Thousand Oaks, CA: Sage, 2001).
3. Adam J. Berinsky et al., "Evaluating Online Labor Markets for Experimental Research: Amazon.com's Mechanical Turk," *Political Analysis* 20, no. 3 (2012).
4. Brad J. Bushman and Angelica M. Bonacci, "You've Got Mail: Using E-mail to Examine the Effect of Prejudiced Attitudes on Discrimination Against Arabs," *Journal of Experimental Social Psychology* 40, no. 6 (2004).
5. "Community Facts," *American FactFinder*, United States Census Bureau, accessed August 6, 2016, http://factfinder.census.gov/faces/nav/jsf/pages/index.xhtml#.
6. Jean C. Deville et al., "Generalized Raking Procedures in Survey Sampling," *Journal of the American Statistical Association* 88, no. 423 (1993).

Bibliography

"4 Ways Baltimore Has A Massive Police Problem." *AJ+*. Accessed August 12, 2016. https://www.youtube.com/watch?v=wC5CneOoe7o.

Abdul-Nabi, Zainab. "Based on the Peace Journalism Model: Analysis of Al-Jazeera's Coverage of Bahrain's Uprising and Syria's Chemical Attack." *Global Media and Communication* 11 (2015): 271–302.

Abu-Lughod, Janet L. *Before European Hegemony: The World System, AD 1250–1350*. New York: Oxford University Press, 1989.

———. *New York, Chicago, Los Angeles: America's Global Cities*. Minneapolis: University of Minnesota Press, 1999.

Ackerman, Spencer. "Is Al Jazeera the Next PBS? Coming to America." *The New Republic*, May 1, 2006. Accessed August 5, 2016. http://www.tnr.com/article/al-jazeera-the-next-pbs.

Adams, Paul C., Steven Hoelscher, and Karen E. Till. "Place in Context: Rethinking Humanist Geographies." In *Textures of Place: Exploring Humanist Geographies*, edited by Paul C. Adams, S. Steven Hoelscher, and Karen E. Till, xiii–xxxiii. Minneapolis: University of Minnesota Press, 2001.

Adriaens, Fien, and Daniel Biltereyst. "Glocalized Telenovelas and National Identities: A 'Textual Cum Production' Analysis of the Telenovelle Sara, the Flemish Adaptation of *Yo soy Betty, La Fea*." *Television & New Media* 13, no. 6 (2012): 551–567.

"Africanews Launches Vision of Unbiased Information, Embracing Diversity." *Euronews*, January 7, 2016. Accessed August 5, 2016. http://www.euronews.com/2016/01/07/africanews-launches-vision-of-unbiased-information-embracing-diversity/.

Agnew, John A. *Place and Politics: The Geographical Mediation of State and Society*. New York: Routledge, 2015.

"AIM Protests Ohio Cable Co.'s Decision to Air Al-Jazeera English Channel." *Accuracy in Media*, March 30, 2007. Accessed August 5, 2016. http://www.aim.org/press-release/aim-protests-ohio-cable-cos-decision-to-air-al-jazeera-english-channel/.

Ali, Lorraine, and Marisa Guthrie. "Why American Cable Systems Won't Carry the Al Jazeera Network." *The Hollywood Reporter*, March 17, 2011.

"Al Jazeera America: Audience." *Allied Media Corporation*. Accessed August 6, 2016. http://www.allied-media.com/aljazeera/america/aljazeera_america_audience.htm.

"Al-Jazeera America Will Have to Work Hard to Win Viewers." *On the Media*, NPR, August 16, 2013. Accessed August 6, 2016. http://www.onthemedia.org/story/312966-inside-al-jazeera-america/transcript/.

"Al Jazeera and Kidnapping Tapes." *Wikileaks*, February 13, 2006. Accessed August 5, 2016. https://wikileaks.org/plusd/cables/06DOHA219_a.html.

"Al-Jazeera Draws Harsh Comments Online." *Sandusky Register*, March 15, 2007. Accessed August 5, 2016. http://www.sanduskyregister.com/2007/mar/16/al-jazeera-draws-harsh-comments-online?similar.

"Al Jazeera Media Network Launches a New Era of Storytelling." Al Jazeera Media Network [press release], September 15, 2014. Accessed August 6, 2016. http://pr.aljazeera.com/post/97562972470/al-jazeera-media-network-launches-a-new-era-of.

"Al Jazeera Media Network Launches a New Era of Storytelling." *Business Wire*, September 15, 2014. Accessed August 5, 2016. http://www.businesswire.com/news/home/20140915005268/en/Al-Jazeera-Media-Network-Launches-Era-Storytelling#.VBbkL-eLGAd.

"Al Jazeera Tells Glassman It's Restructuring to Boost Professionalism and Independence." *Wikileaks*, September 4, 2008. Accessed August 7, 2016. https://wikileaks.org/plusd/cables/08DOHA633_a.html.

"Al Jazeera to Expand Digital Services in US." *Al Jazeera Media Network* [press release], January 14, 2016. Accessed August 5, 2016. http://www.aljazeera.com/news/2016/01/al-jazeera-160113151725873.html.

"Al Jazeera to Launch Dedicated Online Channel." *Al Jazeera Media Network* [press release], October 9, 2013. Accessed August 5, 2016. http://pr.aljazeera.com/post/63541421248/al-jazeera-to-launch-dedicated-online-channel.

Allam, Hannah. "New Al-Jazeera International Channel Sparks Conflict." *Knight Ridder*, March 2, 2006. Accessed August 5, 2016. http://www.commondreams.org/headlines06/0302-08.htm.

Allan, Scott. *News Culture*. 2nd ed. Buckingham: Open University Press, 2004.

Al-Najjar, Abeer I. "How Arab Is Al-Jazeera English? Comparative Study of Al-Jazeera Arabic and Al-Jazeera English News Channels." *Global Media Journal* 8 (2009). Accessed August 5, 2016. http://www.globalmediajournal.com/open-access/how-arab-is-aljazeera-english.pdf.

Alterman, Jon B. "The Challenge for Al Jazeera International." *Transnational Broadcasting Studies* 14 (2005): 143–146.

Ambinder, Marc. "How Al Jazeera Outlasted Donald Rumsfeld." *The Atlantic*, December 10, 2009. Accessed August 5, 2016. http://www.theatlantic.com/politics/archive/2009/12/how-al-jazeera-outlasted-donald-rumsfeld/31587/.

Ammori, Marvin. "TV Competition Nowhere: How the Cable Industry Is Colluding to Kill Online TV." *Free Press Report*, January 2010.

Appadurai, Arjun. "Disjuncture and Difference in the Global Cultural Economy." *Public Culture* 2 (1990): 1–24.

———. *Modernity at Large: Cultural Dimensions of Globalization*. Minneapolis: University of Minnesota Press, 1996.

Atkinson, Claire. "Al Jazeera America Angers Staffers with Shift in Direction." *New York Post*, April 21, 2015. Accessed August 5, 2016. http://nypost.com/2015/04/21/al-jazeera-america-angers-staffers-with-shift-in-direction/.

Bailey, Charles W. "Foreign Policy and the Provincial Press." In *The Media and Foreign Policy*, edited by Simon Serfaty, 179–188. London: Palgrave Macmillan, 1990.

Baker, Edwin C. *Media, Markets, and Democracy*. New York: Cambridge University Press, 2002.

Baker, Liana, and Peter Lauria. "Al Jazeera Inherits Current TV's Distribution Woes." *Reuters*, January 4, 2013. Accessed August 5, 2016. http://www.reuters.com/article/us-currentv-aljazeera-idUSBRE90301I20130104.

Barbrook, Richard, and Andy Cameron. "The Californian Ideology." In *Crypto Anarchy, Cyberstates, and Pirate Utopias*, edited by Petr Ludlow, 363–387. Cambridge, MA: MIT Press, 2001.

Barker, Greg. "Interview with Wadah Khanfar, Director General, Al Jazeera." *PBS*, March 27, 2007. Accessed August 5, 2016. http://www.pbs.org/frontlineworld/stories/newswar/war_interviews.html.

Barker, Kim. *The Taliban Shuffle: Strange Days in Afghanistan and Pakistan*. New York: Anchor, 2012.

Bathelt, Harald, and Armin Gräf. "Internal and External Dynamics of the Munich Film and TV Industry Cluster, and Limitations to Future Growth." *Environment and Planning* 40, no. 8 (2008): 1944.

Bauder, David. "Clinton Media Criticism Buoys Al-Jazeera." *Washington Post*, March 5, 2011. Accessed August 7, 2011. http://www.washingtonpost.com/wp-dyn/content/article/2011/03/04/AR2011030405714.html.

Baum, Matthew A. *Soft News Goes to War: Public Opinion and American Foreign Policy in a New Media Age*. Princeton, NJ: Princeton University Press, 2003.

Bauman, Zygmunt. *Liquid Modernity*. Malden, MA: Polity, 2000.

"BBC and Discovery Communications, Inc. Sign the Deal of the Decade." *BBC* [press release], March 22, 2002. Accessed August 5, 2016. http://www.bbc.co.uk/pressoffice/bbcworld-wide/worldwidestories/pressreleases/2002/03_march/dci_deal.shtml.

Bebawi, Saba. *Media Power and Global Television News: The Role of Al Jazeera English*. London: IB Tauris, 2016.

Beblawi, Hazem, and Giacomo Luciani. *The Rentier State*. New York: Routledge, 1987.

Beck, Ulrich. "The Cosmopolitan Society and Its Enemies." *Theory, Culture & Society* 19 no. 1–2 (2002a): 17–44.

———. *The Cosmopolitan Vision*. Cambridge: Polity Press, 2006.

———. "The Terrorist Threat. World Risk Society Revisited." *Theory, Culture & Society* 19, no. 4 (2002b): 39–55.

Bennett, Stephen E., Richard S. Flickinger, John R. Baker, Staci L. Rhine, and Linda L. M. Bennett. "Citizens' Knowledge of Foreign Affairs." *Harvard International Journal of Press/Politics* 1, no. 2 (1996): 10–29.

Bennett, W. Lance. *News: The Politics of Illusion*. 4th ed. New York: Addison Wesley Longman, 2001.

Bennett, W. Lance. "Toward a Theory of Press-State Relations in the United States." *Journal of Communication* 40, no. 2 (1990): 103–127.

Berinsky, Adam J., Gregory A. Huber, and Gabriel S. Lenz. "Evaluating Online Labor Markets for Experimental Research: Amazon.com's Mechanical Turk." *Political Analysis* 20, no. 3 (2012): 351–368.

Berry, Brian Joe L. "Cities as Systems Within Systems of Cities." *Papers of the Regional Science Association* 13 (1964): 147–163.

Best, Samuel J., Brian Chmielewski, and Brian Krueger. "Selective Exposure to Online Foreign News during the Conflict with Iraq." *International Journal of Press/Politics* 10, no. 4 (2005): 52–70.

Bilton, Ricardo. "Al Jazeera's Distributed Content Unit Generated 2.2 Billion Facebook Video Views in 2015." *Digiday*, January 13, 2016. Accessed August 5, 2016. http://digiday.com/publishers/al-jazeeras-distributed-content-unit-generated-2-2-bil-facebook-video-views-2015/.

Black, Alex. "Al Jazeera Picks BLJ to 'Soften' English Launch." *PR Week*, July 21, 2005. Accessed August 5, 2016. http://www.prweek.com/article/487135/al-jazeera-picks-blj-soften-english-launch.

Boden, Deirdre and Harvey L. Molotch, "The Compulsion of Proximity." In *Now Here: Space, Time and Modernity*, edited by Roger Friedland and Deirdre Boden, 157–176. Berkeley: University of California Press, 1994.

Bollinger, Lee C. "Al Jazeera Can Help U.S. Join Conversation." *Bloomberg*, March 15, 2011. Accessed August 7, 2016. http://www.bloomberg.com/news/articles/2011-03-15/al-jazeera-can-help-u-s-join-conversation-commentary-by-lee-c-bollinger.

Bond, Shannon. "Al Anstey Looks to Rewrite Al Jazeera America Headlines." *Financial Times*, September 28, 2015b. Accessed August 5, 2016. http://www.ft.com/intl/cms/s/0/7bef7300-6304-11e5-a28b-50226830d644.html#axzz3wKB9JM00.

———. "Al Jazeera America Shaken by Defections." *Financial Times*, May 4, 2015a. Accessed August 5, 2016. http://www.ft.com/intl/cms/s/0/4b782a8e-f2a5-11e4-b914-00144feab7de.html#axzz3wkk79FtO.

Booth, Robert. "WikiLeaks Cables Claim al-Jazeera Changed Coverage to Suit Qatari Foreign Policy." *The Guardian* [UK], December 5, 2010. Accessed August 5, 2016. http://www.the-guardian.com/world/2010/dec/05/wikileaks-cables-al-jazeera-qatari-foreign-policy.

Bordelon, Brendan. "Internal Emails Show Al Jazeera English Banning Use of Terms Terrorist, Militant, Islamist." *National Review*, January 27, 2015. Accessed August 5, 2016. http://www.nationalreview.com/corner/397320/internal-emails-show-al-jazeera-english-banning-use-terms-terrorist-militant-islamist.

Bourne, Larry S. *Urban Systems: Strategies for Regulation*. Oxford: Clarendon Press, 1975.

———. James W. Simmons. *Systems of Cities*. New York: Oxford University Press, 1978.

Boyd-Barrett, Oliver. "Media Imperialism Reformulated." In *Electronic Empires: Global Media and Local Resistance*, edited by Daya Thussu, 157–176. New York: Hotter Arnold, 1998.

———. Shuang Xie. "Al-Jazeera, Phoenix Satellite Television and the Return of the State: Case Studies in Market Liberalization, Public Sphere and Media Imperialism." *International Journal of Communication* 2 (2008): 206–222.

Braudel, Fernand. *The Perspective of the World*. London: Collins, 1984.

Brook, Stephen. "Al-Jazeera Is World's Fifth Top Brand." *The Guardian* [UK], February 1, 2005. Accessed August 5, 2016. http://www.theguardian.com/media/2005/feb/01/marketingandpr.broadcasting.

Brooker-Gross, Susan R. "Spatial Aspects of Newsworthiness." *Geografiska Annaler. Series B. Human Geography* 65, no. 1 (1983): 1–9.

Brown, Alan, Jerry Fishenden, and Mark Thompson. *Digitizing Government: Understanding and Implementing New Digital Business Models*. London: Palgrave Macmillan, 2014.

Brown, Dan. "Historical Perspectives on Communication Technology." In *Communication Technology Update and Fundamentals*, edited by August E. Grant and Jennifer H. Meadows, 9–46. Burlington, MA: Focal Press, 2010.

Bucholtz, Mary, Nancy Bermudez, Victor Fung, Lisa Edwards, and Rosalva Vargas. "Hella Nor Cal or Totally So Cal? The Perceptual Dialectology of California." *Journal of English Linguistics* 35, no. 4 (2007): 325–352.

"Buckeye Cable System Adds Al Jazeera English." *Toledo Blade*, March 10, 2007. Accessed August 5, 2016. http://www.toledoblade.com/TV-Radio/2007/03/10/Buckeye-CableSystem-adds-Al-Jazeera-English.html.

Burman, Tony. "Al Jazeera America Has the Odor of Disaster." *Toronto Star*, June 1, 2013. Accessed August 5, 2016. http://www.thestar.com/news/world/2013/06/01/al_jazeera_america_has_the_odour_of_disaster_burman.html.

Bushman, Brad J., and Angelica M. Bonacci. "You've Got Mail: Using E-mail to Examine the Effect of Prejudiced Attitudes on Discrimination Against Arabs." *Journal of Experimental Social Psychology* 40, no. 6 (2004): 753–759.

Buttimer, Anne. "Grasping the Dynamism of Lifeworld." *Annals of the Association of American Geographers* 66, no. 2 (1976): 277–292.

Byers, Dylan. "CNN Moves to Centralize in New York." *Politico*, May 22, 2014.

Cairncross, Fred. *The Death of Distance: How the Communications Revolution Is Changing Our Lives*. Cambridge, MA: Harvard Business Press, 1997.

Calderone, Michael. "Time Warner Cable Will Consider Carrying Al Jazeera's U.S. Network." *Huffington Post*, January 3, 2013. Accessed August 5, 2016. http://www.huffingtonpost.com/2013/01/03/time-warner-cable-al-jazeera-america_n_2404879.html.

Calhoun, Craig. "Cosmopolitanism and Nationalism." *Nations and Nationalism* 14, no. 3 (2008): 427–449.

Carlton, Dennis, and Jeffrey M. Perloff. *Modern Industrial Organization*. New York: Harper Collins College Publishers, 1994.

Casey, Edward S. *The Fate of Place: A Philosophical History*. Berkeley: University of California Press, 1997.

Castells, Manuel. *La question urbaine*. Paris: Maspero, 1972.

———. *The Rise of the Network Society*, vol. 1. 2nd ed. New York: Blackwell, 2010.

———. *The Urban Question: A Marxist Approach*. Translated by Alan Sheridan. Cambridge, MA: MIT Press, 1979.

Chalaby, Jean. K. *Transnational Television in Europe: Reconfiguring Global Communications Networks*. London: IB Tauris, 2009.

Chan-Olmsted, Sylvia M. "Market Competition for Cable Television: Reexamining its Horizontal Mergers and Industry Concentration." *Journal of Media Economics* 9, no. 2 (1996): 25–41.

Circelli, Deborah. "Daytona State College Faces Complaint over Public TV Programming." *Daytona Beach News-Journal*, February 10, 2011. Accessed August 5, 2016. http://www.usasurvival.org/home/ck02.10.11-2.html.

Clausen, Meredith L. "Localizing the Global: 'Domestication' Processes in International News Production." *Media, Culture & Society* 26, no. 1 (2004): 25–44.

Clemons, Steve. "Al Jazeera English to Downsize D.C. Operation." *The Atlantic*, March 30, 2012. Accessed August 5, 2016. http://www.theatlantic.com/international/archive/2012/03/al-jazeera-english-to-downsize-dc-operation/255276/.

"The Colbert Report. Ayman Mohyeldin interview." *Comedy Central*, March 22, 2011. Accessed August 5, 2016. http://www.colbertnation.com/the-colbert-report-videos/378442/march-22-2011/ayman-mohyeldin.

Coleman, Zach. "CNN Fends Off Its Competitors in Foreign Markets." *Atlanta Business Chronicle*, August 8, 1997. Accessed August 5, 2016. http://www.bizjournals.com/atlanta/stories/1997/08/11/story7.html.

"Community Facts." *American FactFinder*. United States Census Bureau. Accessed August 6, 2016. http://factfinder.census.gov/faces/nav/jsf/pages/index.xhtml#.

Control Room. Directed by Juhane Noujaim. 2004. Santa Monica, CA: Lions Gate Home Entertainment, 2004. DVD.

Cook, Timothy E. *Governing with the News: The News Media as a Political Institution*. Chicago: University of Chicago Press, 1998.

"Cre8 Agency Talent at Another Successful Mobile Launch Party." *Cre8 Agency* [press release], October 14, 2014. Accessed August 6, 2016. http://cre8agency.com/cre8-agency-talent-at-another-successful-mobile-launch-party/.

Crowley, Martha, Daniel Tope, Lindsay Joyce Chamberlain, and Roy Hodson. "Neo-Taylorism at Work: Occupational Change in the Post-Fordist Era." *Social Problems* 57, no. 3 (2010): 421–447.

Cunningham, James B. "Dave Marash: Why I Quit." *Columbia Journalism Review*, April 4, 2008. Accessed August 5, 2016. http://www.cjr.org/the_water_cooler/dave_marash_why_i_quit.php?page=all.

Curran, James, Shanto Iyengar, Anker Brink Lund, and Inka Salovaara-Moring. "Media System, Public Knowledge and Democracy: A Comparative Study." *European Journal of Communication* 24, no. 1 (2009): 5–26. Accessed August 6, 2016. doi: 10.1177/0267323108098943.

Currier, Richard C. "Al Jazeera Blocks Anti-Saudi Arabia Article." *The Intercept*, December 18, 2015. Accessed August 6, 2016. https://theintercept.com/2015/12/18/al-jazeera-blocks-anti-saudi-arabia-article/.

Curtin, Michael. "Comparing Media Capitals: Hong Kong and Mumbai." *Global Media and Communication* 6, no. 3 (2010): 263–270.

———. "Conditions of Capital: Global Media in Local Contexts." In *Internationalizing "International Communication,"* edited by Chin-Chuan Lee, 109–133. Ann Arbor: University of Michigan Press, 2015.

———. "Media Capital: Towards the Study of Spatial Flows." *International Journal of Cultural Studies* 6, no. 2 (2003): 202–228.

———. *Playing to the World's Biggest Audience: The Globalization of Chinese Film and Television*. Berkeley: University of California Press, 2007.

———. "Thinking Globally: From Media Imperialism to Media Capital." In *Media Industries: History, Theory, and Method*, edited by Jennifer Holt and Alisa Perren, 108–119. Walden, MA: John Wiley & Sons, 2009.

Da Lage, Olivier. "The Politics of Al Jazeera or the Diplomacy of Doha." In *The Al Jazeera Phenomenon: Critical Perspectives on New Arab Media*, edited by Mohamed Zayani, 49–65. London: Pluto Press, 2005.

Dahl, Jeremy. "I Want My AJE." *Guernica*, May 2008. Accessed August 5, 2016. http://www.guernicamag.com/features/588/limited_access_1/.

Dawson, Trevor. *Building Blocks: Buckeye CableSystem's Communications Revolution, From Printer's Ink to Cable to Fiber.* Lanham, MD: Hamilton Books, 2015.

Day, Patrick K. "Colbert Interrogates John Seigenthaler about Al Jazeera America." *Los Angeles Times*, January 8, 2014. Accessed August 5, 2016. http://articles.latimes.com/2014/jan/08/entertainment/la-et-st-colbert-interrogates-john-seigenthaler-about-al-jazeera-america-20140108.

Deuze, Mark. "National News Cultures: A Comparison of Dutch, German, British, Australian, and US Journalists." *Journalism & Mass Communication Quarterly* 79, no. 1 (2002): 134–149.

———. "What Is Journalism? Professional Identity and Ideology of Journalists Reconsidered." *Journalism* 6, no. 4 (2005): 442–464.

Deville, Jean C., Carl-Erick Särndal, and Olivier Sautory. "Generalized Raking Procedures in Survey Sampling." *Journal of the American Statistical Association* 88, no. 423 (1993): 1013–1020.

Dicken, Peter. *Global Shift: Mapping the Changing Contours of the World Economy.* 5th ed. Thousand Oaks, CA: Sage Publications.

Dickey, Christopher. "The Al Jazeera Revolution." *Newsweek*, May 23, 2013. Accessed August 5, 2016. http://www.newsweek.com/2013/05/22/al-jazeera-revolution-237390.html.

Doorley, Scott, and Scott Witthoft. *Make Space: How to Set the Stage for Creative Collaboration.* Hoboken, NJ: John Wiley & Sons, 2011.

Downey, George. "Making Media Work: Time, Space, Identity, and Labor in the Analysis of Information and Communication Infrastructure." In *Media Technologies: Essays on Communication, Materiality, and Society*, edited by Tarleton Gillespie, Pablo J. Boczkowski, and Kirsten A. Foot, 141–166. Cambridge, MA: MIT Press, 2014.

"Dr. Yaser Bishr." *Digital Media Strategies 2017*, 2016. Accessed August 7, 2016. http://digital-media-strategies.com/speakers/dr-yaser-bishr/.

Duranti, Alessandro. "Husserl, Intersubjectivity and Anthropology." *Anthropological Theory* 10, no. 1–2 (2010): 16–35.

Edge, Abigail. "How Al Jazeera's AJ+ Aims to Engage Millennials." *UK Journalism*, September, 2014. Accessed August 5, 2016. https://www.journalism.co.uk/news/how-al-jazeera-s-aj-aims-to-engage-millennials-/s2/a562464/.

"Egypt Releases Al Jazeera Journalists Fahmy and Mohamed." *BBC News*, September 23, 2015. Accessed August 6, 2016. http://www.bbc.com/news/world-middle-east-34337595.

Ellis, Allan J. "Demand Al Jazeera: How Al Jazeera is Using Social Media to Cover Egypt and Distribute Its Content in the US." *Nieman Journalism Lab*, February 4, 2011. Accessed August 5, 2016. http://www.niemanlab.org/2011/02/demandaljazeera-how-al-jazeera-is-using-social-media-and-hopes-to-use-twitter-to-get-on-us-tv/.

El-Nawawy, Mohammed, and Adel Iskandar. *Al Jazeera: How the Free Arab News Network Scooped the World and Changed the Middle East.* Cambridge, MA: Westview, 2002.

———. Adel Iskandar. *Al-Jazeera: The Story of the Network that Is Rattling Governments and Redefining Modern Journalism.* Cambridge, MA: Westview, 2003.

———. Shawn Powers. "A Conciliatory Medium in a Conflict-Driven Environment?" *Global Media and Communication* 6, no. 1 (2010): 61–84.

———. Shawn Powers. *Mediating Conflict: Al-Jazeera English and the Possibility of a Conciliatory Media.* Los Angeles: Figueroa Press, 2008.

Engelhart, John K. "Ali Velshi on Launching Al Jazeera America and the Future of TV." *MacLean's*, August 12, 2013. Accessed August 5, 2016. http://www2.macleans.ca/2013/08/12/on-launching-al-jazeera-america-engaging-an-american-audience-and-the-future-of-tv/.

Ericson, Erik, and Hamilton, Roger J. "Happy Landings: A Defense of Parachute Journalism." In *From Pigeons to News Portals: Foreign Reporting and the Challenge of New Technology*, edited by David D. Perlmutter and John Maxwell Hamilton, 130–149. Baton Rouge: Louisiana State University Press, 2007.

Esposito, John L., and Ibrahim Kalin, eds. *Islamophobia: The Challenge of Pluralism in the 21st Century.* New York: Oxford University Press, 2011.

"Ex-G. I. Candidate Finds Election Battle All Too Real." *New York Daily News*, July 28, 2008. Accessed August 5, 2016. http://www.nydailynews.com/entertainment/gossip/ex-g-candidate-finds-election-battle-real-article-1.352549.

Fahmy, Mohamed. "How Qatar Used and Abused Its Al Jazeera Journalists." *New York Times*, June 2, 2015. Accessed August 5, 2016. http://www.nytimes.com/2015/06/03/opinion/mohamed-fahy-how-qatar-used-and-abused-its-al-jazeera-journalists.html?_r=0.

Farhi, Paul. "Al Jazeera Channel Cracks the U.S. Dial." *Washington Post*, April 29, 2009. Accessed August 5, 2016. http://www.washingtonpost.com/wp-dyn/content/article/2009/04/28/AR2009042803918.html.

Feeney, Lauren. "What's Al Jazeera's Problem?" *PBS*, April 29, 2009. Accessed August 5, 2016. http://www.pbs.org/wnet/need-to-know/the-daily-need/whats-al-jazeeras-problem/3924/.

Fernandez, Bob. "Al-Jazeera Seeks TV Distribution Deal with Comcast." *Philadelphia Inquirer*, February 25, 2011. Accessed April 28, 2016. http://articles.philly.com/2011-02-25/business/28629801_1_mouthpiece-for-osama-bin-al-jazeera-officials-al-jazeera-english.

Figenschou, Tine U. *Al Jazeera and the Global Media Landscape: The South Is Talking Back.* New York: Routledge, 2013.

———."Content: The Messages of AJE's News." In *Al Jazeera English: Global News in a Changing World*, edited by Phil Seib, 41–56. New York: Palgrave Macmillan, 2012.

———. "A Voice for the Voiceless? A Quantitative Content Analysis of Al-Jazeera English's Flagship News." *Global Media and Communication* 6, no. 1 (2010): 85–107.

Finn, Tom. "Qatar's Support for the Entire Al Jazeera Operation Is in Question, Diplomats Say." *Reuters*, January 27, 2016. Accessed August 6, 2016. http://www.jpost.com/Middle-East/Al-Jazeera-America-closure-marks-a-quieter-Qatar-442972.

Fisher, Alan, and Libby Casey. "Al Jazeera English Foreign News Bureau-Online Broadcast." Filmed July 2, 2012. C-SPAN Video, 43:17. Posted July 2, 2012. Accessed August 5, 2016. https://www.c-span.org/video/?306872-5/al-jazeera-english-foreign-news-bureau.

Fishman, Mark. *Manufacturing the News.* Austin: University of Texas Press, 1980.

Flew, Terry, and Silvio Waisbord. "The Ongoing Significance of National Media Systems in the Context of Media Globalization." *Media, Culture & Society* 37, no. 4 (2015): 620–636.

Florida, Richard. *Cities and the Creative Class.* New York: Routledge, 2005.

———.*Who's Your City? How the Creative Economy Is Making Where to Live the Most Important Decision of Your Life.* Toronto: Vintage Canada, 2010.

———. Charlotta Mellanderand, and Kevin Stolarick. "Music Scenes to Music Clusters: The Economic Geography of Music in the US, 1970–2000." *Environment and Planning*, 42, no. 4 (2010): 785–804.

Folkenflik, David. "Al-Jazeera English Struggles for U.S. Audience." *NPR*, February 24, 2009. Accessed August 5, 2016. http://www.npr.org/templates/story/story.php?storyId=101071599.

Friedmann, John, and Harold G. Wolff. "World City Formation: An Agenda for Research and Action." *International Journal of Urban and Regional Research* 6, no. 3 (1982): 309–344.

Gagliardone, Iginio. "China as a Persuader: CCTV Africa's First Steps in the African Mediasphere." *Ecquid Novi: African Journalism Studies* 34, no. 3 (2013): 25–40.

Gamerman, Ellen. "Al-Jazeera Grows Boldly, Keeps Head Down in D.C." *Baltimore Sun*, January 14, 2005. Accessed August 5, 2016. http://articles.baltimoresun.com/2005-01-14/news/0501140086_1_arab-network-al-jazeera-international-arab-world.

Garnham, Nicholas. "Concepts of Culture: Public Policy and the Cultural Industries." *Cultural Studies* 1, no. 1 (1987): 23–37.

George, Alexander L., and Andrew Bennett. *Case Studies and Theory Development in the Social Sciences.* Cambridge, MA: MIT Press, 2005.

Giddens, Anthony. *Central Problems in Social Theory: Action, Structure, and Contradiction in Social Analysis.* Berkeley: University of California Press, 1979.

———. *The Constitution of Society: Outline of the Theory of Structuration.* Berkeley: University of California Press, 1984.

Gillespie, Tarleton, Pablo J. Boczkowski, and Kristen A. Foot, eds. *Media Technologies: Essays on Communication, Materiality, and Society*. London: MIT Press, 2014.

Golan, Guy. "Inter-Media Agenda Setting and Global News Coverage: Assessing the Influence of the *New York Times* on Three Network Television Evening News Programs." *Journalism Studies* 7 (2006): 323–334.

Goodman, Amy. "Al Jazeera Chief Wadah Khanfar on Obama's Expansion of the Afghan War, US Policy in the Middle East and the Role of Independent Voices in the Media." *Democracy Now*, March 31, 2010. Accessed August 5, 2016. http://www.democracynow.org/2010/3/31/al_jazeera_chief_wadah_khanfar_on.

———. "Media Blackout in Egypt and the U.S.: Al Jazeera Forced Off the Air by Mubarak, Telecommunications Companies Block Its Expansion in the United States." *Democracy Now*, February 1, 2011. Accessed August 5, 2016. http://www.democracynow.org/2011/2/1/media_blackout_in_egypt_and_the.

———. "'Shouting in the Dark': Film Chronicles Bahrain's Pro-Democracy Uprising Against U.S.-Backed Rule." *Democracy Now*, April 6, 2012. Accessed August 5, 2016. http://www.democracynow.org/2012/4/6/shouting_in_the_dark_film_chronicles.

Goodstein, Louis. "Across Nation, Mosque Projects Meet Opposition." *New York Times*, August 7, 2010. Accessed August 5, 2016. http://www.nytimes.com/2010/08/08/us/08mosque.html.

"GOP Congressional Candidate Accuses Al Jazeera of Trying to Kidnap Him in Florida." *Democracy Now*, July 31, 2008. Accessed August 7, 2016. http://www.democracynow.org/2008/7/31/gop_congressional_candidate_accuses_al_jazeera.

Govil, Nitin. "Thinking Nationally: Domicile, Distinction, and Dysfunction in Global Media Exchange." In *Media Industries: History, Theory, and Method*, edited by Jennifer Holt and Alisa Perren, 132–143. Walden, MA: Wiley-Blackwell, 2009.

Greenberg, Josh, Graham Knight, and Elizabeth Westersund. "Spinning Climate Change: Corporate and NGO Public Relations Strategies in Canada and the United States." *International Communication Gazette* 73, no. 1–2 (2011): 65–82.

Greenberg, Morris. *Branding New York: How a City in Crisis Was Sold to the World*. New York: Routledge, 2008.

Greenwald, Glenn. "Al Jazeera Deletes Its Own Controversial Op-Ed, then Refuses to Comment." *The Guardian* [UK], May 21, 2013. Accessed August 5, 2016. http://www.the-guardian.com/commentisfree/2013/may/21/al-jazeera-joseph-massad-retraction.

Grim, Ryan. "Al Jazeera English Blacked Out Across Most Of U.S." *Huffington Post*, January 30, 2011. Accessed August 5, 2016. http://www.huffingtonpost.com/entry/al-jazeera-english-us_n_816030.

Guthrie, Marisa. "Al Jazeera Unit Renews U.S. TV Push." *Broadcasting & Cable*, October 1, 2007. Accessed August 5, 2016. https://www.highbeam.com/doc/1G1-169306612.html.

Hafez, Kai. "Guest Editor's Introduction: Mediated Political Communication in the Middle East." *Political Communication* 19, no. 2 (2002): 121–124.

———. *The Myth of Media Globalization*. Translated by Alex Skinner. Cambridge: Polity Press, 2007.

Hagey, Keach. "Al Gore Sues Al Jazeera America Over Current TV Sale." *Wall Street Journal*, August 15, 2014. Accessed August 5, 2016. http://www.wsj.com/articles/al-gore-sues-al-jazeera-america-over-current-tv-sale-1408125073.

———. "Al Jazeera US Cable Deal Signals New Era." *The National* [UAE], July 15, 2009. Accessed August 5, 2016. http://www.thenational.ae/business/al-jazeera-us-cable-deal-signals-new-era.

———. "Amjad Atallah to Al Jazeera English." *Politico*, May 1, 2011. Accessed August 5, 2016. http://www.politico.com/blogs/onmedia/0511/Amjad_Atallah_to_Al_Jazeera_English.html.

———. Byron Tau. "Al-Jazeera has Fans in Obama W.H." *Politico*, April 17, 2011. Accessed August 5, 2016. http://www.politico.com/news/stories/0411/53339.html.

———. Eliot Brown. "Al Jazeera in Site Hunt: Broadcaster Looks at Former New York Times, Other Offices for U.S. Operations." *Wall Street Journal*, March 11, 2013. Accessed August 5, 2016. http://www.wsj.com/articles/SB10001424127887324128504578348711622224832.

Hallin, Daniel, and Paolo Mancini. *Comparing Media Systems: Three Models of Media and Politics.* New York: Cambridge University Press, 2004.

Hamilton, James T. "The (Many) Markets for International News: How News from Abroad Sells at Home." *Journalism Studies* 11, no. 5 (2010): 650–666.

Hamilton, John M. *Journalism's Roving Eye: A History of American Foreign Reporting.* Baton Rouge: Lousiana State University Press, 2009.

Hampp, Andrew. "Al-Jazeera English Looks to Build Audience Before Ads." *Advertising Age,* June 13, 2011. Accessed August 5, 2016. http://adage.com/article/global-news/al-jazeera-english-build-audience/228094/.

Hardy, Stephen. "Placiality: The Renewal of the Significance of Place in Modern Cultural Theory." *Brno Studies in English* [Masarykova Univerzita, Brno, Czech Republic], (2000): 86–100.

Harvey, David. *The Condition of Postmodernity.* Vol. 4. Oxford: Blackwell, 1989.

——. *Social Justice and the City.* London: Edward Arnold, 1973.

Harvey, Penny, and Harvey Knox. "Ethnographies of Place." In *Understanding Social Research: Thinking Creatively about Method,* edited by Jennifer Mason and Angela Dale, 107–119. London: Sage, 2013.

Havens, Timothy, and Amanda Lotz. *Understanding Media Industries.* New York: Oxford University Press, 2012.

——, Serra Tinic. "Critical Media Industry Studies: A Research Approach." *Communication, Culture & Critique* 2, no. 2 (2009): 234–253.

Helman, Christopher. "Will Americans Tune to Al Jazeera?" *Forbes Magazine,* June 24, 2009. Accessed August 5, 2016. http://www.forbes.com/forbes/2009/0713/comcast-al-qaeda-will-americans-tune-to-al-jazeera.html.

Henning, Christoph. "Distanciation and Disembedding." In *The Blackwell Encyclopedia of Sociology,* vol. 3, edited by George Ritzer, 1188–1189. Malden, MA: Blackwell Publishing, 2007.

Herman, Edward, and Noam Chomsky. *Manufacturing Consent: The Political Economy of the Mass Media.* New York: Pantheon, 2002.

Herman, Edward S., and Robert W. McChesney. *The Global Media: The New Missionaries of Corporate Capitalism.* London: Cassell, 1997.

Hess, Stephen. *International News and Foreign Correspondents.* Washington, DC: The Brookings Institution, 1996.

Higham, John. *Strangers in the Land: Patterns of American Nativism, 1860–1925.* New Brunswick: Rutgers University Press, 2002.

Holt, Jennifer and Alissa Perren, eds. *Media Industries: History, Theory, and Method.* Malden, MA: John Wiley & Sons, 2011.

Holton, Robert J. *Making Globalization.* New York: Palgrave Macmillan, 2005.

Howarth, William. "Reading the Wetlands." In *Textures of Place: Exploring Humanist Geographies,* edited by Paul C. Adams, Steven Hoelscher, and Karen E. Till, 55–83. Minneapolis: University of Minnesota Press, 2001.

Hudson, John. "Andrea Mitchell: What I Read." *The Wire,* April 19, 2011. Accessed August 8, 2016. http://www.thewire.com/business/2011/04/andrea-mitchel-what-i-read/36797/.

Hunter, Glenn. "The Selling of Al Jazeera America." *Front Burner,* October 8, 2014. Accessed August 5, 2016. http://www.dmagazine.com/frontburner/2014/10/the-selling-of-al-jazeera-america/.

Huntington, Samuel P. *The Clash of Civilizations and the Remaking of World Order.* New York: Simon & Schuster, 1996.

"Intro to Design Thinking." Presentation at the annual convention of the Online News Association. San Francisco, CA, September 20, 2012. Accessed online August 7, 2016. https://ona2012.sched.org/event/18HiCGr/intro-to-design-thinking.

Irwin, Neil. "Landlord Snubs Al-Jazeera." *Washington Post,* June 9, 2003. Accessed August 5, 2016. http://www.washingtonpost.com/archive/business/2003/06/09/landlord-snubs-al-jazeera/7d2f9286-5bdf-404a-b30a-69dc6f6260db/.

Iwabuchi, Koichi. "Contra-Flows or the Cultural Logic of Uneven Globalization? Japanese Media in the Global Agora." In *Media on the Move: Global Flow and Contra-Flow,* edited by Daya K. Thussu, 68–83. London: Routledge, 2007.

Iyengar, Shanto, James Curran, Anker Brink Lund, Inka Salovaara-Moring, Kyu S. Hahn, and Sharon Coen. "Cross-National Versus Individual-Level Differences in Political Information: A Media Systems Perspective." *Journal of Elections, Public Opinion and Parties* 20, no. 3 (2010): 291–309.

——. Kyu S. Hahn, Heinz Bonfadelli, and Mirko Marr. "'Dark Areas of Ignorance' Revisited: Comparing International Affairs Knowledge in Switzerland and the United States." *Communication Research* 36, no. 3 (2009): 341–358. doi: 10.1177/0093650209333024.

Jackman, Robert W., and Ross A. Miller. "A Renaissance of Political Culture." *American Journal of Political Science* 40, no. 3 (1996): 632–659.

Jackson, Jasper. "Facebook to Prioritise Posts from Friends Rather than Brands." *The Guardian* [UK], June 29, 2016. Accessed August 6, 2016. https://www.theguardian.com/technology/2016/jun/29/facebook-to-prioritise-posts-from-people-rather-than-brands.

Jacobs, Jane. *Cities and the Wealth of Nations.* New York: Vintage, 1984.

Jacobson, Robert Dale. *New Nativism: Proposition 187 and the Debate Over Immigration.* Minneapolis: University of Minnesota Press, 2008.

James, Brendan. "Al Jazeera America Will Not Recognize Union: NLRB Elections Underway." *International Business Times,* September 29, 2015. Accessed August 6, 2016. http://www.ibtimes.com/al-jazeera-america-will-not-recognize-union-nlrb-elections-underway-2118695.

Jijon, Isabel. "The Glocalization of Time and Space: Soccer and Meaning in Chota Valley, Ecuador." *International Sociology* 28, no. 4 (2013): 373–390.

——. "The Moral Glocalization of Sport: Local Meanings of Football in Chota Valley, Ecuador." *International Review for the Sociology of Sport* (2015). Accessed August 7, 2016. doi: 1012690215572854.

Jones, Timothy M., Peter Van Aelst, and Rens Vliegenthart. "Foreign Nation Visibility in US News Coverage: A Longitudinal Analysis (1950–2006)." *Communication Research* 40, no. 3 (2011): 417–436.

Joyella, Mark. "Watchup Adds Fusion, The Verge, Vox and AJ+." *TV Newser,* January 6, 2015. Accessed August 5, 2016. http://www.adweek.com/tvnewser/watchup-adds-fusion-the-verge-vox-and-aj/251494.

Jurkowitz, Mark, Amy Mitchell, and Katerina E. Matsa. "How Al Jazeera Tackled the Crisis Over Syria." *Pew Research Center,* September 26, 2013. Accessed August 5, 2016. http://www.journalism.org/2013/09/16/how-al-jazeera-tackled-the-crisis-over-syria.

Kamrava, Mehran. *Qatar: Small State, Big Politics.* Ithaca, NY: Cornell University Press, 2013.

Kant, Immanuel. "Perpetual Peace: A Philosophical Sketch." In *Political Writings,* 2nd ed., edited by H. Reiss, translated by H. Nisbet, 93–130. Cambridge: Cambridge University Press, 1991.

Karlsson, Charlie, and Robert G. Picard. "Media Clusters: What Makes Them Unique?" In *Media Clusters: Spatial Agglomeration and Content Capabilities,* edited by Charlie Karlsson and Robert G. Picard, 1–29. Northampton, MA: Edward Elgar Publishing, 2011.

Keane, Michael. "Once Were Peripheral: Creating Media Capacity in East Asia." *Media, Culture and Society* 28, no. 6 (2006): 835–55.

Khalidi, Rashid. *Resurrecting Empire: Western Footprints and America's Perilous Path in the Middle East.* Boston, MA: Beacon Press, 2004.

Khamis, Sahar. "The Role of New Arab Satellite Channels in Fostering Intercultural Dialogue: Can Al Jazeera English Bridge the Gap?" In *New Media and the New Middle East,* edited by Phil Seib, 39–52. London: Palgrave Macmillan, 2007.

Khanfar, Wadah. "Al Jazeera Banned: The Revolution America's Missing." *The Daily Beast,* February 4, 2011. Accessed August 5, 2016. http://www.thedailybeast.com/articles/2011/02/04/al-jazeera-banned-the-revolution-americas-missing.html.

Kim, Young Mie, and Michael McCluskey. "The DC Factor? Advocacy Groups in the News." *Journalism* 16, no. 6 (2015): 791–811.

Kincaid, Cliff. "How Al-Jazeera Kills Americans." *Accuracy in Media,* Feburary 28, 2011. Accessed August 5, 2016. http://bigjournalism.com/aim/2011/02/28/how-al-jazeera-kills-americans/.

Kirell, Andrew. "Al Jazeera America Beat MSNBC for 2 Hours in the Key 25–54 Ratings Demo." *Mediate*, March 31, 2015. Accessed August 5, 2016. http://www.mediaite.com/tv/al-jazeera-america-beat-msnbc-for-2-hours-in-the-key-25-54-ratings-demo/.

Klinefelter, Quinn. "Al Jazeera TV Gets Toe-hold in Toledo." *Voice of America*, March 31, 2007. Accessed August 5, 2016. http://www.voanews.com/english/news/a-13-2007-03-29-voa53.html.

Kludt, Tom, and Brian Stetler. "Al Jazeera America to Shut Down in April." *CNN Money*, January 13, 2016. Accessed August 5, 2016. http://money.cnn.com/2016/01/13/media/al-jazeera-america/.

Koblin, John. "Al Jazeera America, Its Newsroom in Turmoil, Is Now the News." *New York Times*, May 5, 2015. Accessed August 5, 2016. http://www.nytimes.com/2015/05/06/business/media/al-jazeera-network-in-turmoil-is-now-the-news.html?_r=1.

Kovessy, Peter, and Shabina S. Khatri. "Al Jazeera Launches Digital Channel AJ+ in Bid to Woo Younger Viewers." *Doha News*, September 15, 2014. Accessed August 6, 2016, http://dohanews.co/al-jazeera-launches-digital-channel-aj-bid-woo-younger-viewers/.

Kraidy, Marwan. *Hybridity, or the Cultural Logic of Globalization.* Philadelphia: Temple University Press, 2005.

Krätke, Stefan. *Medienstadt. Urbane Cluster and globale Zentren der Kulturproduktion.* Opladen: Leske & Budrich, 2002.

———. Peter J. Taylor. "A World Geography of Global Media Cities." *European Planning Studies*, 12, no. 4 (2004): 459–477.

Kreiss, Daniel, and Mike Ananny. "Responsibilities of the State: Rethinking the Case and Possibilities for Public Support of Journalism." *First Monday* 18, no. 4 (2013). doi: 10.5210/fm.v18i4.4323.

Krugman, Paul. *Geography and Trade.* Cambridge, MA: MIT Press, 1991.

———. "What's New About the New Economic Geography." *Oxford Review of Economic Policy* 14, no. 2 (1998): 7–17.

La Guerre, Liam. "Al Jazeera Pays Boston Properties $45M For Midtown Lease Termination." *Commercial Observer*, February 4, 2016. Accessed August 5, 2016. https://commercialobserver.com/2016/02/al-jazeera-pays-boston-property-45m-for-midtown-lease-termination/.

Landry, Charles. *The Creative City: A Toolkit for Urban Innovators.* London: Earthscan, 2000.

Larkin, Brian. *Signal and Noise: Media, Infrastructure and Urban Culture in Nigeria.* Durham, NC: Duke University Press, 2008.

Lefebvre, Henri. *The Production of Space.* Translated by Donald Nicholson-Smith. Oxford: Blackwell, 1991.

Lerner, Daniel. *The Passing of Traditional Society: Modernizing the Middle East.* Glencoe, IL: Free Press, 1958.

Leroy and Clarkson. "Homepage." Accessed August 7, 2016. http://www.leroyandclarkson.com/.

———. "Would You Like to Know More? Al Jazeera America Launch Campaign." Accessed August 8, 2016. http://www.leroyandclarkson.com/work/ajam-launch.

Levine, David M. "The Fox News Revolution." *Adweek*, October 3, 2011. Accessed August 5, 2016. http://www.adweek.com/news/television/fox-news-revolution-135385.

Lippmann, Walter. *Public Opinion.* London: Transaction Publishers, 1991.

Lotz, Amanda. *The Television Will Be Revolutionized.* New York: New York University Press, 2007.

Lynch, Marc. *Voices of the New Arab Public: Iraq, Al-Jazeera, and Middle East Politics Today.* New York: Columbia University Press, 2006.

MacMillan, Robert. "Al Jazeera Fights 'Myths' in North American Push." *Reuters*, February 17, 2009. Accessed August 5, 2016. http://www.reuters.com/article/aljazeera-idUSN1738968120090218.

MacNicol, Glynnis. "Even President Obama Is Watching Al Jazeera." *Business Insider*, January 29, 2011. Accessed August 5, 2016. http://www.businessinsider.com/egypt-crisis-obama-al-jazeera-2011-1.

Malone, Scott. "Talking Heads Block Al-Jazeera TV in U.S.-Zucker." *Reuters*, February 7, 2011. Accessed August 6, 2016. http://blogs.reuters.com/mediafile/2011/02/07/talking-heads-block-al-jazeera-tv-in-u-s-zucker/.

Manly, Lorne. "Translation: Is the Whole World Watching?" *New York Times*, March 26, 2006. Accessed August 8, 2016. http://www.nytimes.com/2006/03/26/arts/television/translation-is-the-whole-world-watching.html?_r=0.

Marash, David. "TV News Creates Ignorant Americans." *Milwaukee Journal-Sentinel*, April 13, 2008. Accessed August 5, 2016. http://www.jsonline.com/news/opinion/29558064.html.

———. "Why Can't You Watch Al Jazeera English?" *Television Quarterly* 37, no. 3/4 (2007): 46–50.

Marshall, Alfred. *Principles of Economics*, 8th ed. London: Macmillan, 1920.

Mason, Rowena. "Al Jazeera English Focused on its American Dream." *The Telegraph* [UK], March 23, 2009. Accessed August 5, 2016. http://www.telegraph.co.uk/finance/news-bysector/mediatechnologyandtelecoms/5039921/Al-Jazeera-English-focused-on-its-American-dream.html.

Massey, Doreen. "Politics and and Space/Time." *New Left Review* 196 (1992): 65–84.

———. *Space, Place and Gender*. Minneapolis: University of Minnesota Press, 1994.

———. *World City*. Malden, MA: Polity, 2007.

Massing, Michael. "Digital Journalism: The Next Generation." *New York Review of Books*, June 25, 2015. Accessed August 5, 2016. http://www.nybooks.com/articles/archives/2015/jun/25/digital-journalism-next-generation/.

Matias, Yossi. "More Spring Cleaning." *Google Official Blog*, September 28, 2012. Accessed August 5, 2016. https://googleblog.blogspot.com.es/2012/09/more-spring-cleaning.html.

Mato, Daniel. "Miami in the Transnationalization of the Telenovela Industry: On Territoriality and Globalization." *Journal of Latin American Cultural Studies* 11, no. 2 (2002): 195–212.

Mattelart, Armand. *The Invention of Communication*. Translated by Susan Emanuel. Minneapolis: University of Minnesota Press, 1996.

"Mayor Bloomberg Announces Eight Initiatives to Strengthen the Media Industry in New York City." *NYC Economic Development Corporation* [press release], July 7, 2009. Accessed August 5, 2016. http://www.nycedc.com/press-release/mayor-bloomberg-announces-eight-initiatives-strengthen-media-industry-new-york-city.

Mazzarella, William. *Shoveling Smoke: Advertising and Globalization in Contemporary India*. Durham, NC: Duke University Press, 2003.

McChesney, Robert. *Rich Media, Poor Democracy: Communication Politics in Dubious Times*. Urbana: University of Illinois Press, 1999.

McDonald, Frank, Qihai Huang, Dimitrios Tsagdis, and Heinz Josef Tüselmann. "Is There Evidence to Support Porter-Type Cluster Policies?" *Regional Studies* 41, no. 1 (2007): 39–49.

"Media. NYC. 2020. Final Report." *NYC Economic Development Corporation*, 2009. Accessed August 6, 2016. http://www.nycedc.com/sites/default/files/filemanager/Industries/Media_EmergTech/MediaNYC2020_Report.pdf.

Miladi, Noureddine. "Satellite TV News and the Arab Diaspora in Britain: Comparing Al-Jazeera, the BBC and CNN." *Journal of Ethnic and Migration Studies* 32, no. 6 (2006): 947–960.

Miles, Hugh. *Al Jazeera: How Arab TV News Challenges America*. New York: Grove Press, 2005.

Mitchell, Timothy. *Rule of Experts: Egypt, Techno-Politics, Modernity*. Berkeley: University of California Press, 2002.

Mitchell, William J. *City of Bits: Space, Place and the Infobahn*. Cambridge, MA: MIT Press, 1995.

———. *Ethnographies of Place*. Cambridge, MA: MIT Press, 1995.

Moores, Shaun. *Media, Place and Mobility*. New York: Palgrave Macmillan, 2012.

Moran, Theodore H. "Foreign Direct Investment." In *The Wiley-Blackwell Encyclopedia of Globalization*, edited by George Ritzer. Oxford: Wiley-Blackwell, 2012. Accessed August 5, 2016. http://onlinelibrary.wiley.com/doi/10.1002/9780470670590.wbeog216/full.

Morley, David. "Communications and Transport: The Mobility of Information, People and Commodities." *Media, Culture & Society* 33, no. 5 (2011): 743–759.

———. "For a Materialist, Non-media-centric Media Studies." *Television & New Media* 10, no. 1 (2009): 114–116.

Morris, Jan. *The Great Port: A Passage Through New York*. New York: Oxford University Press, 1969.

Mosco, Vincent. *The Political Economy of Communication*. London: Sage, 1996.

Nasr, Assem. "Al-Jazeera and the Arab Uprisings: The Language of Images and a Medium's Stancetaking." *Communication, Culture & Critique* 7, no. 4 (2014): 397–414.

Neff, Gina. "The Changing Place of Cultural Production: The Location of Social Networks in a Digital Media Industry." *Annals of the American Academy of Political and Social Science* 597, no. 1 (2005): 134–152.

Negroponte, Nicholas. *Being Digital*. New York: Vintage, 1996.

Neuman, W. Russell. *The Future of the Mass Audience*. Cambridge: Cambridge University Press, 1991.

Noam, Eli M. *Media Ownership and Concentration in America*. Oxford: Oxford University Press, 2009.

Noonan, Caitriona. "The BBC and Decentralisation: The Pilgrimage to Manchester." *International Journal of Cultural Policy* 18, no. 4 (2012): 363–377.

Nordenstreng, Kaarle. "Three Theses on the Imbalance Debate." In *Politics of News: Third World Perspective*, edited by Jaswant S. Yadava, 24–39. New Delhi: Concept Publishing Company, 1984.

Norris, Pippa, and Ronald Inglehart. *Cosmopolitan Communications: Cultural Diversity in a Globalized World*. Cambridge: Cambridge University Press, 2009.

Nye Jr., Joseph S. "Soft Power." *Foreign Policy* 80 (1990): 153–171.

Otterman, Sharon. "Students Take Time to Reflect on Bin Laden." *New York Times*. City Room Blog, May 3, 2011. Accessed August 6, 2016. http://cityroom.blogs.nytimes.com/2011/05/03/students-take-time-to-reflect-on-bin-laden/.

Parker. "Francophone Africa Is the New Land of Opportunity for the French Media Industry." Translated by Lova Rakotomalala. *Global Voices*, June 15, 2015. Accessed August 5, 2016. https://globalvoices.org/2015/06/12/francophone-africa-is-the-new-land-of-opportunity-for-the-french-media-industry/.

Parks, Carla. "BBC World News Channel in 30m American Homes." *Ariel* [BBC internal news website], April 14, 2014. Accessed August 5, 2016. http://www.bbc.co.uk/ariel/27487105.

Pattison, Pete. "Revealed: Qatar's World Cup 'Slaves'." *The Guardian* [UK], September 25, 2013. Accessed August 5, 2016. http://www.theguardian.com/world/2013/sep/25/revealed-qatars-world-cup-slaves.

Pedelty, Mark. *War Stories: The Culture of Foreign Correspondents*. London: Routledge, 1995.

Perlberg, Steven. "Al Jazeera America Has Its First Major Shake-Up." *Wall Street Journal* [blog], April 14, 2014. Accessed August 5, 2016. http://blogs.wsj.com/cmo/2014/04/14/al-jazeera-america-layoffs/.

Pintak, Lawrence. "Interview with Nigel Parsons, Managing Director of Al Jazeera International." *Transnational Broadcasting Studies* 15 (2005): 262–267.

Poggi, Jeanine. "Al Jazeera America One Year Later: Is Gaza the Turning Point?" *Advertising Age*, August 8, 2014. Accessed August 5, 2016. http://adage.com/article/media/al-jazeera-america-year-gaza-a-turning-point/294495/.

Pompeo, Joe. "Al Jazeera America: A Unicorn Is Born." *New York Magazine*, July 11, 2013a. Accessed August 5, 2016. http://nymag.com/daily/intelligencer/2013/07/al-jazeera-america-a-unicorn-is-born.html.

———. "The Last Time Al Jazeera Had a Big American Strategy, It Was Rejected." *Politico*, July 15, 2013b. Accessed August 5, 2016. http://www.capitalnewyork.com/article/media/2013/07/8531884/last-time-al-jazeera-had-big-american-strategy-it-was-rejected.

———. Hadas Gold, and Peter Sterne. "Al Jazeera America Shutting Down." *Politico*, January 13, 2016. Accessed August 5, 2016. http://www.capitalnewyork.com/article/media/2016/01/8587929/al-jazeera-america-shutting-down.

Porter, Michael E. "Location, Competition, and Economic Development: Local Clusters in a Global Economy." *Economic Development Quarterly* 14, no. 1 (2000): 15–34.

Portes, Alejandro. "On the Sociology of National Development: Theories and Issues." *American Journal of Sociology* 82, no. 1 (1976): 55–85.

Powell, Walter W., Kenneth W. Koput, James I. Bowie, and Laurel Smith-Doerr. "The Spatial Clustering of Science and Capital: Accounting for Biotech Firm-Venture Capital Relationships." *Regional Studies* 36, no. 3 (2002): 291–305.

Powers, Shawn. "The Geopolitics of News: The Case of the Al Jazeera Network." PhD diss., University of Southern California, Los Angeles, 2009.

———. "The Origins of Al Jazeera English." In *Al Jazeera English: Global News in a Changing World*, edited by Phil Seib, 5–28. New York: Palgrave Macmillan, 2012.

———. Mohamed El-Nawawy. "Al-Jazeera English and Global News Networks: Clash of Civilizations or Cross-Cultural Dialogue?" *Media, War & Conflict* 2, no. 3 (2009): 263–284.

Pratt, Andy C. "Hot Jobs in Cool Places. The Material Cultures of New Media Product Spaces: The Case of South of the Market, San Francisco." *Information, Communication & Society* 5, no. 1 (2002): 27–50.

———. "Microclustering of the Media Industries in London." In *Media Clusters: Spatial Agglomeration and Content Capabilities*, edited by Charlie Karlsson and Robert G. Picard, 120–135. Northampton, MA: Edward Elgar Publishing, 2011.

Price, John. "A Tale of Two Cultures: A Comparison of EU News Reporting by Brussels-Based and National-Based Journalists." In *Public Communication in the European Union: History, Perspectives and Challenges*, edited by Chiara Valentini and Giorgia Nesti, 217–236. Newcastle, UK: Cambridge Scholars Publishing, 2010.

Proshansky, Harold M., Abbe K. Fabian, and Robert Kaminoff. "Place-Identity: Physical World Socialization of the Self." *Journal of Environmental Psychology* 3, no. 1 (1983): 57–83.

———. William H. Ittelson, and Leanne G. Rivlin. "The Influence of the Physical Environment on Behavior: Some Basic Assumptions." In *Environmental Psychology: Man and His Physical Setting*, edited by Harold M. Proshansky, William. H. Ittelson, and Leanne G. Rivlin, 27–37. New York: Holt, Rinehart & Winston, 1969.

Punathambekar, Aswin. *From Bombay to Bollywood: The Making of a Global Media Industry.* New York: New York University Press.

"Qatar Court Upholds Poet's Jail Sentence." *Al Jazeera English*, October 21, 2013. Accessed August 6, 2016. http://www.aljazeera.com/news/middleeast/2013/10/qatar-court-upholds-sentence-against-poet-20131021123723850815.html.

"Qatari Poet Final Verdict Expected in February." *Al Jazeera English*, January 27, 2013. Accessed August 6, 2016. https://www.youtube.com/watch?v=ME15QDcGw94.

"Qatari Poet's Life Sentence Cut to 15 Years." *Al Jazeera English*, February 24, 2013. Accessed August 6, 2016. https://www.youtube.com/watch?v=_Zr1dkd5mks.

Quenqua, Douglas. "Al Jazeera Steps Up Efforts to Establish Presence in US." *PR Week*, January 13, 2003. Accessed August 15, 2016. http://www.prweek.com/article/168049/al-jazeera-steps-efforts-establish-presence-us.

Raboy, Marc. "Media Pluralism and the Promotion of Cultural Diversity." *A Background Paper for UNESCO*, December 10, 2007. Accessed August 6, 2016. http://media.mcgill.ca/files/unesco_diversity.pdf.

Radia, Kirit. "Sec. of State Hillary Clinton: Al Jazeera is 'Real News', U.S. Losing 'Information War'." *ABC News*, March 2, 2011. Accessed March 3, 2016. http://blogs.abcnews.com/politicalpunch/2011/03/sec-of-state-hillary-clinton-al-jazeera-is-real-news-us-losing-information.html.

Rahimi, Shadi. "How AJ+ Reported from Baltimore Using Only Mobile Phones." *Poynter*, May 1, 2015. Accessed August 6, 2016. http://www.poynter.org/news/mediawire/341117/how-aj-reported-from-baltimore-using-only-mobile-phones/.

Rantanen, Terhi. "The New Sense of Place in 19th-Century News." *Media, Culture & Society* 25, no. 4 (2003): 435–449.

Rao, Shakuntala. "Glocalization of Indian Journalism." *Journalism Studies* 10, no. 4 (2009): 474–88.

"RE: [Fwd: Re: [Fwd: Interview Request—Al Jazeera]]" *Wikileaks: The Global Intelligence Files*, December 3, 2009. Accessed August 5, 2016. https://wikileaks.org/gifiles/docs/28/280821_re-fwd-re-fwd-interview-request-al-jazeera-.html.

Reich, Zvia. "The Impact of Technology on News Reporting: A Longitudinal Perspective." *Journalism & Mass Communication Quarterly* 90, no. 3 (2013): 417–434.

Reid, Alastair. "Beyond Websites: How AJ+ is Innovating in Digital Storytelling." *Journalism. co.uk*, April 17, 2014. Accessed August 6, 2016. https://www.journalism.co.uk/news/ beyond-websites-how-aj-is-innovating-in-digital-storytelling/s2/a564811/.

Rheingold, Howard. *The Virtual Community: Homesteading on the Electronic Frontier.* Cambridge, MA: Addison Wesley, 1993.

Rieder, Rem. "Can Al Jazeera America Flourish?" *USA Today*, January 27, 2014. Accessed August 6, 2016. www.usatoday.com/story/money/columnist/rieder/2014/01/27/can-al-jazeera-america-flourish/4938253/.

Riegert, Kristina. "Pondering the Future for Foreign News on National Television." *International Journal of Communication* 5 (2004): 1567–1585.

Rinnawi, Khalil. *Instant Nationalism: McArabism, Al-Jazeera, and Transnational Media in the Arab World.* Lanham, MD: University Press of America, 2006.

Robertson, Roland. "Globalization: Time-Space and Homogeneity-Heterogeneity." In *Global Modernities*, edited by Mike Featherstone, Scott Lash, and Roland Robertson, 25–44. London: Sage, 1995.

———. "Situating Globalization: A Relatively Autobiographical Intervention." In *Global Themes and Local Variations in Organization and Management: Perspectives on Globalization*, edited by Gili S. Drori, Markus A. Höllerer, and Peter Walgenbach, 25–36. New York: Routledge, 2014.

Robinson, James. "New Boss Is Determined to Keep the Faith at Al-Jazeera." *The Guardian* [UK], June 7, 2008. Accessed August 5, 2016. http://www.theguardian.com/media/2008/ jun/08/television.mediabusiness.

Roettgers, Janko. "Al Jazeera's AJ+ Gets Its Own Apple TV App." *Variety*, January 19, 2016. Accessed August 5, 2016. http://variety.com/2016/digital/news/ajplus-apple-tv-app-1201682896/.

———. "Close to Half of All U.S. Households Subscribe to Netflix, Amazon Prime or Hulu Plus." *GigaOm*, June 6, 2014. Accessed August 5, 2016. https://gigaom.com/2014/06/06/close-to-half-of-all-u-s-households-subscribe-to-netflix-amazon-prime-or-hulu-plus/.

Rosenau, James N. *Distant Proximities: Dynamics beyond Globalization.* Princeton, NJ: Princeton University Press, 2003.

Rosenberg, Emily S. *Transnational Currents in a Shrinking World.* Cambridge, MA: Harvard University Press, 2014.

Roudometof, Victor. "The Glocal and Global Studies." *Globalizations* 12, no. 5 (2015): 774–787.

"Rumsfeld in Heated Conversation with Al Jazeera." *Al Jazeera English*, October 4, 2011. Accessed August 5, 2016. https://www.youtube.com/watch?v=tiTaAhOW5Is.

Sabbagh, Dan. "Al-Jazeera's Political Independence Questioned Amid Qatar Intervention." *The Guardian* [UK], September 30, 2012. Accessed August 5, 2016. http://www.theguardian. com/media/2012/sep/30/al-jazeera-independence-questioned-qatar.

Said, Edward. *Orientalism.* New York: Vintage, 1979.

Sakr, N. "Challenger or Lackey? The Politics of News on Al-Jazeera." In *Media on the Move: Global Flow and Contra-Flow*, edited by Daya K. Thussu, 117–132. London: Routledge, 2007.

Samuel-Azran, T. "Al-Jazeera, Qatar, and New Tactics in State-Sponsored Media Diplomacy." *American Behavioral Scientist* 57, no. 9 (2013): 1293–1311.

———. *Al-Jazeera and US War Coverage.* New York: Peter Lang, 2010.

Sanger, David E. "Under Pressure, Dubai Company Drops Port Deal." *New York Times*, March 10, 2006. Accessed August 5, 2016. http://www.nytimes.com/2006/03/10/politics/10ports. html?pagewanted=all&_r=0.

Sassen, Saskia. "Global City: Introducing a Concept." *Brown Journal of World Affairs* 11, no. 2 (2005): 27.

———. *The Global City: New York, London, Tokyo.* Princeton, NJ: Princeton University Press, 2001.

"Scenesetter for Senator Kerry's Visit to Qatar." *Wikileaks*, February 8, 2010. Accessed August 5, 2016. https://wikileaks.org/plusd/cables/10DOHA52_a.html.

"ScheduALL." *Al Jazeera English Channel: A Case Study*, 2008. Accessed August 5, 2016. http://www.scheduall.com/casestudy/aljazeera.html.

Schiller, Herbert I. *Communication and Cultural Domination*. New York: International Arts and Sciences Press, 1976.

———. *Mass Communications and American Empire*, 2nd ed. Boulder: Westview Press, 1992.

———. *Mass Communication and American Empire*. Boston: Beacon, 1969.

———. "Not Yet the Post-Imperialist Era." *Critical Studies in Mass Communication* 8 (1991): 13–28.

Schudson, Michael. "The News Media as Political Institutions." *Annual Review of Political Science* 5, no. 1 (2002): 249–269.

———. "The Objectivity Norm in American Journalism." *Journalism* 2, no. 2 (2001): 149–170.

Scott, Allen J. *The Cultural Economy of Cities: Essays on the Geography of Image-Producing Industries*. London: Sage, 2000.

Seamon, David. *A Geography of the Lifeworld: Movement, Rest and Encounter*. New York: St. Martin's Press, 1979.

Seib, Philip. *The Al-Jazeera Effect*. Washington, DC: Potomac Books, 2008.

———. "Hegemonic No More: Western Media, the Rise of Al-Jazeera, and the Influence of Diverse Voices." *International Studies Review* 7, no. 4 (2005): 601–615.

———. ed. *Al Jazeera English: Global News in a Changing World*. New York: Palgrave Macmillan, 2012.

Shafer, Jack. "What's More Rare, a Unicorn or an Al Jazeera America Viewer?" *Reuters*, July 9, 2014. Accessed August 5, 2016. http://blogs.reuters.com/jackshafer/2014/07/09/whats-more-rare-a-unicorn-or-an-al-jazeera-america-viewer/.

Sherman, Alex, and Christopher Palmeri. "Current TV Said to Fetch $500 Million from Al Jazeera." *Bloomberg*, January 4, 2013. Accessed August 5, 2016. http://www.bloomberg.com/news/articles/2013-01-03/al-jazeera-news-network-acquires-current-tv-to-expand-in-u-s-.

Shoemaker, Pamela J. and Stephen Reese. *Mediating the Message: Theories of Influences on Mass Media Content*, 2nd ed. New York: Longman, 1996.

Shrikhande, Seema. "Competitive Strategies in the Internationalization of Television: CNNI and BBC World in Asia." *Journal of Media Economics* 14, no. 3 (2001): 147–168.

Shryock, Andrew. "Introduction: Islam as an Object of Fear and Affection." In *Islamophobia/Islamophilia: Beyond the Politics of Enemy and Friend*, edited by Andrew Shryock, 1–28. Bloomington: Indiana University Press, 2010.

Sinclair, John. "The Hollywood of Latin America: Miami as Regional Center in Television Trade." *Television & New Media* 4, no. 3 (2003): 211–229.

Spangler, Todd. "Cord-Cutting Alert: Pay-TV Business Declines for First Time During Q1." *Variety*, May 11, 2015. Accessed August 5, 2016. http://variety.com/2015/biz/news/cord-cutting-alert-pay-tv-business-declines-for-first-time-in-q1-1201492308/.

Sparks, Colin. "China's Media in Comparative Perspective." *International Journal of Communication* 4 (2010): 552–66.

Sparrow, Bartholomew. "Tocqueville and Political Communication in America." In *Politics, Discourse, and American Society: New Agendas*, edited by Roderick P. Hart and Bartholomew Sparrow, 1–18. Lanham, MD: Rowman & Littlefield, 2001.

Sreberny, Annabelle. "The Global and the Local in International Communications." In *Media and Cultural Studies: Keywords 2006*, rev. ed., edited by Meenakshi G. Durham and Douglas M. Kellner, 604–625. Malden, MA: Blackwell, 2006.

Steinberg, Brian. "Al Jazeera America's New Chief Hopes to Change Network's Image." *Variety*, November 2, 2015. Accessed August 6, 2016. http://variety.com/2015/tv/news/al-jazeera-america-al-anstey-1201631317/.

Stephens, John. "Sierra Madre Residents Gather to Celebrate and Discuss the Death of Osama Bin Laden." *Sierra Madre Patch*, May 2, 2011. Accessed August 6, 2016. http://patch.com/california/sierramadre/sierra-madre-residents-react-to-death-of-osama-bin-laden.

Stetler, Brian. "In Qatar, Hillary Clinton Meets with Al Jazeera Staff." *New York Times*, February 16, 2010.

Storper, Michael. "Globalization, Localization and Trade." In *The Oxford Handbook of Economic Geography*, edited by Gordon L. Clark, Meric S. Gertler, and Maryann P. Feldman, 146–165. Oxford: Oxford University Press, 2000.

———. Anthony Venables. "Buzz: Face-to-Face Contact and the Urban Economy." *Journal of Economic Geography* 4, no. 4 (2004): 351–370.

Straubhaar, Joseph. *World Television: From Global to Local.* Los Angeles: Sage, 2007.

Stroud, Shawn. "The Rise of Al Jazeera: The Need for Greater Engagement by the U.S. Department of Defense." *Military Review* (July–August 2014): 63–70.

Talley, Wayne K. *Port Economics.* New York: Routledge, 2009.

Taylor, Peter J. *World City Network: A Global Urban Analysis.* London: Routledge, 2004.

———. P. Ni, Ben Derudder, M. Hoyler, J. Huang, and Frank Witlox. *Global Urban Analysis: A Survey of Cities in Globalization.* London: Routledge, 2012.

Tehranian, Majid. "Peace Journalism in West Asia." *Global Media Journal: Mediterranean Edition* 1, no. 1 (2005): 71–73.

Telhami, Shibley. *The World Through Arab Eyes.* New York: Basic Books, 2013.

Tereshchuk, David. "Al Jazeera: Management Style Echoes Country-of-Origin." *Huffington Post,* May 21, 2015. Accessed August 5, 2016. http://www.huffingtonpost.com/david-tereshchuk/al-jazeera-management-sty_b_7377190.html.

Terzis, Georgios. "The EU Correspondent." *Journalism* 9, no. 4 (2008): 537–550.

Tewksbury, David. "What Do Americans Really Want to Know? Tracking the Behavior of News Readers on the Internet." *Journal of Communication* 53, no. 4 (2003): 694–710.

"The Flow of News." Zurich: The International Press Institute, 1953.

"The Humble Hero." *The Economist,* May 18, 2013. Accessed August 5, 2016. http://www.economist.com/news/finance-and-economics/21578041-containers-have-been-more-important-globalisation-freer-trade-humble?fsrc=nlw|hig|5-16-2013|5722602|34886579|.

"The 'War on Terror' 10 Years On." *Frost Over the World.* Al Jazeera English, October 1, 2011. Accessed August 6, 2016. https://www.youtube.com/watch?v=4S3pBzaK4d4.

Thussu, Daya K. "Introduction." In *Media on the Move: Global Flow and Contra-Flow,* edited by Daya K. Thussu, 1–8. London: Routledge, 2007a.

———. "Mapping Media Flow and Contra-Flow." In *Media on the Move: Global Flow and Contra-Flow,* edited by Daya K. Thussu, 10–29. London: Routledge, 2007b.

Tong, Jingrong. "The Importance of Place: An Analysis of Changes in Investigative Journalism in Two Chinese Provincial Newspapers." *Journalism Practice* 7, no. 1 (2013): 1–16.

Toonkel, Jessica. "Al Jazeera to Launch English Language Digital Streaming Service in U.S." *Reuters,* July 21, 2016. Accessed August 5, 2016. http://ca.reuters.com/article/technologyNews/idCAKCN1012PF.

Trollbäck + Company. "Al Jazeera America: Light + Voice." Accessed August 6, 2016. http://trollback.com/al-jazeera-america/.

Tryhorn, Chris. "Staff Shakeup at Al-Jazeera English." *The Guardian* [UK], November 20, 2009. Accessed August 5, 2016. http://www.guardian.co.uk/media/2009/nov/20/staff-shakeup-al-jazeera-english.

Tsing, Anna L. *Friction: An Ethnography of Global Connection.* Princeton, NJ: Princeton University Press, 2011.

Tuan, Yi-Fu. "Geography, Phenomenology, and the Study of Human Nature." *Canadian Geographer* 15, no. 3 (1971): 181–192.

———. *Topophilia: A Study of Environmental Perceptions, Attitudes, and Values.* Englewood Cliffs, NJ: Prentice-Hall, Inc., 1974.

"Tubular Labs Ranks the Top Video Brands and Influencers in December 2015." *Business Wire* [press release], January 19, 2016. Accessed August 6, 2016. http://www.businesswire.com/news/home/20160119005795/en/Tubular-Labs-Ranks-Top-Video-Brands-Influencers.

Tunstall, Jeremy. *The Media Were American: U.S. Mass Media in Decline.* New York: Oxford University Press, 2008.

———. "Part IV: International-Regional-National: The National Media System as the Lead Player." *Global Media and Communication* 3, no. 3 (2007): 321–324.

Turner, Fred. *From Counterculture to Cyberculture: Stewart Brand, the Whole Earth Network, and the Rise of Digital Utopianism.* Chicago: University of Chicago Press, 2006.

———. *The Frontier in American History.* Mineola, MN: Dover Publications, Inc., [1893] 2010.

Ure, Andrew. *The Philosophy of Manufactures; or, An Exposition of the Scientific, Moral, and Commercial Economy of the Factory System of Great Britain.* London: C. Knight, 1835.

Volkmer, Ingrid. "Deconstructing the 'Methodological Paradox': Comparative Research Between National Centrality and Networked Spaces." In *The Handbook of Global Media Research*, edited by Ingrid Volkmer, 110–122. Malden, MA: Wiley-Blackwell, 2012.

Waisbord, Silvio. "McTV: Understanding the Global Popularity of Television Formats." *Television & New Media* 5, no. 4 (2004): 359–383.

———. *Reinventing Professionalism: Journalism and News in Global Perspective.* Cambridge: Polity Press, 2013.

Wallace, Aurora. *Media Capital: Architecture and Communications in New York City.* Urbana: University of Illinois Press, 2012.

Wallerstein, Immanuel. *The Modern World System: Capitalist Agriculture and the Origins of the European World Economy in the Sixteenth Century.* New York: Academic Press, 1974.

Warren, James. "Al Jazeera America Digital Workers Vote to Go Union." *Poynter*, October 6, 2015. Accessed August 6, 2016. http://www.poynter.org/2015/al-jazeera-america-digital-workers-vote-to-go-union/377175/.

Wemple, Erik. "Former Al Jazeera Employee Sues Network, Alleging Anti-Semitism, Anti-Americanism." *The Washington Post*, April 28, 2015. Accessed August 6, 2016. https://www.washingtonpost.com/blogs/erik-wemple/wp/2015/04/28/former-al-jazeera-employee-sues-network-alleging-anti-semitism-anti-americanism/.

Wengraf, Tom. *Qualitative Research Interviewing: Biographic Narrative and Semi-Structured Methods.* Thousand Oaks, CA: Sage, 2001.

Wessler, Hartmut, and Manuel Adolphsen. "Contra-Flow from the Arab World? How Arab Television Coverage of the 2003 Iraq War Was Used and Framed on Western International News Channels." *Media Culture Society* 30 no. 4 (2008): 439–461.

"What Is White Privilege? Here's What People on the Street Have To Say." *AJ+*, December 12, 2014. Accessed August 8, 2016. https://www.youtube.com/watch?v=aQK8H0z-irM.

Wheelock, Bob, and Libby Casey. "Al Jazeera's U.S.-Based News Channel." Filmed February 8, 2013. C-SPAN Video, 43:17. Posted February 8, 2013. Accessed August 6, 2016. http://www.c-span.org/video/?310901-4/al-jazeeras-usbased-news-channel.

"Where News Audiences Fit on the Political Spectrum." *Pew Research Center*, October 21, 2014. Accessed August 6, 2016. http://www.journalism.org/interactives/media-polarization/table/overall/.

Whitaker, Brian. "Al-Jazeera Causes Outcry with Broadcast of Battle Casualties." *The Guardian* [UK], March 25, 2003. Accessed August 6, 2016. http://www.guardian.co.uk/media/2003/mar/24/broadcasting.Iraqandthemedia.

Whyte, William. *City: Rediscovering the Center.* New York: Doubleday, 1988.

Wilkerson, David B. "Al Jazeera English Makes Case to Comcast." *MarketWatch*, March 1, 2011. Accessed March 8, 2016. http://www.marketwatch.com/story/al-jazeera-english-makes-its-case-to-comcast-2011-03-01.

Williams, Raymond. *The Long Revolution.* Orchard Park, NY: Broadview Press, 2001.

Winkler, Joe. "Al-Jazeera Publishes, Pulls, then Reposts Joseph Massad Piece." *Jewish Telegraph Agency*, May 22, 2013. Accessed August 6, 2016. http://www.jta.org/2013/05/22/arts-entertainment/al-jazeera-publishes-pulls-then-reposts-joseph-massad-piece.

Winseck, Dwayne. "The State of Media Ownership and Media Markets: Competition or Concentration and Why Should We Care?" *Sociology Compass* 2, no. 1 (2008): 34–47.

Winsor, Ben. "Al Jazeera America Has an Ambitious Plan for Its Future in the US." *Business Insider*, September 18, 2014. Accessed August 6, 2016. http://www.businessinsider.com/al-jazeera-americas-plan-towards-profit-2014-9.

Wolff, Michael. "Who Will Buy Al Gore's Current TV?" *USA Today*, November 12, 2012. Accessed August 6, 2016. http://www.usatoday.com/story/money/business/2012/11/04/michael-wolff-currenttv/1677303/.

Worth, Robert F. "Al Jazeera No Longer Nips at Saudis." *New York Times*, January 4, 2008. Accessed August 6, 2016. http://www.nytimes.com/2008/01/04/world/middleeast/04jazeera.html?pagewanted=all.

———. David D. Kirkpatrick. "Seizing a Moment, Al Jazeera Galvanizes Arab Frustration." *New York Times*, January 27, 2011. Accessed August 8, 2016. http://www.nytimes.com/2011/01/28/world/middleeast/28jazeera.html.

Wu, Haoming Denis. "Investigating the Determinants of International News Flow: A Meta-Analysis." *International Communication Gazette* 60 (1998): 493–512.

———. "Systematic Determinants of International News Coverage: A Comparison of 38 Countries." *Journal of Communication* 50, no. 2 (2000): 112–130.

Youmans, William L. "Al Jazeera English After the Arab Spring: The Changing Politics of Distribution in the United States." In *Al Jazeera English: Global News in a Changing World*, edited by Phil Seib, 57–78. New York: Palgrave Macmillan, 2012a.

———. "The Debate Over Al Jazeera, English in Burlington, VT." *Arab Media & Society* 13, May 21, 2011. Accessed August 6, 2016. http://www.arabmediasociety.com/articles/downloads/20110601113558_Youmans_Burlington_VT.pdf.

———. "The Media Economics and Cultural Politics of Al Jazeera English in the United States." PhD diss., University of Michigan, 2012b.

Zaheer, Srilata. "Overcoming the Liability of Foreignness." *Academy of Management Journal* 38, no. 2 (1995): 341–363.

Zak, Dan. "K Street: The Route of All Evil, or Just the Main Drag?" *Washington Post*, Feburary 5, 2012. Accessed August 6, 2016. http://www.washingtonpost.com/lifestyle/style/k-street-the-route-of-all-evil-or-just-the-main-drag/2012/01/26/gIQAAnKdsQ_story.html.

Zaller, John. *The Nature and Origins of Mass Opinion*. Cambridge: Cambridge University Press, 1992.

Zayani, Mohamed. "Arab Media, Corporate Communications, and Public Relations: The Case of Al Jazeera." *Asian Journal of Communication* 18, no. 3 (2008): 207–222.

———. "Introduction." In *The Al Jazeera Phenomenon: Critical Perspectives on New Arab Media*, edited by Mohamed Zayani, 1–46. London: Pluto Press, 2005.

———. Sofiane Sahraoui. *The Culture of Al Jazeera: Inside an Arab Media Giant*. Jefferson, NC: McFarland, 2007.

Zelizer, Barbie. "Journalists as Interpretive Communities." *Critical Studies in Media Communication* 10, no. 3 (1993): 219–237.

Zettl, Herbert. *Television Production Handbook*. Stamford, CT: Cengage Learning, 2011.

Zurawik, David. "What Al Jazeera America's Death Means to TV News." *Baltimore Sun*, January 15, 2016. Accessed August 6, 2016. http://www.baltimoresun.com/entertainment/tv/z-on-tv-blog/bs-ae-zontv-al-jazeera-20160115-story.html.

Index

Huntington, Samuel, 28, 45
Hyatt, Joel, 114, 119, 128, 136
Hybridity, 9, 18, 34, 65, 151–153, 156, 171, 175, 179

India, 2, 52, 54, 112, 177, 178
India TV, 178
Indonesia, 2
industrial clustering, 12–15, 23, 29, 30, 48–51,
    53–55, 66, 74, 157, 172, 175, 176
Information sovereignty, 24
Innovation and Incubation Group, 142, 147
Inside Story, 110, 122
Instagram, 44
International Crisis Group, 85
Intersubjectivity, 63
Interview booking, 85
iOs, 145
Iraq, 1, 26, 31, 35, 63, 86, 91, 98, 99, 132, 166
Ireland, 40
Islam, 17, 27, 28, 30–33, 36, 42, 78, 137, 146,
    154, 182
Islamophobia, 6, 32, 33, 146
Israel, 26, 33, 83, 129–131, 182
iterative proportional fitting modeling (IPF), 187
Ivory Coast, 178
Ixonos, 158
Iyengar, Shanto, 32

Jacobs, Jane, 12

K Street, 69, 70
Khan, Riz, 72, 82, 109
Khan, Suhail, 86
Khanfar, Wadah, 6, 41, 42, 76, 78, 89, 99, 100,
    141, 182
Kincaid, Cliff, 33
Kraidy, Marwan, 9n
Krätke, Stefan, 12, 14, 53, 176
Krugman, Paul, 49n

Latin America, 3, 108, 110, 141, 176
Lawrence, Colin, 40
Lawrie, Phil, 40
Lawson & Associates, 71
Lebaron, Joseph, 36, 42n
Lefebvre, Henri, 11
Leroy & Clarkson, 127
Let Haiti Live, 84
Lewis, Avi, 85
Libya, 26, 95–97
Life (magazine), 117
Linkedin, 122, 186
localization, 8, 14, 15, 19, 46, 49, 108, 137, 171,
    173, 175

location theory, 149
locationality, 46, 59, 150, 166, 176
London, 50, 61, 65, 72, 73, 76, 80, 109, 117, 122,
    161
Look (magazine), 117
Los Angeles, CA, 41, 50, 53, 82, 107, 110
Lotz, Amanda, 44
Luke, Matthew, 129–131
Lynch, Marc, 18

Maddow, Rachel, 92
Mahmud, Osman, 129–130
*Make Space: How to Set the Stage for Creative
    Collaboration*, 157
Mancini, Paolo, 30, 35, 81
Mandela, Nelson, 140
Manhattan, 19, 27, 113, 114, 127, 162
Marash, Dave, 21, 33, 72, 74, 75
Maryland, 79, 83
Massachusetts, 103
Massad, Joseph, 121
Massey, Doreen, 56–58
Master Control Room (MCR), 74
Material culture, 15, 16, 71, 98
McCain, John, 87, 96, 97, 101
McChrystal, Stanley, 82n, 87
McDonalds, 112
McGinnis, Marcy, 122, 134, 135
media capitals, 7, 9, 13, 15, 18, 19, 23, 46, 48–55,
    55, 57, 58, 65, 67, 88, 111, 116, 117, 127,
    159, 167, 169, 171, 173, 175–179
media imperialism, 10, 23, 24, 171
media industries/industry, 7, 9, 12–15, 19, 41, 48,
    49, 50–52, 95, 117, 123, 126, 127, 153, 162,
    168, 171, 173, 175, 178, 182, 186
Media Matters, 85
media nationalism, 22, 25
media-politics, 7, 14, 66, 69, 71, 72, 79–83, 85–89,
    91, 93–95, 97, 98, 100, 101, 103, 108, 109,
    111, 167, 168
media-politics rationale, 66, 71, 72, 79, 101
Mehta, Jigar, 150, 157
Menlo Park, CA, 158
Merleau-Ponty, Maurice, 63
methodological nationalism, 7, 9–11, 175
MHz, 78, 79, 88
Miami, FL, 52, 110, 176
Mic, 159
Microsoft Word, 156
Middle East, 1, 3, 12, 17–19, 22–23, 26–27, 29–31,
    64, 70, 72, 82–83, 96, 100–101, 129–132,
    137, 146, 166
Minneapolis, MN, 107
Minty, Riyaad, 152
MIPCOM, 142
Mitchell, Andrea, 92
Mohyeldin, Ayman, 83, 93, 94